SOME SIMPLE RULES FOR

STAYING OK

* Don't try to overcome unpleasant feelings by using willpower.
* Don't try to get your way by getting angry.
* Don't play games by giving and taking "emotional trading stamps."
* Don't send the message "YOU'RE NOT OK" to your children.
* Don't waste time on unfulfilling activities.
* Don't withdraw from encounters with threatening people.

THE AUTHORS WHO TAUGHT US I'M OK—YOU'RE OK SHOW US HOW TO STAY THAT WAY!

"Another fine book...Highly recommended reading for all!"
—Ray H. Roseman, M.D., co-author of *Type A Behavior and Your Heart*

"Bright examples and persuasive common-sense details...By self-help standards this is the most theoretically sound."
Kirkus Reviews

Other Avon Books by
Thomas A. Harris, M.D.

I'M OK—YOU'RE OK

STAYING OK

AMY BJORK HARRIS
and THOMAS A. HARRIS, M.D.

AVON
PUBLISHERS OF BARD, CAMELOT, DISCUS AND FLARE BOOKS

A portion of this work originally appeared in *Redbook*.
Grateful acknowledgment is made for permission to reprint:
Excerpts from *Type A Behavior and Your Heart* by Meyer Friedman, M.D. and Ray H. Rosenman, M.D. Copyright © 1974 by Meyer Friedman, M.D. Reprinted by permission of Alfred A. Knopf, Inc.
"Karpman Drama Triangle" from "Fairy Tales and Script Drama Analysis" by Stephen B. Karpman. Reprinted by permission of the author from *Transactional Analysis Bulletin*, vol. 7, no. 26, 1968.
Excerpts from *Games People Play* by Eric Berne. (Grove Press, Inc., 1964.) Reprinted by permission of Random House, Inc.
Excerpt from "Six Gifts to Make Children Strong" by Ruth Stafford Peale from the August 1974 issue of *Reader's Digest*. Reprinted by permission of *Reader's Digest*.

AVON BOOKS
A division of
The Hearst Corporation
1790 Broadway
New York, New York 10019

First Avon Printing, March 1986

AVON TRADEMARK REG. U. S. PAT. OFF. AND IN
OTHER COUNTRIES, MARCA REGISTRADA, HECHO EN
U. S. A.

Printed in the U. S. A.

WFH   10   9   8   7   6   5   4   3   2   1

In Memory of Our Parents

Ruth Josefina Nyberg Bjork
Eric Johannes Bjork

Lula Jenkins Harris
William Milton Harris

Contents

Illustrations

Foreword

Thomas A. Harris, M.D.

It seems appropriate to write a bridge between *I'm OK—You're OK*, published sixteen years ago, and *Staying OK*. The first book, the only book we have written until now, is our basic manual, what Dr. Eric Berne called "the first layman's guide" to Transactional Analysis, the system he originated. In August 1972 Webster Schott, writing in *Life* magazine, stated, "When an idea finds its time and voice it takes on force. Transactional Analysis is the idea. Now is the time. *I'm OK—You're OK* is the voice." We believe *now* is still the time and that TA is as useful today as it was sixteen years ago when the book was written. If you have not already read it we hope you will, for it contains a detailed description of the principles upon which the present book rests. For those who have not read it, the basics will be reviewed briefly in the first chapter.

Although I am retired from my practice, I continue now, as I have throughout my lifetime, to look for better ways to understand what builds and motivates persons along with practical ideas for the enrichment of life. I am as enthusiastic as ever about Transactional Analysis, which I believe is the best system yet devised to understand and explain behavior from a psychological point of view. Though extensive research in brain physiology continues to produce remarkable insights into the mystery of the mind, TA remains an effective tool anyone can use to gain practical insight into one's own behavior and how to change if one chooses.

At the time *I'm OK—You're OK* was written it contained

the culmination of thirty years of my own search, research, and practice as a psychiatrist. It also contained the collected observations, anecdotes, scholarship, and writing skills of Amy, who has been my partner in marriage and vocation through nearly thirty years. The widespread enthusiasm generated by that one volume was evidence, to us, that the ideas contained in it were not only motivating, but worked! Fifteen million copies are in print and the book has been translated into eighteen foreign languages as well as Braille. Thousands of remarkable letters have brought reports of exultation, confirmation, and change. Letters continue to arrive from people in every walk of life, from prisoners and priests, professors and students, women and men, eighty-year-olds and eighteen-year-olds, Muslims and Christians, from kibbutzim and convents, from rich and poor, scientists and blue-collar workers, patients and therapists.

In a four-to-one ratio, letter writers asked for additional information and applications of TA in problem solving. Many of the applications contained in this book have grown from the questions posed in these letters and from formulations by participants in seminars and workshops that Amy and I and our colleagues have conducted over the years. We particularly thank former staff members employed in my practice as well as others who participated in the teaching programs of the Harris Institute of Transactional Analysis. Their enthusiasm and creative thinking, combined with our own, comprise many of the ideas contained in this book. We especially thank Dr. Craig Johnson, Larry Mart, Robert Miller, and the late Connie Drewry, who died in 1981 after a long, brave battle against cancer. I write the above acknowledgments in the past tense because the institute was discontinued following my retirement.

Also we appreciate TA colleagues Dr. Gordon Haiberg, Dr. Hedges Capers, Dr. Robert Goulding and Mary McClure Goulding, Bill Collins, Joseph Concannon, Dr. Stephen Karpman, Jacqui Schiff, John Defoore, Mary Joe Hannaford, Mary Boulton, and the late Warren Cheney. Through the years a wealth of stimulating ideas and encouragement has come also from our friends, notably Thomas E. Smail, Jr., Judge Wyatt Heard and Heidi Frost Heard, Dr. Baxter

Geeting, Corinne Geeting, Carol Jean Noren, Merrill Heidig, and Lou Foley. We gratefully acknowledge the valuable information we gained from the staff of St. Helena Hospital and Health Center in Deer Park, California, and from many colleagues, including Richard Frink, M.D., Founder and Principal Investigator of the Sacramento Heart Research Foundation.

Particularly do we thank Amy's brother the Rev. Elvin E. Bjork, pastor of the Lutheran Church of the Good Shepherd of Salem, Oregon, our own pastor Dr. Robert R. Ball of Fremont Presbyterian Church in Sacramento, our friend Father Henry Doherty of Lenoir, North Carolina, and Dr. Elton Trueblood, who was the first to suggest we write a book, which eventually became *I'm OK—You're OK*. Special thanks to Eva Hewlin, friend and faithful helper in our home. We also thank our children for their patience, love, and wisdom beyond their years, sometimes beyond ours.

We deeply appreciate the assistance of our former editor at Harper & Row, Harold E. Grove. After his retirement we were exceedingly fortunate to work with our present editor, Ann Bramson. We are especially grateful to her for her irresistible affirmation, hospitality, and gracious persistence, which kept us moving toward the completion of this book. Finally, we thank the thousands of readers of *I'm OK—You're OK* who took the time to write us and to urge us on.

As I stated in the preface of *I'm OK—You're OK*, Amy's writing made possible the effective presentation of ideas in that book, which brought such a remarkable response. I now leave it to her to do the first-person presentation of the material in *Staying OK*. Amy is a Special Fields Teaching Member in the International Transactional Analysis Association, her special field being Communications. She attended Eric Berne's San Francisco Social Psychiatry Seminars and was a co-founder with me of the institute. She was also a member, with me, of the board of the ITAA. In recent years she has become well known, not only as a writer but also as a lecturer in both the theory and application of TA.

Because Amy will be writing in the first person, the style, sensitive insight, humor, philosophy, and personal examples she brings to this work will be uniquely hers. This work is, nonetheless, a combined effort, for we have been in constant collaboration through the intervening years, melding ideas and experiences into one fairly unified approach. At this time in my life, after decades of treating severely ill people and counseling others with the ordinary problems of ordinary people, I gladly leave the creative, culminating effort, the reporting of our experience, and the writing to her.

One person who recognized Amy's contribution was Dr. Berne, who at the time of the publication of *I'm OK—You're OK*, wrote the following statement for the book jacket, only a brief part of which was used. Because we treasure it as an expression of his ongoing support, which came to us in frequent letters and other statements of encouragement until his death in 1970, I include it here, in full:

> I am grateful to Dr. Harris and his colleagues for doing a job that needed doing. In this book he has clarified the principles of Transactional Analysis with cogent and easily understood examples, and has related them to broader considerations, including ethics, in a thoughtful and skillful way. I am sure that many people of all ages will find it instructive, broadening and helpful, and also readable and enjoyable.
>
> Naturally I feel honored that Dr. Harris has taken such an interest in the subject and has done so much with it, and that our association has proven so useful for both of us. I am particularly happy to see the influence of Mrs. Harris and the Harris children come through very clearly in the book, an excellent precedent, I think, for others who write about people, and even for others who write about animals and plants and sticks and stones.

STAYING OK

1

If I'm OK and You're OK, How Come I Don't Feel OK?

After the door slams, the glass breaks, the siren growls, the interview chills, after someone else gets the promotion, after a stabbing thought about what we forgot to do, after talking too much, after a look in the mirror, after a lot of things, we beat ourselves nearly to death. Why did I have to say that? Why didn't I keep my mouth shut? Why wasn't I a better parent? Why didn't I speak up? Why don't I just drop dead?

Alone with our feelings, in the dark of the night or the surreal light of day, the punishing voice of regret often plays like a broken record, if only, if only, if only. If only I could take back my words, erase it all, and start over.

When our daughter Gretchen was six years old, her persistent begging for something she couldn't have finally provoked me to angry words. She stopped begging and went to sit on the floor, tears brimming in her big blue eyes. In a few moments she was back.

"You were mad at me. You shouted at me," she said.

"That's right, I did," I replied. "But do you know what you were doing that finally made me shout at you?"

Weary of reasons, she turned her wet, wistful face square at mine and said, "Oh, Mama, sometimes we have to start all over."

And we did, and my face got wet, too. How often had I not felt just that way, a little girl again, wanting to be close once more, with another chance? I was proud of her persistence and awed by her words. Had she not stated something universal and ultimate? Do we not all, from time to time, wish we could start over?

The wonderful thing about being young is that if we had it to do all over again we could. Many of us aren't young anymore, and our history follows us around like a patient dog, nudging us for attention, and dropping long white hairs on the carpet of life. If we tell it to go lie down, it is soon back. The past is forever with us, the bad with the good, and all the feelings that accompanied both. Good feelings from the past are the golden, nostalgic moments that every so often fill our chests to bursting. The more common intrusions from the past, however, are bad feelings, sad feelings, little-girl or little-boy feelings of wanting and wishing and not getting.

Painful feelings erode self-esteem. We may wake up feeling like a million dollars, but sometimes it takes only a second for a frown, a slight, a remembered failure, to reduce us to zero, and the zero may last all day. We may have read rows of books on behavior, motivation, and spiritual uplift. We may have insight, foresight, and hindsight. All this can go out the window in an instant when someone pushes a "hot" button, or when tragedy strikes, and feelings surge along every nerve fiber, preempting all the voices of reason that could give us hope and reassure us that life can be good again. Most of us are acquainted with the symptoms— weariness, depression, apathy, sleeplessness, sighs, too much to do, no taste for doing it, disorganization, sadness, loss of enthusiasm, loneliness. Emptiness.

The good news is that though we cannot stop the bad feelings from coming, we can keep them from staying. This is a book not only about how to get rid of bad feelings, once they have arrived, but also how to get good ones. It is a book about loving, talking, listening, wanting, getting, giving, deciding where we're going, and enjoying the trip. It is the only trip we will take, and we can make it a good one despite our own imperfections and the imperfect world in which we live.

What "I'm OK—You're OK" Means

Although the millions of people who have read *I'm OK—You're OK* know what we mean by the title, we have come to realize there are a great many others who are familiar with the title only. Popularity has pitfalls. In time the title became a slogan with all the twists and twits that slogans attract. Seen only as a slogan, stenciled on sweatshirts and bumper stickers, the notion that "everybody is OK" doesn't quite seem to fit the truth. What we *know* is that sometimes we feel not OK, sometimes we act not OK, and certainly there are plenty of other people who act or feel worse than we.

Recently we received a letter from a woman who had been encouraged by a friend to read the book in 1969, the year of publication. She wrote:

> What she was telling me about the ideas it contained was drowned out by my interpretation of the title, from which I gathered presumptuously that the ideas expressed a somewhat laid-back philosophy suggesting that if people would just "cool it" and accept one another, the world would be a better place. Since I didn't quarrel with such an attitude, and because it didn't seem very helpful to me, I "shelved" your book. Until recently. I was in 1969 *very* ready to consider the ideas actually contained in *I'm OK—You're OK;* but presumption and what I think is a misleading title (however appropriate when one knows the meaning) have delayed for 16 years my use of some exceedingly significant ideas. . . . All the same I wonder whether you've encountered this response over the years from other tardy readers. Implicit in all this is my sense of gratitude to someone for having produced such a simple, beautifully coherent and useful exposition of a subject horrendously complex.

Others who at the outset felt the title was "flip" or "pop" also changed their minds. Among them was the late eminent neurosurgeon Dr. Wilder Penfield, whose pioneering work on memory mechanisms will be referred to in this chapter. In a letter written to us in December 1973, he stated:

> I have been reading your book, *I'm OK—You're OK*. It was given to me by another surgeon who is also a member with me of the American Philosophical Society. . . . Let me congratulate you. The title seemed to me first to suggest that your approach was a superficial one. I apologize now for that misconception.

Because we want to be responsive to our readers, and because the present book gains much of its recognition by virtue of the fact that it is written by the authors of *I'm OK—You're OK,* we feel it important to clarify misconceptions. We feel it a necessary siding on the track before taking you to the destination of this book, how to handle bad feelings, produce good ones, and live life to the fullest.

One of Four Life Positions

"I'm OK—You're OK" can best be understood when it is compared with the position of early childhood, "I'm Not OK—You're OK." We believe all children make this preverbal conclusion during the first or second year of life in the setting of a world of giants, the most significant being their parents, upon whom they depend for everything, food, care, nurture, life itself. This decision, permanently recorded, is a product of the situation of childhood, in which the critical reality is dependency.* In early childhood, a period we designate as the first five years of life, thousands of events and perceptions, among them intense feelings, were recorded in the little person's brain and are available for replay throughout his life. If in the present we find ourselves in a situation of dependency, we become a "child"

*The other two positions, "I'm Not OK—You're Not OK" and "I'm OK—You're Not OK," will not be discussed in this book but were explained at length in *I'm OK—You're OK,* pp. 60–77. Both are variations of the first position "I'm Not OK—You're OK." (All page numbers pertaining to *I'm OK—You're OK* refer to the Avon Books edition, New York, 1973.)

again, feeling the very same feelings we did when we were little. We not only remember that child, we *are* that child. We may again feel "I'm Not OK and You're OK." Much of our life consists of attempts to rise above, circumvent, prove, or disprove this early decision. To help get the feel of the predicament, we will refresh your memory.

What It Is to Be a Child

Objectively, a grownup looking at a baby sees an awesome, infinitely precious miracle of creation. Unless genetically impaired, the baby is indeed perfect. Perfectly OK. What is relevant to understanding feelings, however, is the *subjective* view of the child, his interpretation of experiences in which he participates in childhood. However perfect he is, he is little and his parents are big, he is helpless, they are not. Most significant, he is totally dependent on them. It is hard to be objective, even as grownups, when we need somebody that much.

Can we be objective about what the child feels? We cannot interview an infant or recall our own view of life in the first two years, the critical time during which the "I'm Not OK—You're OK" position was decided. However, we can observe the little person and the situation in which he lives. He is small, clumsy, uncoordinated, without words to express his feelings, and totally dependent on big people to set up the situations that produce good feelings for him.

Consciously, we recall the good, most of the time. Yet the "happy childhood" is a myth, not because there was a total absence of happiness in childhood but because there was no way the child could control the environment to make the good feelings last. Play was interrupted by bedtime, mud had to be washed off, spilling the milk brought irritable disapproval, running free as the wind down the hill ended in skinned knees, mother's rocking was terminated by the ring of the telephone, squeezing the cat produced claws, mispronunciation brought correction, intriguing explorations of the body sometimes brought abrupt interruption, and running into the street ended with a rough retrieval.

In the best of situations, with the best-intentioned parents, the child had no way to assure that good feelings would continue. Powerlessness, the total dependence on others, left the child with the on-again-off-again experience of great glee and the sudden cessation of what felt so good. One way to figure this out was to make a decision about it: "You are in charge; I am not." "You are OK—I am not."

The helplessness of the little person is compounded by his lack of knowledge about a vast, strange, new, sometimes terrifying world. As grownups we forget what our point of view was as small people, how things looked and seemed. Years ago we spent a week vacationing at the White Sun Guest Ranch in Palm Desert, California. Our lodging was a snug, rough-hewn cottage, decorated with a Southwest Indian motif. After bedtime, the first night, Gretchen, then age nine months, awoke screaming. I turned on the light in the girls' bedroom, picked her up from her crib, and held her. Her uncharacteristic screaming continued as hard as ever. I thought she had been bitten by something, and searched both her body and her bed for evidence. I found nothing. I finally was able to calm her, and I rocked her and soothed her until she dozed. I turned the light off and laid her back in the crib. In the process she awoke and again began screaming. For more than an hour the holding, calming, dozing, continued. Yet every time I laid her down her terror returned.

Once more I laid her down, this time putting my head near hers in the crib, humming, as if to go to sleep with her. Then I saw what she saw. On the wall was a handcrafted tin mask with grotesque features and with eyes made of faceted red glass. Outside the window was a neon sign that flashed on and off, lighting up the mask with regularity, and causing the red eyes to glow horribly on, off, on, off. When the lights of the room had been on, the mask had not seemed so scary. But from her crib, in the dark, from *her* point of view, the scene was terrifying.

I picked her up again and turned on the light, and we went to examine the mask. "We will put it away in the drawer," I said, and did. "The mask is gone, Gretchen," I assured her. "It will not hurt you. It is only a decoration, a silly-looking face. It looked scary in the dark, but it won't be scary anymore. I won't let it scare you anymore." After more rocking and reassuring I again laid her down. She stared steadily at the blank wall for a long while, the pink and dark gray still alternating from the neon light, and finally she fell asleep. There was no way to understand her terror until I saw what she saw. The mask did not frighten me. I knew what it was. She did not.

When we are grown we forget what we once saw, how scary life could be, how helpless we were. We even forget we made a decision, "I'm Not OK—You're OK." Yet once the decision is made, it is recorded forever. Because the assumption is a true impression of what life is like for the child, he attempts to maintain the integrity of his conclusion. Even though his assumption about himself and others seems unfavorable it has great staying power, because it is a decision based on sound early mental processes seeking practical and successful adaptation. Inadequate data, but good data processing. Though the "assumptive reality" that the child constructs may contain some wrong assumptions, it is nonetheless *reality* to him.

We believe there is ample evidence to conclude this is the preverbal assumption of *all* small children.* Why, then, do some children appear more self-assured, more OK, than others? Why do some seem to be little princesses and princes almost from the start? Why are some outgoing, bright, curious, pleasant, self-assertive, and happy most of the time, while others are sulky, whiny, or terrified most of the time? Why are some childhoods more happy than others? Is it because the happy children never concluded "I'm Not OK—You're OK"? We do not believe so. We believe the behavior of happy children is a result of unconditional love and straight, consistent, caring parental instructions and demonstrations of how to think and solve problems. Thinking and doing produce knowledge and mastery, *despite* the original decision! Mastery, too, is recorded and is replayed with accompanying feelings of self-confidence. Yet even confident children have their Not OK moments, as do grownups.

There is another way to be objective about how the little

*See *I'm OK—You're OK*, pp. 60–67.

child felt about himself. This is the replay of our own recorded feelings when we find ourselves in a situation of
dependency and helplessness—when a superior has us in a
corner, when we run out of ideas to solve a problem, when
we are tired, when we're broke, sick, or old, when we are
misunderstood, when we do our best and it still isn't good
enough, when we are judged unfairly, when our best-laid
plans turn sour because of the whim of someone more powerful than we. Most people experience a feeling markedly
different from "I'm OK—You're OK" in such circumstances. The existence of a feeling of "I'm Not OK" is an
indication that the original position of helplessness and dependency was recorded early in childhood and is available
for replay in the present.

There is ample evidence for the existence of the first half
of the equation, "I'm Not OK." We can feel it just as plain!
Also we can observe its expression in little children—tears,
rage, shyness, fear, frustration. Why did we conclude, then,
that these others, "they," our parents, were OK if they were
centrally involved in that which produced our frustration?
Where does the "You're OK" come from? *They* were OK
because they were the child's primary source of lifegiving
physical and emotional contact, which we call *stroking*.

Redeciding

What was once decided can be redecided. Our childhood
position was arrived at preverbally and was based on feelings
about how life seemed to us then. The "I'm OK—You're
OK" position is based less on feelings than on conscious
thought, faith, and the wager of action. It is a decision to
reject our childhood assumption and to assert that we are
no longer helpless, dependent children. If is a statement not
of evaluation but of acceptance. It is a statement of belief
in the worth of persons, ourselves included. It does not
mean that everybody is perfect or that all actions are good.
It does not mean that all actions have the same merit, or
that all persons are the same. It does mean that we treat
people as persons and not things, willing to regard them in
the best possible light, open to what can be regardless of

what has been. It means we view ourselves in the same way. Goethe stated the possibility of the "I'm OK—You're OK" position: "When we treat a man as he is, we make him worse than he is. When we treat him as if he already were what he potentially could be, we make him what he should be."

"I'm OK—You're OK" is an amendment of our constitution. Many good and novel actions may ensue. It does not mean the earlier decision is erased, for it was recorded and every so often it replays. But our later decision is recorded, too. The more conscious we become of this new way to look at ourselves and others, the more readily we are able to change the nature of our daily transactions, our greetings, our attitudes, our reaction to stress, and the way we handle feelings. Our guiding star is the faith that something better can exist between persons in this world than the combative and manipulative exchanges that threaten to destroy us today.

What Is Transactional Analysis?

Having attended to the clarification of the meaning of "I'm OK—You're OK," we now wish to be responsive to persons who do not know what Transactional Analysis is. We trust that those of you who are already familiar with the basics of TA will be patient with a brief review. We simply do not know a better or more precise way to understand or discuss behavior than TA. Nor do we know how to say anything novel about handling feelings without using TA tools. The next few pages of this chapter and a brief section in Chapter 3, describing transactions, are the only places in this book where basics will be reviewed. For those not acquainted with TA, an understanding of these basics is essential to a correct understanding of all that follows. For instance, when we write of Parent Stoppers and Parent Shrinkers, we do not mean we are against parents, yours or ours. Quite the opposite! Even TA old-timers may derive new insights. Emerson said, "We are far from having exhausted the significance of the few symbols we use." TA's symbols are three circles, representing the three parts of the personality of every person, Parent, Adult, and Child, words which we will define forthwith.

A *transaction* is the basic unit of behavior: You say or do something to me, and I say or do something back. *Transactional Analysis* is determining what part of the three-part you initiated the transaction and what part of the three-part me responded.

You Are More Than a Child

Thus far we have written mostly about the part of the personality which in TA we call the *Child,* the recorded experience of that little person we once were. It is a state of being, a state in which we may appear in the present, felt by ourselves and observed by others.

In the 1950s TA's founder Dr. Eric Berne was treating a patient who was a lawyer. At one point the lawyer said, "Right now I feel like a little boy." And he looked like a little boy, the way he was sitting, his vocabulary, his facial expression. Soon the treatment began to center on the question "Who's talking now, the lawyer or the little boy?" They were two different people. About six months later Berne introduced his observation that still another person made his appearance in the present. That was a person who was very much like the man's father, a parental person who appeared in a nurturing, sometimes critical way.

TA is based on the observation that all of us are three persons in one. Sometimes we act as the little child we once were, sometimes in a parental way copied from what we observed our parents do, and sometimes as an objective data processor, thinking, analyzing, predicting, estimating probabilities, making decisions, and solving problems. We are in one or another of these states at any given time. We can change from one person to another in a moment. Everything about us changes—our physiology, voice tone, respiration, perspiration, vocabulary, and gestures. These states are not roles, but realities. The state is produced by the playback of recorded events in the past involving real people, real times, real places, real decisions, and real feelings.

We represent these states by three circles, signifying *Par-*

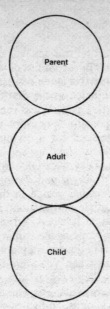

Figure 1
Three-Part Structure of the Personality

ent, Adult, and *Child* (Figure 1). These three words, defined, form the basic language tools of TA. Thoreau once said, "Beware of all enterprises that require new clothes." In a similar vein, many people are wary of a system that requires new words. Yet in order to communicate meaning it is essential to agree upon definitions. The thousands of letters we received from readers of *I'm OK—You're OK* confirmed that meaning had been communicated, and we shall use these words in exactly the same way we did in that book. An impressive slogan used in a TRW advertisement is "Getting an idea from one place to another is as important as getting an idea." Ideas travel on words. We therefore review the following definitions of Parent, Adult, and Child, always capitalized.

The Parent

The Parent is made up of recordings of what the little person saw mother and father (or parent substitutes) do during a period we have designated as the first five years of life. It also includes what they said. It was recorded unedited, for the child was in no position to question the powerful people upon whom he depended for everything. Because of his dependency, he made assumptions and attributed to his parents magic qualities. They were OK, no matter what. In the Parent is recorded a *taught* and *demonstrated* concept of life. Traditions and values reside in the Parent, although values, as well as other information, may need updating later in life. The Parent is dated. What your parents think today may not be the same as the Parent in your head. They may have changed. The Parent may not even be what they actually said and did when you were little, but what you *assumed* about what they said and did.

The Parent is unerasable. The Parent is both nurturing and critical, if your parents, in fact, were both. The Parent is the history of your early environment, events that really happened, not an abstraction like "super-ego." The Parent is unique. Yours is different from mine. The Parent is both a state and an influence. From this vast source of data comes information into our thought processes to influence decisions. Or we can "come on" Parent, and act just as mother or father did, even to the finer points of the same gestures and voice tone. The Parent is a recording. We do not think with it, we merely play it back.

One of the most powerful ways in which the Parent enters our lives in the present is the "internal dialogue" in which we hear the same applause, warnings, accusations, and punishments we heard when we were toddlers. The person in us who is at the other end of the dialogue is the Child, the preschooler in our heads. We can feel as bad today as we did then, when negative recordings in either Parent or Child are activated, and we hear the internal, unceasing voices of regret or accusation, if only, if only, if only, why did you, why did you, why didn't you? It is probable people cannot hurt our feelings unless they arouse our Parent, which then accuses us internally. An oppressive Parent does not mean we had cruel parents. They could have been angels, but to the little person, when the Parent was recorded, they were giant angels, and may not always have seemed to be angels, either.

Parent is, in some respects, a problematic word, for, even though it has a unique meaning in TA, it nonetheless has intrinsic semantic power. We have tried to think of a less inflammatory word, but have not been successful. Neither are we eager to alter a now well-known structure, Parent-Adult-Child.

Perhaps inflammation has a benefit. It takes a certain amount of psychic upset to power a fresh examination of our hallowed dogmas and crippling misconceptions. *Parent*, despite the above-mentioned semantic shading, is an apt name for the authority in our heads, for it was derived essentially from what mother and father or their substitutes said and did. The significant distortion, however, is that it was *we ourselves* who internalized them, and we were unable to do the job objectively—unable to comprehend that they were only human and not God—because of our dependency, the inescapable situation of childhood.

As we begin to recognize the distortion, and as we begin to feel compassion for ourselves instead of continual self-castigation, we also begin to feel capable of compassion for our parents, who are, or were, in the same boat as we. They had a Child, too.

The Child

A great deal has been written already in this chapter about what it is to be a child. The child's experience was recorded in the same way the Parent was recorded. It consists of the child's responses to what the parents said and did. The Child is a permanent recording of internal events in response to the external events of the first five years of life. The most potent internal events were *feelings*. These feelings frequently replay in the present when we are put in a situation similar to that of the little person, when we are cornered, dependent, unfairly accused, clumsy, uninformed. If we are confronted today by parental-type accusers, we may be transported *back there* once again. Old tapes are always ready to roll, be they Parent or Child.

The Child includes our instincts and biological urges, genetic recordings, our physical selves, curiosity, and intuition. It contains joy as well as sadness. Whereas the Parent is filled with demands, directions, and dogma, the Child is filled with desire. The Child is where the "want to," the motivation, is. Much of what we *have* to do is an adaptive response to the Parent. What we *want* to do originates in the Child. The Child, like the Parent, is both an influence and a state. When we are *in* the Child state we act and look like the little person we once were. The Child is the most delightful part of our personality, or can be, if it is free to be inventive, creative, and spontaneous. The Child can also be a problem part of our personality if it is fearful, intimidated, or selfish. The referee between the demands of the Parent and the desires of the Child is the third part of the personality, the Adult, which thinks, solves problems, and mediates.

The Adult

At about ten months of age, perhaps earlier, the little person has developed motor control and strength sufficient to enable him to begin to explore things on his own. Soon he crawls, he climbs, he walks, he runs! He has entered the glorious age of major motion. He also is thinking, adding a novel *thought concept of life* to the Parent-taught concept of life and the Child-felt concept of life. He begins to construct his own understandings. He begins to separate himself from mother and learns how to say *no*. He has his own intentions and his own reasons. As his vocabulary grows, he begins to ask *why*. All of these individuating activities are products of that growing part of his personality we call the *Adult*. The Adult reasons, thinks, predicts, and figures out how to do things. In time the Adult begins to consider consequences. Whereas the Child provides the "want to," the Adult provides the "how to," borrowing heavily from what he learned from his parents. Good parents encourage the building of the child's Adult capabilities, praise him for his observations about life, and applaud his questions as to why the rain falls, the smoke rises, and his shadow leans over.

The Adult is not only a functional part of the personality, but also a state, observable by others in the present. A person in the Adult state appears thoughtful, rational, and in the here and now. We can usually tell which state a person is in by looking. Body language, vocabulary, and gestures are clues to each state. The Adult grows from the child's innate curiosity. Both Adult and Child are internally derived, whereas the Parent is externally derived. One of the important functions of the Adult is to update the Parent. A secure youngster is one who finds that most Parent data is reliable: "They told me the truth!"

The functions of all three states will appear in the following chapters. For a more detailed explanation of Parent, Adult, and Child, we encourage you to review Chapter 2 of *I'm OK—You're OK*.

This Is a Recording

Startling realism is conferred on the foregoing descriptions by the findings of the late Dr. Wilder Penfield of McGill University. His hundreds of experiments in evoking artificial recall by applying a galvanic probe to the exposed brains of persons undergoing surgery for focal epilepsy provide convincing evidence that the past is recorded in time sequence and in detail.* He discovered that the electrode probe evoked one single recollection after another, not a mixture of memories or a generalization. He discovered the memory record continued intact even after the subject's ability to recall it had disappeared. His experiments led to four con-

*Wilder Penfield, "Memory Mechanisms," *AMA Archives of Neurology and Psychiatry,* 1952, Vol. 67, pp. 178–198, with discussion by L. S. Kubie et al.

clusions of great significance to the understanding of feelings.*

　　1. The brain functions as a high-fidelity recorder of the events of our lives, the most deterministic of which occurred in early childhood. These recordings are in sequence and continuous. "Whenever a normal person is paying conscious attention to something," said Penfield, "he simultaneously is recording it in the temporal cortex of each hemisphere."

　　2. The *feelings* which were associated with past experiences also are recorded and are *inextricably locked* to those experiences.

　　3. Persons can exist in two "places" at the same time. You can be physically present with someone in the here and now, but your mind can be miles and years removed. One of our problems in relationships is that "something" removes us from the present and we are not with whom we're with.

　　4. These recorded experiences and *feelings associated with them* are available for replay today in as vivid a form as when they happened, and they provide much of the data that determines the nature of today's transactions. Events in the present can replicate an old experience and we not only remember how we felt, but we feel the same way. We not only remember the past, we relive it. We are there! Much of what we relive we don't remember.

Did you ever wonder what became of that little boy, that little girl, you once were, the little person with the missing tooth and tousled hair that you look at in the family photo album? One look in the mirror tells you that you have changed. The cells of your skin and body tissue have died and been replaced millions of times. Not so with brain cells. Neuroscientist Dr. Gary Lynch, of the University of California at Irvine, states that "somehow the cells and the proteins that constitute cell membranes in your brain are

I'm OK—You're OK, pp. 25–33.

being broken down and replaced, and yet the traces [memories] you stored as a child are still there."* It seems a reasonable assumption, therefore, that brain cells, though "refurbished," are permanent. If brain cells are destroyed by injury or advancing age, they are not replaced, although their function in some cases may be taken over by other cells. Most of us have most of the brain cells we had when our brains had developed their full complement. These include the cells that existed when we opened our eyes in the delivery room, took our first steps, learned our first words, first felt curiosity, glee, shame, fear, belonging, rejection, and the all-consuming feeling of panic when we felt ourselves to be lost and out of control. Childhood events and the feelings that were produced by them were recorded in electrochemical neural pathways. They are still there. Though the encoding does not stop at the end of childhood, the circuitry so elaborately built in those early years is the basic wiring to which everything else is connected. We still *are* that little person, the Child, even though we have become much more.

Facts About Feelings

Why do things that bother us not seem to bother others at all? Why are some people "up" all the time and others "down"? How can one person drop the aquarium on the parquet floor of the boss's office and live to laugh about it when someone else would simply die along with the fish? Four facts help us find answers.

1. *Every person is unique.* We come into life with our own particular genetic coding, containing instructions for our one-of-a-kind fingerprints, how we're to look, function physically, and, to a degree, function mentally. Also our histories are unique. They, too, are recorded permanently and in great detail in the brain. Everyone is born into a different situation. Even the situations of brothers and sisters

*Richard Restak, M.D., *The Brain,* Bantam, New York, 1984, pp. 189–190.

are unique. A mother had four children in rapid succession.
As we watched her dealing with the ever-increasing demands of the tots, we asked, "Jean, how do you do it?"
She replied, amused, "With each one I just lower my standards." In that home, as in all families, each sibling has a
unique history, a singular place in the birth order, differing
standards, and differing external realities. This unique history of early experience is permanently recorded.

Because of our uniqueness, we handle the problems and
pleasures of life differently. For example, if a man's mother
died when he was four years old, it is probable that all
experience of loss throughout life will be more painful for
him than for others. Losing a mate, losing a job, misplacing
a credit card, any kind of loss would probably produce more
desperation for him than for someone who had not so suffered as a child. There are mitigating circumstances, of
course: how the reality of her death was reported and understood, who became his new "mother," what his father was
like, generally the feeling of security that he did or did not
have.

Sights, sounds, and smells affect us differently because
of our uniqueness. For example, if you see a red car today,
your "red-car circuits" hum with all the previous impressions
you have had of red cars. If your first teenage romance was
with someone who drove a red convertible, the sight of a
red car today might flood you with happy feelings. If, however, you had a head-on collision in a red car and ended up
in a body cast for eight months, the sight of a red car today
would probably produce markedly different feelings from
those of the person with the romance. The earliest memories
are the most powerful. Little red wagons produce richer
memories than big red cars, and jelly beans than caviar.

As our history is unique, so are our perceptions and
feelings. A car backfires. Five people react five different
ways on the basis of their past experience. It was a gun! A
balloon popping. A bomb. A firecracker. A car backfiring.
Penfield in the course of his experiments discovered "the
subject feels again the emotion which the situation originally
produced in him, and is aware of the same interpretation,

true or false, which he himself gave to the experience in the first place. Thus, evoked recollection is not the exact photographic or phonographic reproduction of past scenes or events. It is reproduction of what the patient *saw and heard and felt and understood"* [italics added].*

Because our feelings are unique, our best attempt to describe feelings with words is never quite adequate, although it is one way we can attempt to share ourselves with others. If you tell a friend you're sad, he can know approximately what you mean by *sad*. He knows what *sad* means to him, but he can't know *exactly* how you feel, because he can't get into your memory banks. Putting words to feelings is perhaps like trying to sing a picture or paint a song. Nonetheless, expressing ourselves with words, despite their limitations, is one of the ways we help each other. If we didn't have words, our mutual assistance would be limited indeed.

2. *Feelings are real*. Feelings are direct, indisputable knowledge. We gain most of our knowledge about the world second-hand through reports of others. Through the abstraction of words we can have proximate knowledge about history, mathematics, geography, or current news bounced off orbiting satellites. We can infer, guess, dispute, and wonder whether or not this information is true. But *feelings* are primary, personal knowledge. When we are in the grip of feelings, we know it! That is, most people know it. Some people were told, in effect, not to feel their feelings. If children report how they feel and are told it is "wicked" to feel that way, or if a parent says, "what's a kid like you got to be sad about?" they may decide to keep their feelings to themselves, to "hold it all in." If expressions of feelings are always negated or twisted, children may become afraid to trust their own perceptions, and begin not to *feel* feelings at all. Later in life they may be "unfeeling" people. One woman, who described herself as unfeeling, said, "When I think of my childhood, I can't remember a thing." Childhood was loaded with feelings. If she was not supposed to

*Penfield, op. cit.

have feelings, her childhood was buried along with the feelings she was not supposed to have. She did, however, acknowledge she had a feeling of emptiness.

Feelings are neither good nor bad, in an ethical sense. They are events, facts of our existence. What we do about them may be good or bad. But the feelings themselves cannot be judged by ethical standards. They occur to us unbidden. We may decide on a given day that we are not going to feel anger anymore. We may decide to love everybody, and not have any hateful feelings ever again. Then all of a sudden, out of the blue, we are furious. Something has occurred to us. We may not have the slightest notion what produced the fury. But the feeling is real. It is an event. *Subjectively,* feelings *feel* good or bad. Feelings are particularly bad when they decommission the Adult and we compound our misery by doing one dumb thing after another.

3. *We can change our feelings.* We can't do this directly by a resolution or meditate our way into a state of lasting bliss. The only way we can change feelings is through knowledge of their origin followed by a change in *behavior*. Much of this book will be devoted to explaining how this is done.

4. *Everyone was once a child.* Our experience today is filtered through the events and feelings of childhood, recorded in detail. We cannot have a feeling today that is "disconnected" from similar feelings recorded in the past, the most intense of which occured to us in the first five years of life. This does not mean that today's feelings are not real, or that we are to discount them by claiming "they're just an old recording." We are today who we once were. The Not OK feelings that resulted from the dependency and helplessness of our early years are recorded and ready to roll when we face situations of dependency and helplessness in the present. If we feel ashamed, for instance, the "ashamed circuits" fire, and we not only remember we were once ashamed, we relive, we *are* the same ashamed small person we once were. We feel the same feeling we once had; thus the powerful, cumulative effect feelings have on us in the present.

Sorting Yourself Out

We reveal ourselves today. We do this in transactions. We learn what our parents were like in our early years as our Parent is observed. The same is true for the Child and Adult. TA is a superb sorting device, whereby we learn to identify our own Parent, Adult, and Child and discover how each is revealed in today's transactions. Swiss psychiatrist Paul Tournier likened the mind to a messy drawer, which every so often has to be dumped on the bed and sorted out. This total emptying can be likened to classical psychoanalysis. It takes a long time to examine every item and put it back where it belongs, and during the analysis the use of the drawer is significantly interrupted. In TA we force down a couple of dividers and start putting things in their place, into three sections, Parent, Adult, and Child. The advantage is we have the use of the drawer. This process is similar to rebuilding a railroad bridge one tie at a time. The trains can keep running, and finally there is an entirely new bridge.

This is the work of Transactional Analysis. The goal of TA is the strengthening and emancipation of the Adult through a clear identification of "what part of me is coming on" and an assessment as to whether or not this information is true, reasonable, and appropriate to today's reality. The purpose is not to do away with the Parent or the Child, but to be free to examine these bodies of data. The Adult, to paraphrase Emerson, "must not be hindered by the name of goodness, but must explore if it be goodness." Or badness, for that matter, as in the early decision "I'm not OK." The ultimate goal of TA is to enable a person to have freedom of choice. "To say that we are free," said Will Durant, "is merely to mean that we know what we are doing." This freedom makes possible the creation of new options beyond the limiting influences of the past.

The goal of this book is to use the tools of TA to handle bad feelings and to produce good ones. Good feelings produce energy to fuel our trip through life. Many people, beset by bad feelings, are running on empty. Frustration, dependency, and confusion can indeed overwhelm us, undermine our plans, fracture the relationships we long for, and send us into the deep despair of feeling totally insignificant. When we were three we were at the mercy of others. That was a past reality. The present reality is that we are not totally helpless even though we may *feel* we are.

The most common cause of negative feelings is the failure to live up to the conditions we originally assumed had to be met to be OK, those important *ifs* that constitute what Kant called the "handful of maxims which govern our lives."

2

You Can Be OK If

Most of us were raised, I love you if . . . I love you if, if, if . . . I love you if you bring good grades home. I would love you if you make it through high school. Boy, would I love you if you go through college. Oh, would I love you if I could say, my son, the doctor. And we . . . literally end up believing that we can buy love with good behavior, or rewards or whatever . . . and then they marry somebody who says, I love you if you buy me a mink coat. If we would raise the next generation of children with *unconditional love* and firm consistent discipline, not punishment, those children would never be afraid of life, nor of death, and we would never have to make films and write books about "death and dying."*

This statement by Dr. Elisabeth Kübler-Ross both confirms and confounds. Many people, particularly certain types of achievers, will hear the ring of truth in the conditions she enumerates. Social approval most certainly is conditional, and which "society" we seek approval from is determined largely by what our parents approved of. Whether we seek acceptance in the church, in business and professions, in the "jungle out there," or the underworld, depends largely on which society our parents valued. We join an organization and, at the outset, learn the by-laws, both written and un-

*Elisabeth Kübler-Ross, "To Live Until You Die," NOVA, WGBH Educational Foundation, 1983, pp. 19, 20.

written: "If you're going to make it here, this is what you must do."

"Making it" is the goal. Measurement is the gauge. Many of our "best people" go through life measuring up, desperate for approval, and, like the Good Guys and Sweethearts in the next chapter, are forever preoccupied with the anxious question "How'm I doing?" The paradox is that it generally takes achievers to make such observations about achievement. Would Dr. Kübler-Ross have derived such an insight had she not herself been an achiever, for whatever reason she became one?

The question follows: Is it wrong for parents to expect things of their children? We believe not, but before we explain why, it is necessary to make a distinction between *explained* expectations and *assumed* expectations.

The critical fact of early childhood is *dependency*. Unable to make fine distinctions or to understand reasons for their parents' sometimes shifting expectations, small children construct an "assumptive reality" about themselves and their surroundings.* Everything from genealogy, to birth order, to illness, to the world situation feeds into these assumptions. What the child assumes may be incorrect, but for him it is *reality*. His most deterministic assumption was "I'm Not OK—You're OK."

Having perceived his predicament, the little person looks to his parents for clues as to what he can do to please them, whom he regards as OK. To the child they are magic people, big, powerful, comforting, frightening sometimes, and, of primary significance, *needed*. However they treat him, he needs them.

Some years ago we read an account of a murder trial of a father who had beaten his four-year-old daughter to death over a twenty-four-hour period because she had "not minded him." The mother had participated in the relentless, horrible punishment administered with belts and whips. One of the

---

*Thomas A. Harris, "The Developing Child and His Assumptive Reality," paper presented at the American Ortho-Psychiatric Association, February 24, 1951.

most pathetic accounts in the entire proceeding was of the little girl, after about the twentieth hour, weak and dying, approaching her father for help to undo the clasps of her overalls so she could go to the bathroom. She came to her tormentor because she *needed* him, and he was her father.

In the best and worst of circumstances the need of childhood prevails. Because the child has nowhere else to go, he forces his perceptions into the molds of his need, and distortion in thinking, or incorrect assumptions, are not only possible, but probable.

In the beginning the infant gets what he wants by crying, yet it may not be long before he receives the message, in words or actions, that a crying baby is a bad baby. So he figures out new ways to get his needs met, to make mother smile. Whatever he does, if it works, he continues doing it.

As his sensory equipment matures he fine-tunes his perception to pick up clues as to how he can please his parents, or at least get their attention. His eyes search their faces for needed approval or dreaded disapproval. Not all at once, but little by little, the child pieces together a comprehension of his reality, and decides what he must do to be OK. As the puzzle takes shape he makes a series of decisions, and these decisions become the basis for his life script.

You Can Be OK If

Kübler-Ross suggests it is possible to raise children with unconditional love. From a parent's point of view, this ideal may seem within reach. From a child's point of view, it is not, for even survival depends on conditions: keeping mother around, being picked up, fed, and cared for. When the infant becomes a toddler the parent's life-saving *don'ts* are conditional to the child. You will stay alive if you don't run into the street, stick a bobby pin in the socket, get into the medicine cabinet, drink Lysol, or play with the butcher knife. The child does not understand these activities as life-threatening for he does not know what *life-threatening* means. Even if these dangers were behind lock and key, as they should be, a little child, fired by curiosity, gets into the darndest places. Therefore, he needs powerful verbal as well as physical restraints. When a child tries dangerous adventures and is restrained or punished, *he* understands them to mean he has done wrong: he is not OK. He *has* done wrong, but the assumption *he is not OK* is incorrect. Yet this is how he feels.

Thus his decision "I can be OK if I mind mother" becomes a *fact of conditional love*. A bit of his self-assertion has had to go in order to preserve his life. Parents may try to circumvent the predicament by (1) keeping all dangers out of the child's way, which they should, or (2) explaining everything. The problem with the first solution is that, besides being nearly impossible, it fails to implant firm conditional no's in the child's mind, necessary to his survival. Mother will not be there every moment, and it only takes a second to grab a danger. Besides, the implanted no's become useful prohibitions as the child's tether lengthens. It is not safe to leave home without them. The second solution, explaining everything, is all right after the child has learned language. Before he has adequate words, however, involved explanations may confuse, rather than help. Many of the child's assumptions are made preverbally, most particularly the assumption I'm Not OK— You're OK.

The child himself constructs some of his internal no's, even if they were not spoken or demonstrated by his parents. Transactional Analysts Robert and Mary Goulding write:

We believe that many injunctions were never even given! The child fantasizes, invents, misinterprets, thereby giving himself his own injunctions. When a brother dies, a child may believe his own jealousy of his brother magically caused the death, because the child does not understand pneumonia. Then, in guilt, he may give himself a *Don't Be* injunction. If a beloved father died a child may decide never to be close to anyone again. He gives himself a *Don't Be Close* injunction in an effort to avoid reexperiencing the pain he experienced at his father's

death. In effect he says, "I'll never love again and then
I won't ever have to be hurt again."*

A child is not built in a day, and neither are his decisions,
although one-time traumas, such as the above, *can* produce
certain sudden decisions. Most decisions follow an accumulation of signals or experiences. It takes more than one
mistake by a parent to produce a conclusion in the child.
His early assumptions are tentative and do not become firm
without repeated reinforcement.

A little girl runs up the sidewalk every day to meet her
daddy on his return from work. Every day their greeting
ritual is repeated. He picks her up, kisses her, and tells her
she is his little princess. Then one day he doesn't arrive.
She is disappointed, but still believes in her daddy. The
greeting ritual is restored the next day and continues as ever
for many weeks. Then one day he arrives home angry, for
reasons of his own, and he brushes past her, refusing to
pick her up. She is disappointed again, but still believes in
her daddy. The ritual is restored the following day and
continues as before. Then one day daddy arrives home in-
toxicated. When she rushes to him, he tells her to go away,
grow up! and stop bothering him. Even this behavior may
not produce a decision, but trust begins to erode and is
edged with anxiety. The bad scene is repeated on another
day, and still another day. On x hour of y day of z year, the
little girl's trust topples under the accumulated disappoint-
ments, and she decides: "I will never trust daddy again."
Or "I will never trust daddy$s$ again." Or "I will never trust
men."

The child's trust is tenacious because his need is great.
Therefore, a child can survive many "bad" incidents before
he makes a "get away from" decision. We emphasize this
to put parents' minds at ease. Though it takes one straw to
break a camel's back, there must be a fairly large stack there
already.

In the best of conditions and with the best-meaning par-

*Robert and Mary Goulding, *Changing Lives Through Rede-
cision Therapy,* Brunner Mazel, New York, 1979, pp. 39–40.

ents the child's first assumptions are conditional. Later in childhood the parents' actions and words may communicate unconditional love, but the recordings of early preverbal events are not thereby erased. *If* remains a fulcrum in a person's life, and even though it produces troublesome feelings, it also provides stability, predictability, and safety, providing it does not shift about, as in the case of conflicting double messages, which will be discussed later in this chapter.

Don't Messages

Don't messages are more powerful than *do* messages, even though positive action is often attempted to overcome the negatives. We are indebted to the Gouldings for their clear summary of the kinds of *don't* messages a child internalizes as injunctions. They are the result either of wrong assumptions, as in the case of the boy whose brother died of pneumonia, or of correct interpretations of what mother and father actually said or did. Implicit or explicit, the message is "I will love you if you don't. . . ." State the Gouldings, "Injunctions are messages from the Child ego state of the parents, given out of circumstances of the parents' own pains: unhappiness, anxiety, disappointment, anger, frustration, secret desires."* Few parents are free from painful feelings and the perplexing (to the child) behavior that accompanies them. Therefore, on the basis of repeated "charged" behavior, children make decisions of the *don't* variety:

1. *Don't,* period. This message is given by fearful, overprotective parents, who are unable to give positive affirmation to any of the child's wants, dangerous or not. "Run out and tell Johnny that whatever he's doing, don't." Life is one big NO, paralyzing curiosity and creativity. Both parents and children are care-ful, that is, full of care.

2. *Don't be.* This is the most lethal message, according

*Ibid., pp. 34–35.

to the Gouldings, stating in one way or another, "I wish you had never been born." "What would we ever do without the children?" heard literally, raises a real possibility of life "without the children." The message can be communicated by consistent nonattention to the child, speaking as if he weren't there, or saying, "Remember all the fun we had before the kids came?" What is the child to do with such a statement?

3. *Don't be close*. This decision may grow from loss, the death of a parent or sibling, or cruelty at the hands of parents.

4. *Don't be important*. Belittling a child's accomplishments, shh-ing him every time he speaks before grownups, "who do you think you are?" may lead a child to make this decision.

5. *Don't be a child*. "Daddy's gone; now you must be mother's little man." "Grow up!" And there goes childhood.

6. *Don't grow*. Parents often hate to see their youngest child leave babyhood/childhood/home or enter into the threatening (to them) age of adolescence. "Stay as sweet as you are." "You'll always be Daddy's little girl." Baby talk may persist into adulthood with grown women retaining the name "Tootsie" or "Baby" and grown men being called by the diminutive of their names, Bobby, Jimmie, Chuckie, or "Junior." This is a clue, and not conclusive, for some men break loose and even get to the White House. Little-boy and little-girl names also are used to express endearment. In the South, where parents' names are often passed through several generations, diminutive names are used to make distinctions between generations. *Dallas* has three John Ross Ewings. Father was Jock, son is J.R., and grandson is John Ross. Thinking of *Dallas*, perhaps the "don't grow" message *does* persist whenever a person is not called by his real name, for whatever reason the nickname is used.

7. *Don't succeed*. Father plays chess with his son, and one day son beats him. Father doesn't play chess with him anymore. Perfectionism also frustrates success. "If you can't do it right, don't do it at all."

8. *Don't be you*. According to the Gouldings this "is

most frequently given to the child who is the 'wrong' sex"—
a boy when a girl was wanted, and vice versa. Don't be
you; be my fantasy of you.

9. *Don't be sane and don't be well.* Children who get
strokes for being sick, attention for being "emotionally upset," whose therapists are changed "just when they are getting well," decide the way to get love is to stay the way
they are, sick or upset.

10. *Don't belong.* An immigrant family who talked dis-
paragingly about "Amerikanare" as outlanders, forbade their
children to join Boy Scouts and Girl Scouts or participate
in school sports. The parents did not feel they belonged,
and passed the message on to their children.

11. Other *don't* messages are: Don't trust, don't think,
don't show your feelings, don't have your feelings (you're
not hungry, you're sleepy), and don't enjoy. Also you don't
deserve it, you'll never get it, you'll lose it if you do, you'll
regret it, you'll pay for it, and you have more than you
deserve.

Do Messages

People are generally not aware of the foregoing negative
"secret" injunctions. *Do* messages are in awareness. The
child heard them "in so many words" or inferred them from
what the parents said or did. The child believes he can be
OK *if* he can do one or more of the following:

1. Be perfect. "What's the *B* for?" asks father of son
whose report card shows five A's and one B.

2. Be best. "Winning isn't everything, but losing isn't
anything."

3. Try hard. "The boy simply isn't performing up to his
potential."

4. Please me. "Unless you do the things that please me,
I'm not going to like you."

5. Hurry up. "The early bird catches the worm."

6. Be strong (and don't show your feelings).

When a person cannot succeed in these positive attempts, the earlier *don't* decisions are confirmed. I can't be perfect; therefore, I won't make it. I can't be best; therefore, I won't be important. I can't try any harder; therefore, I won't be well. I can't please you; therefore, I won't be me, or I won't be, period. I can't hurry any faster; therefore, I won't grow up. I can't be strong and not show my feelings; therefore, I won't have any feelings.

Conflicting Double Messages

Children thrive when "what to do" messages are consistent and harmonious. This is not always the case. However well-intentioned parents are, they frequently communicate mixed messages that confuse the child.

We receive signals from six primary sources: Mother's (1) Parent, (2) Adult, (3) Child, and Father's (4) Parent, (5) Adult, and (6) Child. (Figure 2.) We internalize messages from these six sources by recording them in our own Parent, where they remain the rest of our lives. The most potent messages are the parents' feelings, those things they said and did when *their* Child was hooked.

That all six sources are at all times in harmony is as unlikely as a unanimous vote in the UN. Essential to our understanding of disharmony is that there often is a distinct conflict of interest among the six sources. Parents are not so much misunderstood as understood all too well. Henry Kissinger stated, "The diplomat believes that an international conflict derives from misunderstanding. Therefore he seeks a verbal formula to overcome it. The statesman believes that conflict derives from a difference of interest and confrontation positions. Therefore he tries to change the realities on the ground."*

We cannot change the "realities on the ground," the recorded communications from our three-part mother and our three-part father. Though we hold to the belief that "my parents meant well," which most parents do, it is essential

Time, April 1, 1974, p. 26.

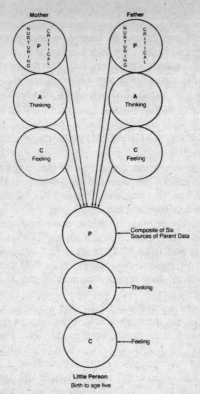

Figure 2
Six Sources of Parent Data

we see the double messages for what they were and are: *conflict*. Children see and experience communications from all three parts of the personality in both parents: Parent nurturing and criticizing, Child feeling, and Adult problem solving. Father had his set of variables. Mother had hers. They had their own internal conflicts, and each may have disagreed with the other. All of this mixed externality was recorded in the little person's Parent, a cauldron of human need and hope. From all this he has to choose. Who was right? What was right?

The parents' conflict becomes the child's conflict, *and* confusion. Eager to please, the child attempts to follow both the instructions of the parents and the feelings they express, even if there is discord. If, when he does his very best, he is still wrong, he despairs in the double bind, "Damned if you do, and damned if you don't." As a little person, he has neither the power nor understanding to confront the conflict, and assumes it is his own fault. By examining the P-A-C of our parents we can return the conflict to the place it belongs, then choose which Parent messages to live by and which set of values enhances our lives in the present. As grownups we no longer need our parents for *survival*. When the messages were recorded, we did.

We Are Not Wholly Determined

Our assumptions about the external world, most significantly, mother and father, became a part of us. But only a part. We also have a Child and an Adult, and in these two parts of our personality lies our capacity for feeling, novelty, and creative thinking. The Child has its own desires and intentions, and the Adult has made choices based on signals not only from the Parent but also from the Child and from the Adult's appraisal of incoming data from the outside world. Parent messages which may have evoked automatic child responses lose their "knee-jerk" quality once we have become aware of them, thereby increasing the number of neuronal connections or associations. We are not wholly determined, and therein lies our hope for change.*

Tournier tells of a patient who related to him her experience with another therapist, a psychoanalyst:

> My psychoanalyst's moral neutrality was a great help to me in relieving me of the weight of formalism that had been crushing me. But I remember the no less lively feeling of liberation I had one day when I was talking with you, when I realized once more that I was personally

*See "Does Man Have a Free Will?," *I'm OK—You're OK*, pp. 86–88.

responsible for an act for which the psychoanalyst had always said I was not responsible. It was as if a road out of my illness was being opened out in front of me. You see, as long as I was not responsible for anything, there was nothing I could do to help myself get out of it. It was as if I was locked into it by its very inevitableness!*

A man working his way out of a depression discovered a great part of his difficulty had roots in the conflicting Parent messages: (1) always be best and (2) always be nice. His attempt to be both had driven him into a corner, and all exits seemed blocked. The competitive spirit that drove him was continually at war with the unacceptable aggressive spirit required to make it: Nice people are not aggressive. He was burdened with the painful certainty that, no matter what he did, it wouldn't be right.

Though an examination of the conflicting Parent messages helped him recognize the source of some of his difficulty, *the most liberating discovery was that he, too, had participated in his choices*. He said, "I don't want to be treated like a bouncing ball. There is more to me than that. I enjoyed being best. They wanted things for me but I also wanted things for myself. I made decisions and I also made mistakes." He said it was more demeaning to believe he was only a mechanism caught in a cause-and-effect series of events than to acknowledge his complicity in the decisions that had led him to where he was. Accepting responsibility for at least a part of the past made it possible to have power over the future. Although the various *do* and *don't* messages we have described are useful clues to help us change, they are not conclusive. At each juncture of life we have had choices to make, regardless of what our parents told us or showed us. We have said both *yes* and *no*.

We become hopelessly entangled in unhelpful formulations if we attempt a percentage analysis of how much of our behavior is determined and how much is free. If we go *only* with determinism, we come to the awful conclusion

*Paul Tournier, *The Person Reborn*, Harper & Row, New York, 1966, p. 121.

there is nothing we can do. We need anticipate neither praise nor blame. It couldn't have happened otherwise. Life, so understood, becomes mindless, terrifying, and without hope. If, on the other hand, we discount deterministic factors altogether, we are also deluded, and can only conclude that everything about us is our own fault. Then, instead of the helplessness of the determinist, we have overwhelming guilt, which, unrelieved, can cut the nerve of effort so cleanly that we give up our efforts to change and merely exist.

Therefore, when we examine the ifs we live by, we should do so with a generous spirit, toward both ourselves and our parents. They had their reasons, their ifs, their needs, fears, and complexities. If we adopt a wholly negative attitude toward the Parent we fail to recognize the positive life-preserving and life-enhancing gifts we received from our parents, if, in fact, we did.

Also, bad luck must be factored into the question. When we were little were our parents the victims of catastrophe, poverty, disease? What did we make of it? What did they do about it? How is misfortune internalized in our Parent? The uncontrollable must be taken into account, not only in the past, but also in the present. Did your home blow away in a tornado? Was your son killed in Vietnam? Are you depressed because you have lost your job in a plant layoff? Are you a victim of criminal assault? There are aspects of our lives over which we have little, if any, control. That was true also for our parents even though we, as little children, saw them as magic and all-powerful.

As our problems are not all our own doing, neither is our good fortune. A "self-made" man may look over his ledger sheets, his factories and fields and claim that it was because he got up at 6 A.M. every day and toiled without ceasing that he succeeded in life. He may further judge the poor because they are lazy or unimaginative. The truth is there are millions who get up at 6 A.M. and toil without ceasing—looking for water and wood and a morsel to eat—and they have little to show for it, perhaps a cardboard hut, a few utensils and a little huddle of bewildered children with sad eyes and swollen bellies. *They* were born in Bangladesh, not in Boston. There are many other givens about which we have absolutely nothing to say. Does it make a difference that we are male or female? Black or white, or a mixture of both? That our parents were Jewish or Muslim or Christian or none of the above? If we are legitimate or not? If we were born blind or deaf?

Difficult givens weigh heavy on us. But there is more yet to *get* in the novel present and future. The good news is that we can think! Thinking itself produces novelty. We not only can consider the past but can look to the future. We can put ourselves, our parents, and our children in historic perspective, seeing everyone as having had a part in creative causation. We cannot control everything but we can control some things. If we are a part of the problem, we can also be a part of the answer. This is the creative challenge of being, feeling, and staying OK.

Examining Our Parents' P-A-C

At one time in my life, faced with a difficult choice, I drew P-A-C diagrams of my parents, seeking information about what my mother and father would have done, and what contribution to the subject came from the Parent, Adult, and Child of each. There were positive instructions as well as cautions, those same kinds of "beware" messages parents give their children to protect them. Apart from discovering new information about the content of my Parent, the most significant insight I derived was that *they said a lot of things* about a lot of subjects throughout my childhood and later in life. They also *did* a lot of things. Could any one simple statement summarize all of that, what Willa Cather's character Jim Burden called "my own infinitesimal past"? Would you like a few-word summary to represent everything you have said to your children? Would it be accurate?

A variation of the P-A-C diagram is to draw the Parent, Adult, and Child as cylinders, adding a dimension of quantity. Parents who say little to their children, who do not participate in their lives, or are not around, do not leave a long cylinder of information to examine. The more information in the Parent the more we have to examine, not only for conflict, but also for useful information about how to live. Analyzing this information may help us in day-to-day decisions—taking a different job, buying a house, getting married, taking a stand on a moral issue. What would dad's Parent say? What would his Child feel? What would his Adult decide to do? What about mom's Parent, Adult, Child? Then, what about yours?

Is It Wrong to Have Expectations of Children?

Thus far we have been dealing with destructive, impossible, internalized *assumptions* of what the child must do or not do to be loved. The child himself has made these decisions, based on his own interpretation of reality in a state of dependency and need.

Parents may well wonder what they *can* say or expect or require that will build happy children, secure in self-esteem and rewarded by mastery. We do not believe it is wrong to have expectations of children, provided they are clear and based in reality, which includes the needs and abilities of the child. To expect nothing is a form of discounting, a way of saying "no point in challenging you," leading the child to assume he doesn't have what it takes. Mastery is rewarding in and of itself. The baby figures out how to retrieve a rolling ball. A child learns to open the door by himself or to print his name. His parents may have helped him by showing him how, but once the task is mastered, the child wants to do it himself. A little boy, held up to the light switch and allowed to turn the lights on and off, was asked, "What makes the lights go on?" *"I* do," he said proudly.

Much of the child's assumption about what to do and what to master is derived from observing his parents. Children want to do what their parents do. If a parent plays the piano, the child will want to, even if his first efforts are tuneless and banging. "Do as I do" is clearly a potent message. "Do as I say" is also needed. Language is uniquely human and makes thinking possible. We cannot, for instance, show a child how to behave on the playground (we will not always be there with him). But we can *tell* him. Particularly potent is the message wherein saying and doing agree.

Jacqui Schiff, a pioneer in treating adolescent schizophrenia, stresses the importance of three messages parents should give children: (1) You can solve problems. (2) You can think. (3) You can do things. She states:

> A frequent mistake in parenting occurs when the children are not offered enough "what to do" messages. Almost inevitably children will incorporate "don't" messages. . . . A good rule to practice is, whenever children are told what not to do, they should also be told what to do. This will build their confidence in their own OK-ness and capacity to solve problems, will establish a structure for testing limits, and will teach thinking.*

Happy Achievers

Achievement that brings joy to the child grows from unconditional acceptance before the act, and not the other way around. Knowing he is loved, he will want to please his "lovers," to "show and tell," to bring home reports of his day in the world. He is especially happy if his behavior brings the reward of parental stroking.

Even if the child has assumed a conditional "I can be OK, if" I finish my assignment, do my chores, behave properly, he is happy if the "promised" stroking is delivered. The contract then is complete. "I made you proud of me" is thus experienced as another form of mastery.

*Jacqui Schiff, *Cathexis Reader*, Harper & Row, New York, 1975, pp. 33, 34.

Unhappy Achievers

When children do what is expected of them, they feel betrayed if stroking is withheld. This is done in a variety of ways and for a number of reasons the parent may feel are "good":

1. Stroking is withheld so "you won't get a swelled head." Because the child receives no stroking he does not learn to accept it later in life, nor does he learn to say "thank you" graciously. In his discomfort he says, in Berne's laconic expression, "Shucks, 'twarn't nothing," knowing full well it *was*.

2. "Don't rest on your laurels." Some parents withhold praise, pushing the carrot still further out as an incentive for greater achievement. The child goes through life climbing topless mountains and feeling the despair of bottomless pits, because the anticipated reward never comes. He doesn't stop trying, but his anger and frustration build until he is consumed by them, often to the point of hostility.

3. Achievements are not understood, and thus discounted. John brings home a trophy for winning a high-school debate on the best way to ease the international trade imbalance. He overhears his mother tell a friend, "John always was a good talker," with no understanding of his achievement at grasping this complex subject at such a young age.

4. You didn't do it right (my way). A man works years to become a medical doctor, then specializes in psychiatry. "Do you still practice medicine?" his mother asks. It's great you became a doctor, but did you have to become a psychiatrist? The Parent message here is, "Don't be you; be my fantasy of you." My son, the surgeon.

5. It isn't perfect. Susan and Jennie work several days to redecorate their room, including a new paint job. On being called in to examine their finished product, father looks it over as they await his praise. "You missed a spot up there on the ceiling" is his only comment.

6. Strokes are stolen. A young man receives "the most

outstanding student award" and great applause from the audience. After the ceremony his mother says, "You see, I have prayed for you all my life. You must give God all the glory." Does God *need* all that glory? The young man needs at least a little of it. What is communicated is that mother needs the glory. Gratitude is genuinely expressed only when it is not demanded. Children learn to say "thank you" by hearing parents say "thank you."

7. Strokes are tarnished. Gold stamps from peer admirers or other strangers to the family turn to brass as a parent downplays, "What do *they* know about anything, those people." Or "It is nice you did so well at Siwash College. If only you had gone to Harvard like your cousin Fred."

8. Accomplishment is belittled. Joseph works his way through college, and despite a full-time job, manages to win a scholarship to Oxford, then proceeds to be named a teaching assistant in cultural anthropology at a small New England college. Says his father, "Imagine little Joey Muldoon, back there with all those high-fallutin' folks. My goodness. Did you hear about George Wilson, just been made assistant manager at Sears. Now *there's* a job for you!"

9. You weren't best. "The silver medal is very nice, but with a little more effort you would have had the gold. Maybe next time."

You can be OK, if what? There is no pleasing some parents or the Parent in some people's heads. Life for eternal strivers is a fruitless struggle to get something that isn't there. The insight that can relieve the pressure is that some parents' needs were so great they were not able to reward their children. Parental strokes (external and internal) are sweet, probably the sweetest, but in their absence we can look elsewhere for rewards—in our daily relationships, from our friends, from our own realization that *we did a good job*. We did our best, and our best is good.

We started this chapter with a statement by Dr. Kübler-Ross, who implied there could be another way for parents to raise children, the way of unconditional love. We shall return to this subject in Chapter 14, "Building Children." Before we attempt an answer to the significant question,

"What is good parenting?" it is essential that we know a great deal more about ourselves. In the next chapter we will show how the past "replays in the present," in fact, replaces the present by an ongoing "inward talk with ourselves," an old dialogue that robs us of the awareness of the persons around us, the persons we so desperately need to stay OK, and also the persons who need us, most assuredly our children.

3

The Internal Dialogue

Searching for something as simple as a dialogue in the brain's ten trillion synaptic connections is like looking for two bees saying "good morning" in a newly-hung swarm. Yet it is there, an ongoing inward talk made up of recordings of the thousands of exchanges between you and your parents, verbal and nonverbal, both comforting and castigating, self-justifying and self-defeating. The dialogue also is dated and most often plays just below the level of awareness, like a radio with the volume set low. When we *do* become aware of it and, in fact, enter into it, we slip from the here and now into a past reality and temporarily leave whomever we're with. It is particularly disruptive to relationships if we depart in the middle of a conversation. Staying OK with people generally means staying around. Understanding how the internal dialogue absents us is essential, therefore, to maintaining complementary transactions, which will be described in this chapter.

What is the nature of our recorded internal talking? Our earliest "conversations" as infants were sights and sounds. The look on mother's face and the tone of her voice were primary communicators long before words were understood. Touch, too, was a primary communicator. In fact, until recent years the tactile, skin-on-skin stimulation between mother and child has been emphasized as the main form of stroking experienced by the newborn. We now know that all sensory systems are "go" at birth, and the newborn sees and hears acutely in the bonding process between mother and child immediately after birth.

When mother smiles, the memory is stored. How we made mother smile was our contribution to the dialogue. It is an often-repeated "conversation" because mother's smile, signaling the arrival of food or stroking, meant survival. In speaking of the inner dialogue, therefore, we refer not only to words but to the total interplay of visual and auditory sensations we once felt and *recorded*. These sensations included words, but the earliest and most deterministic recordings were preverbal. These recordings replay in the present. When your beloved frowns at you over his oatmeal, *your* feelings come not only from a present disapproving look but from all the disapproving looks or nonsmiling events of your life, with a contribution, perhaps, from your oatmeal data bank: cold, lumpy, sticky, daily. Your brain replays the old exchange: Parent-like frown registers; Child feelings follow.

This "oatmeal" scene reminds us of one of our favorite cartoons. The setting is the dinner table. A mean-faced father and a mean-faced mother, along with a mean-faced big sister, are all glaring at shame-faced little brother. Says father, "You're the only person in the world I know who makes a crunchy sound eating whipped cream." Exchanges like that, mean faces and all, are recorded. Their replay is what we mean by the internal dialogue.

When the internal dialogue replays in the present, the Child and Parent carry on as they once did, the Parent ten feet tall and the Child two feet tall. An indication that such inner talk is recorded is that we do in fact talk to ourselves or inadvertently spit out phrases or words that are hurled into our awareness in mutters, self-reproaches, and epithets: Stupid! Now you've done it! Idiot!

Have you ever been talking to yourself inside your car as you waited for a light to change and then suddenly become aware the driver of the car alongside you was looking at you? What part of you was talking? What part became aware you were being observed?

Willie Stark's driver in *All the King's Men* regularly sputtered "B-b-b-b-as-tuds, bas-tuds, bas-tuds" as he caromed his boss's big Cadillac through the traffic of Mason City. Who was talking? And to whom? Whether we spit epithets outward, as Willie's driver did, or inward, as we often do when we hear a voice, our own, giving sound to an accusation, such as *"Now* you've done it!" the origin is the old internal dialogue.

Sometimes the internal talk might better be likened to the babble of voices at a political convention. The words aren't clear, but the images are: placards printed CONNECT-ICUT, TEXAS, WASHINGTON, PUERTO RICO, CALIFORNIA. We get flashes of scenes and sounds from first grade, the state fair, Sunday school, the dentist's office, first memories. Sights, sounds, images, and smells in the present trigger old exchanges, sometimes glorious, sometimes ghastly, sometimes just vaguely depressing.

The internal dialogue can best be understood as a shift of awareness from the here and now (Adult perception) to the there and then (the old setting of the original parent-child dialogue).

On occasion we hear internal applause. Good boy! Good girl! Our parents' compliments certainly weren't lost on us. Especially cherished, they were recorded on primary memory circuits and reinforced every time we behaved in such a way that they would say them again.

Because, however, we were little, dependent, untrained, and unsocialized, and because we crunched our whipped cream, much parental response was correcting, *assumed* to be blaming, if not in fact blaming, and negative: Bad boy! Naughty girl! For many children growing up was one humiliation after another: "Not *those* socks," "Pipe down, sit up, bend over." What does "Your face is dirty" mean to a two-year-old boy? Or "You're not old enough to drink coffee!" Is the child's age his fault? He may assume so. Thus, I'm not OK.

Three centuries ago Pascal wrote, "Man is so made that by continually telling him he is a fool, he believes it, and by continually telling it to himself he makes himself believe it. For man holds an inward talk with his self alone, which it behoves [sic] him to regulate well."*

Our childhood shamings and blamings are far worse than

*Blaise Pascal, *Pensées*, #535, p. 144.

any tirade that can be delivered to us in the present. *We believe that no one can hurt us, more specifically hurt our feelings, unless they are able to hook our Parent, which then accuses us internally.* Eleanor Roosevelt said, "No one can make you feel inferior without your consent." That is, without your Parent's consent. We have unique vulnerabilities, unique histories, and a unique Parent.

This explains why some criticisms run off us like water off a duck's back and other criticisms cut us to the heart. If you are self-conscious about your nose, all it takes to make you want to flee the scene is someone staring at it in fascination. Long noses run in my family, physiognomically, not functionally, speaking. Heidi, at age ten, asked me, "Mother, did everyone have long noses in your era?" In my family noses are OK, so the remark cracked me up. I did give *era* a second thought, having something to do with *ancient,* and went to the mirror to check for wrinkles. In Tom's family noses were an issue, though I think his nose is perfectly fine on his handsome face. He thinks it is too small, hearing the tape roll, "Son, why is your nose so small?" My mother thought being tall was better than being short, that tallness meant one had been well-nourished and well-mothered. She probably also took into account the fact that tall people, more often than short people, communicate power and leadership. Though shorter than I, and not unaware of genetics, she nonetheless said to me once when I was a grown woman, "I don't know why you are so short. You were so tall when you were little." We all have our "other voices, other rooms." The internal dialogue is unique, bathroom-personal, and ready to remove us from the present even if we're in the middle of a conversation.

One of the most helpful features of TA is that its circle symbols can be used to diagram conversations, allowing us to "see" what we say and what part of us said it. We can also diagram what happens when the internal dialogue takes over and removes us from the scene. At this point a brief review of transactions is useful.

Talking Pictures: Transactional Diagrams

When two people are talking there are six people present: the Parent, Adult, and Child of each. The basic unit of conversation is the transaction: I say or do something to you, and you say or do something back. The purpose of Transactional Analysis is to determine which part of me, Parent, Adult, or Child, produced the stimulus and which part of you responded. Because we can visualize a transaction on the diagram, two rules of communication may be stated in the following way:

1. *When vectors of stimulus and response are parallel on the diagram, the transaction is complementary and theoretically can go on forever.*

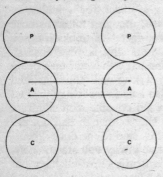

Figure 3a
A-A Complementary
     Transaction

Stimulus: "What are you doing after lunch?"
Response: "I'm going to be working on an agenda for the board meeting."

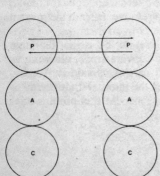

Figure 3b
P-P Complementary
     Transaction

Stimulus: "His wife works, you know."
Response: "Oh, *that* explains it!"

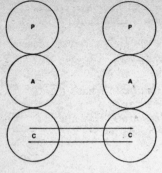

Figure 3c
C-C Complementary
   Transaction

Stimulus: "You sure are a lot
   of fun to be around."
Response: "I'd like to get
   myself around you more
   often."

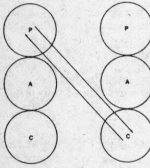

Figure 3d
P-C Complementary
   Transaction

Stimulus: "You sure know how
   to louse things up, Potts."
Response: "I'm sorry, sir."

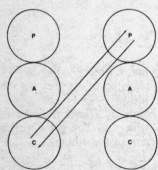

Figure 3e
C-P Complementary
   Transaction

Stimulus: "Don't get near me.
   I have this whole report to
   finish by noon. Go have
   coffee with everybody
   else." (Poor me.)
Response: "Why do you
   always leave things to the
   last minute?"

2. *When vectors of stimulus and response cross each other on the transactional diagram, communication stops.*

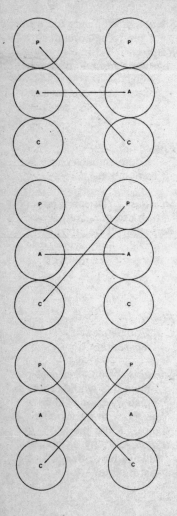

Figure 4a

Stimulus: "What's the day today?"
Response: "Day after yesterday."

Figure 4b

Stimulus: "I'm full."
Response: "Clean your plate!"

Figure 4c

Stimulus: "Mary, will you clean up this office. It's filthy!"
Response: "What's the matter with you? You got a broken arm or something?"

Figure 4
Examples of Crossed Transactions

We communicate not only with words but with body language: gestures, facial expressions, tone of voice, and rapidity of speech.

Stimulus: "You doing anything important?"
Response: "Whatta *you* think?"

This could be either a complementary or crossed transaction depending on what the person is doing: calling the White House, making love, finding a fuse box, or petting the cat. Also significant is how well the persons know each other and whether the tone of voice communicates humor, mockery, silliness, or sternness.

Many transactional configurations are possible. For other transactions, including duplex transactions, where communication is taking place at two levels at the same time, see *I'm OK—You're OK,* pages 89–122.

Another type of transaction is the *cutting-out* transaction. It is also called the *discounting* transaction because the person who is "cut out" feels discounted, or, literally, "I don't count." This is a transaction wherein the internal dialogue interrupts and removes us from the person we are with.

Discounting

Nothing is more unsettling than discovering the person you are talking to isn't listening. Worse yet is when you respond stupidly because *you* haven't been listening. A hairdresser reported, "This woman I was working on was talking away and among other things she told me was that her father had died, and I blurted out, 'Fantastic!' She gave me this horrible look and said, 'You don't listen to a thing I say.' Why do I do that?"

Joe meets Mac, an old acquaintance, in front of the laundromat one Saturday morning (Figure 5). Joe says, "Hi, Mac," and Mac says, "Hi, Joe." "You're looking good." "Not bad yourself." These exchanges are represented by Vectors 1 and 2, Adult-Adult. They are designated *Adult* because they are socially-agreed-upon ritual exchanges that

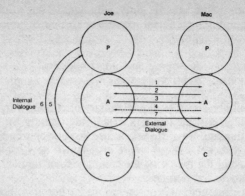

Figure 5
The Discounting Transaction

get a conversation going. When someone asks, "What's new?" the complementary response is not a detailed account of every new thing that has happened since the last encounter. The anticipated response is something on the order of "Oh, not much, what's new with you?" We ease into substance. During the ritual we make a fast computation of how far we will go with the conversation, depending on tone of voice, speed of delivery, facial expression. If someone is obviously "on the run" we probably will decide against telling that person the latest complication in our love life. Thus ritual greetings serve a purpose of predicting. They also are a stroke exchange. If we receive no greeting at all, we feel ignored, discounted, unloved.

Then Joe asks, "Been doing any traveling lately?" (Vector 3.) Mac answers: "As a matter of fact we have. This summer we took the kids to Europe, last chance before they all fly the coop, even got to Cairo and rode camels up to the pyramids . . . and finally ended up in Scotland at my father's ancestral home, and . . ."

At some point in Mac's travelogue (Vector 4), Joe cuts out (Vector 5). The likelihood is that his departure from the here and now originates in some feeling of dis-ease or anxiety in the Child. Or he may be bored, which also is an unpleasant feeling. He therefore turns his attention from his friend to himself. He becomes *self*-conscious. The "make Mother smile" engram in his brain is firing fast and he shoots up a "felt" question, *How'm I doing? How'm I doing, Ma . . . me a good guy who is friendly and asks people about themselves . . . and being outgoing and interested in others. . . .*

Then, while Mac is talking about his travels, which for all Joe knows might include some absolute catastrophes, Joe listens for the Parent reply (Vector 6). Sometimes the reply is positive: *That's my boy. That's it, son, ask him some more questions, be interested* (Joe's freeze-dried smile is in place all the while) *and remember his children's names. . . .* And sometimes negative: *What a place to get caught . . . the laundromat. . . . What kind of a man does the laundry . . . oh, well, stand up tall . . . and look cool . . . RELAX!!! . . . You sure his name is Mac?*

At last, after a series of unconsciously spoken *greats* and *wows* and *wonderfuls,* Joe comes back to the here and now and says to Mac, "That's really terrific, uh, Mac. (Vector 7). By the way, you been doing any traveling lately?" What happens next depends on the nature of their friendship. If Mac cares about Joe he may say, "Hey, something bugging you, Joe? You haven't heard a thing I said?" If not, he will likely walk away sore, forget his wash, or tell Joe to get lost.

The Parent-Child dialogue is all that Joe is aware of during the time Mac is talking. He cannot listen to his Parent and Joe at the same time. When the internal dialogue is running, the Adult is turned off. It is as if there is a switch in the head with two settings: playback and compute. We can only do one thing at a time.

Playing old tapes and computing incoming data are mutually exclusive, even though it is possible for some people to switch back and forth rapidly. It takes a split-second pause to get the Adult working again after the Parent has played its piece. A certain political figure, known to have a sizable and frequently used library of Parent tapes, was speaking about colleges. His Adult was relating certain fiscal problems, which presumably caused the pressure to build sufficiently so that he switched to Parent with an emphatic "It's high time that..." (clichés are Parent and used to underscore). Then there was a short but perceptible pause while he got back to what he was saying. He had gone somewhere else and had "lost his place."

Some people cut out in the middle of a conversation because they are "sick with worry." It is as if they had to leave the room to go lie down. Kierkegaard called the "self-tormented person an absentee, an enfeebled person." Have you ever said, "I'm not myself today"? If not yourself, then who? Another phrase that describes our "absenteeism" is "I'm beside myself." Who is *myself* and who is standing beside? Where do we go when we are absent? People who cut out go somewhere and that somewhere is a past reality recorded in the original situation of childhood. The past becomes, *is*, the present and is not only recalled but relived. *We are there,* and, depending on our unique history, we experience torment, fear, a desperate need to feel significant or to live up to those conditions that we once decided must be met in order to be OK.

Good Guys and Sweethearts

Among the most-tormented absentees are Good Guys and Sweethearts.* Their behavior is one of the best examples of how the internal dialogue works. A Good Guy (male) or Sweetheart (female) is *a parent-dominated person with a depressed Child; who is depressed because of stroke deprivation; who is deprived of strokes because of frequent unawareness or nonregistry of external stimuli; and who is unaware because Adult function is persistently preempted by the internal Parent-Child dialogue*.

Though the names given these basically well-meaning people may seem amusing, their lives are filled with sadness. They are often depressed because they are unaware of the people in their lives. Because their awareness is

*Amy Harris, "Good Guys and Sweethearts," *Transactional Analysis Journal*, January 1972.

constantly inward, replaying old tapes of *shoulds, shouldn't haves, musts,* and *or elses,* their eyes do not see the smiles of other people, their ears do not hear praise, and their spirits are dying from stroke starvation.

Even so, the Good Guy (hereafter used in most instances to refer to both men and women) keeps trying and sets up as many transactions as possible to gain approval, which he seldom feels he gets. He may have ninety-nine people telling him he's great, but he spends all of his energy attempting to get a compliment, even a crumb, from that one aloof person who doesn't seem to like him. He wears a sweatshirt that on the front reads *How'm I doing?* and on the back *Try harder.* He has no standard of what is *enough.* One hundred per cent is good for starters.

The Good Guy's continual *How'm I doing?* makes it impossible for him to maintain an authentic query of "How are you doing?" He may ask this of another person (he *does* know good manners) as Joe did, but the moment the other person begins his response he cuts out to handle his internal agenda. Therefore, he continually discounts others, who end up not thinking of him as a good guy at all, thwarting all his elaborate efforts to get their esteem.

The Good Guy is not with the person he's with. There is gratification only if there is an important third party looking on: Mom and Dad, or some other significant authority, either present or remembered. What is said to another frequently is a ricochet transaction designed to impress someone else in the room. If you are a Good Guy, you may feel the frustration of not having a third party looking on and approving in a situation such as walking down Park Avenue in New York City and meeting a genuine VIP, who happens to actually know you and calls you by name. And no one else is along. What dreadful anguish that no one was there to observe. What a waste! It would almost have been better if it hadn't happened at all. To whom can you tell such an unlikely story, as fishy as "the big one that got away"?

Good Guys can't enjoy the flowers and trees at the family picnic and keep the conversation going with "If only Henry and Henrietta were here." Good Guys can't enjoy the sunset because they are so busy taking pictures of it to show the folks back home. (Good Guys wear two Nikons and a zoom lens. Sweethearts carry Instamatics.) The here-and-now is thus preempted by the there-and-then (Parent comparisons) or the if-and-when (Child wishes).

Good Guys have many people in bed with them for approval of their sexual performance: the guys at the poker club, the women at the Jazzercise class, the village priest, or the members of their therapy group; sometimes even Mom and Dad and Aunt Matilda. The Good Guy wears his sweatshirt to bed.

There are a number of ways to spot a Good Guy. The following are useful tools for self-examination:

Good Guys Can't Remember Jokes and Names

You go to a party and there are two solid hours of joke telling and the next day you can't remember one. That is because while the joke is being told you are busy trying to remember the one you are going to tell next before someone else starts in. This is in response to the Parent reminder: *Be the life of the party.* There is a great deal of discomfort switching back and forth: tuning in the Adult intermittently to hear the joke that is being told, hoping you can remember it, and then back to your own joke catalogue. Good Guys forget punch lines.

Also, Good Guys have trouble with introductions. You are being introduced to Susie Smith and you say, "Hi, Susie. . . ." *Names are important, remember hers, show her how responsive and attentive you are* . . . and a split second later your mind goes blank. Or at the very moment someone's name is being stated in the course of the introduction, the Parent booms, DON'T FORGET HER NAME, drowning it out.

Push-Button People

The phone rings. Will we serve on the clean-up committee for the school bazaar? "I'll be glad to," we say cheerfully, even though we are already weeks behind on the fifteen other commitments we took on in the same automatic way. Good Guys and Sweethearts can't say no. They are afraid to turn down an invitation to a party they don't want to go to because they are afraid that if they do they will not be asked again to go to a party they don't want to go to.

The mother of fifteen-year-old pregnant-out-of-wedlock Mary wrings her hands in unbelieving despair: "I can't understand what happened. Mary has always been such a good girl. She has always done just as we said. She has been so easy to mold. She has never talked back to us. She has never said *no*." Good Guys and Sweethearts were never given permission to discriminate. It is therefore important to please everybody. Don't think. Don't question. Therefore, whether they want to or not, they adapt to the needs of every person on earth as well as their panting partners in the back seats at drive-ins.

If You Can't Say Something Good, Don't Say Anything at All

A Good Guy does not have permission to say anything bad. If one were to draw a horizontal number line, with a zero in the middle, and all the plus numbers to the right, and all the minus numbers to the left, one would find that the Good Guy's vocabulary must always fit on the plus side. Therefore, verbal resources are impoverished 50 per cent. The only way to make distinctions is by the use of superlatives. Every party he goes to is a good party. If he indeed goes to a good party, the only way to distinguish it from all the other good parties is to say it was a *really* good party, or a *really, really* good party. Other Good Guy words are: very, great, super, best friend, very best friend, the most, the mostest. Good Guys and Sweethearts struggle with letter sign-offs. Instead of *Love*, which is direct and expressive, they write *All my love* or *With all my love* or *Lovingly* or *Most lovingly*. When they write to their parents it is not enough to say *Dear Mom and Dad;* instead it becomes *Dearest Mom and Dad*. Thus Mom and Dad become one of many sets of parents, which is not far from the truth.

Good Guys surround themselves with Parent-dominated people.

Pressure

Some Good Guys have a unique style of letter writing. They underline words, sometimes whole sentences. If a whole sentence is underlined certain words in it must be double-underlined. Or triple, sometimes. Or they use stars, and double stars. Or little black boxes. Or rows of exclamation points. *I really mean it; don't I?* If you turn the paper over, you may see how much pressure the Good Guy is under. The lines used in the underlining nearly come through the page. *How'm I doing? Harder, harder!*

Pressure is the body language of de*press*ion or re*pression*. A Good Guy has a knot on the third finger where he holds his pencil. If Good Guys smoke they inhale clear down to their toes. Or they bite their fingernails. These activities cut back or press down or thwart their need to retaliate, for retaliation is not permitted. After all, it was assumed and recorded, "You Can Be OK, *If* You Are Good." Therefore, the only permissible response to adverse people (Parents whom they seek out) is to *placate*. It is as if Good Guys spend their life locked in a cage with an enormous tiger, their Parent, and all they know to do is walk backward, saying, "Nice pussy, pussy, pussy." With the Child's eyes at all times on the tiger Parent, and with total preoccupation with the Parent-Child dialogue, the Adult is disengaged. (Anyone else can see the tiger is fifty years old, toothless and slowing down. Also the lock on the cage has grown rusty. Escape is possible.) The Good Guy does not see what may be obvious to others because his seeing apparatus, the Adult, is not working for him.

His Child, however, is busy filling his emotional trading-stamp book: one stamp for every lap around the cage. He cashes in every so often for free, self-destructive prizes (free of guilt, that is; I have earned this misery and am entitled to it): headaches, ulcers, sleeplessness, or even thoughts of suicide. The guilt his goodness has provoked in so many people (because he invited them to use him and they obliged) results in many floral tributes at his untimely funeral along with the Resolutions in Memoriam duly noted in the minutes of the fifty-five organizations in which he served faithfully, if not effectively. His epitaph is "Pardon me for not getting up."

Occasionally the Good Guy asserts himself by spewing righteous indignation at some vague, abstract enemy that can't strike back—society, the world nowadays, or government bureaucracy. Sometimes he displaces his anger and hurts his children when they are little and can't fight back. His rare blow-ups discharge the build-up of anger inside, which on occasion is expressed, to "everyone's astonishment," in physical violence. Generally, however, he does his best to hide it: *You Can Be OK If You Are Nice.* Therefore, he works all the time at being a *good* guy. He aims to please. He carries his own luggage because he is worried what the Sky Cap will think if his tip isn't right. Or cleans up the house before the housekeeper comes. Or goes to a doctor when deathly ill and says in response to "How are you feeling today?," "Fine, thank you." He tends to do everything himself. He has difficulty asking for help. He doesn't want to be a bother.

Are Bad Guys Better?

The desirable alternative to a Good Guy is not a Bad Guy but an OK Person. A few comparisons may clarify the difference. Good Guys live much of the time in the past; OK People live in the present. Good Guys operate in accordance with an unexamined Parent standard of goodness; OK People live by an updated standard of goodness, developed by the Adult, which may accept or reject Parent standards in the light of new data and an awareness of the novel present. Good Guys tend to respond automatically; OK people think before they respond. Good Guys are predictable; OK People are surprising. Good Guys are useful; OK People, though they, too, may be useful, are also enjoyable. Good Guys smile a lot; OK People laugh and cry as well as smile.

Change Is Possible

The prognosis for Good Guys is generally good because the many social techniques they have learned to please the Parent can be turned to stroke-producing and constructive purposes with real people in the here and now. Once the preempting internal Parent-Child dialogue is tuned out (though it can never be erased), total computer capacity can be given to awareness of others in every transaction. They can learn to *be with* people and to stay with them. The once onerous load of responsibility can be changed to respondability. Love, once a blurred and fearful imperative—*You should love everybody!*—becomes transformed to the ability to see another person's Child.

A cured Good Guy does not necessarily stop being good; but he may choose where he invests his goodness. His Child intuitively knows it is impossible to please everybody, but in the past he has not dared refuse anybody nor known how to discriminate. Once his Adult is emancipated he is free to compute the thousands of signals people send out, and, on the basis of this heretofore blocked-out data, he can predict which people are trustworthy and which people are not. Therefore he can modify his behavior and choose where to invest his life. His choices may involve some risk, but there is Adult protection based on realities he has never noticed before.

In the next chapter we shall explain how to reduce the power of the internal dialogue so we can enjoy life in the present free from the tyranny of the past.

4

Handle Feelings Through Trackdown

We cannot turn off the internal dialogue by will power. If we determine that persistent self-consciousness is wrecking our relationships, we will not get rid of it by a fierce resolution, "I will not be self-conscious anymore!" By noon of the first day of our new start, our Child is apt to shoot a question to the Parent, "How'm I doing, being outgoing and rid of my self-consciousness?" and we're back in the old dialogue.

However determined we are to change, the old dialogue intrudes into the present unsummoned, cutting us off from the here and now and transporting us back to early childhood, when we were on the receiving end of continuing parental instructions, admonitions, criticisms, and cautions, *along with the attendant assumptions we made about them.* How much of every day are we actually back there? Many years ago a black writer stated he resented the amount of time, moments and minutes, adding up to hours every day, when his consciousness was totally preoccupied with his blackness, time stolen by feelings of difference, the stares of uncaring persons, or the nonlooks that ignored him altogether—all of that and his own confusing assumptions of what being black meant. Black children today who are told from the beginning that "black is beautiful" will assuredly have a different self-consciousness than this man, depending, of course, on what they actually experience in a society where actions do not always match words.

Internal jolts to our self-esteem, if they could be seen,

might be likened to the muscle spasms of a person suffering from a tic. Nothing progresses very long without the hated interruption by involuntary muscle contractions, calling attention to something "wrong with me," something "different about me," something Not OK about me. How much of our waking time is filled by the preempting reminder "I'm Not OK"? Reducing this time is the purpose of Trackdown, the basic tool for handling feelings.

As noted in Chapter 3, we do not hurt today unless something in the present triggers a Parent recording. Each of us has unique vulnerabilities, because our Parent and Child are unique, and in these bodies of data our personal history is stored. Many people continually suffer from some *felt* shortcoming: they are too short or too tall. Their ears are too big or too little. They are too fat or too thin. Too large-bosomed or too small-bosomed. Significant is the word *too*. Generally our notions about how we should be are not specific. How tall, short, fat, thin, poor, rich, buxom would be about right? Parental messages were experienced often as vague criticisms without specific standards as to what would be exactly right. A person related the no-win confusion thus: If you are early to a meeting, you are anxious. If you are late, you are unthoughtful. And if you are exactly on time, you are compulsive.

We are generally unaware of many of the parental injunctions and commands recorded in childhood. Our first awareness of internal dis-ease is *feelings*. By starting with the *known* of feelings, we can work backward to the unknown of early Parent messages that provoke feelings in the internal dialogue that intrudes into our present transactions.

Three benefits are produced by the Trackdown process. One, we obtain immediate relief from painful feelings because the Trackdown is a problem-solving procedure requiring the Adult. When we switch to the Adult, the Parent and Child tapes stop rolling, and the internal talk is stopped, at least while we are doing the Trackdown. When we are busy working things out, we stop feeling stupid. Two, we begin to build a source of knowledge about what our Parent contains. Most of us do not consciously remember the painful Parent messages recorded in our first five years. We choose to remember the happy times and block out the humiliations and despair experienced during the years of our childhood dependency. Three, we are brought to a point of decision about *what we can do differently* so that the same old feelings do not continually plague us. New feelings grow from new actions, which ultimately are the purpose of Trackdown. We cannot change the past, but we can change in the present.

The Seven Steps of Trackdown

To do this exercise it is necessary to deal with a *real* feeling, our own. Also, we are tracking down *bad* feelings, for they are what give us problems. We can track down good feelings, too, but a more appropriate way to deal with good feelings, it would seem, is ENJOY!

Step 1: I hurt. This is a necessary first acknowledgment. Many of us were taught to deny feelings: You don't either hate your teacher. A toothache is nothing to cry about. Cheer up, you're crying over spilled milk. Don't be a baby! Cultural conditioning also affects our ability to acknowledge feelings. Men, more often than women, were told not to show feelings. Not showing feelings leads often to the denial that they exist. Yet *feelings are real* and, as our former associate Dr. Craig Johnson says, "Feelings leak!" One way or another they leak *out*, through body language, or *in* to our bodies, producing ulcers, headaches, muscle tension, indigestion, or depression. Reality is our most important therapeutic tool. Feelings are a primary reality, direct knowledge of our inner life, and acknowledging them is our first step to change.

Step 2: Which part of me hurts? This is a rhetorical question because, by the definition we invite you to use, it is the Child who hurts. We make this question a conscious step of Trackdown in order to put ourselves in touch with that little boy, that little girl we once were. (Stop a moment, and remember how you looked at five years old, how you looked *up* to the important people around you, how they looked *down* at you. Imagine, earlier still, how it was to be a toddler, when what was at eye level were table tops, the knees of big people, the dog's big white teeth, the hot embers in the fireplace, automobile grills, water fountains. Recreate the situation of your childhood in order to aquaint yourself with that little person. Get out a photograph album. How did you look? Who were you then? What ever happened to that little boy, that little girl? He or she is as alive as ever, recorded in the trillions of neural pathways that existed then and now.) *That* little person is who hurts today as he or she did in the original transactions and experiences of bumps and falls, shamings and blamings, and all the civilizing, socializing rearing that admonished us against bad manners and running into the street.

Step 3: What word best describes my hurt? It may take a while to come up with the most specific word. Commonly discovered feelings are: stupid, ugly, "my fault," scared, mad, bad, "had," harried, ashamed, lonely, worried, unwanted, embarrassed, accused, and guilty. Sometimes our self-impressions seem more like conclusions about "how we *are*" than how we feel: I am a failure. I am not a lovable person. I'm a "bad seed." I'm a case of nerves. That's the way I am. If these kinds of statements, or conclusions, come to mind, it is important to dig for the feelings underlying them. Statements of "how I am" tend to discourage further effort at self-understanding. What's the point of trying to change if that's how I *am?* That may be the way one feels about oneself, but the case is not closed. An old decision, made without adequate data and under duress, requires an appeal, and a new decision.

Step 4: What happened, in the recent present, to trigger this feeling? Feelings, like dreams, are sparked by specific events in the very recent past, a crossed transaction, a disapproving look, a Parent putdown, a look at reality (like the overdrawn bank account), a phone call, no phone call, physical pain, seeing someone else having fun or getting the promotion you wanted. Remembering some long-gone difficulty can produce bad feelings, too, but we believe even such remembering is triggered by some recent event. The possibilities of event-feeling connections are as varied as individuals and their unique histories. What makes one person sad may make another happy. If the power goes off in an elevator holding six people, the likelihood is none of the six will have feelings exactly like the others. They may all share some feeling in common, as initial fright, but soon their individual proclivities appear. The first becomes hysterical. The second soothes and says optimistically, "It's probably a blown fuse from a temporary overload." The third blames fate: "Wouldn't you know it would happen to me?" The fourth feels resourceful and asks if anyone has a flashlight or a match so they can find the phone in the elevator. And the fifth makes a pass at the sixth who, depending on her or his feelings, is accommodating or shocked.

The here-and-now triggers of old feelings are frequently transactions with another person. Who said what? In what tone of voice? With what facial expression? What did you say? Reconstruct the moment when you first became aware of your hurt. Two Trackdowns at the end of this chapter will demonstrate in detail how this is done.

Step 5: What is your Parent saying to you and how is your Child responding? At this point in the Trackdown visualize your Adult standing to one side, fine-tuning the old reruns of Parent-Child exchanges. Can you step back into the Child and listen for Parent admonitions? In your first Trackdown this may take some time, several minutes, perhaps longer. As you become good at it, you can do a Trackdown in seconds. The point of the Trackdown is to become aware of the recordings, for once you know them and can see them for what they are—archaic and assumed—they lose some of their power to overwhelm, even though they cannot be erased.

An example of such a recording is *Now You've Done It!* This internal judgment is often heard by someone whose Parent demands perfection. Failure of any kind is the unforgivable sin. Not one mistake is allowed. Not one risk may then be taken. *You had your chance and you blew it.* The underlying demand is to be perfect. One mistake is experienced as total failure. Perfectionism cuts the nerve of effort: "If you can't do it right, don't do it at all!" Sometimes nothing at all is accomplished despite elaborate plans.

One woman's Trackdown of a sad feeling evoked the Parent statement, "I don't care how hard you try, people will disappoint you." A Trackdown of a feeling of pressure evoked the admonition, "Never miss an opportunity." What triggered the feelings of the woman who did this Trackdown was driving home in rush hour after a difficult day at the office, thinking of what to prepare for dinner for her family of five, and seeing a billboard proclaiming the challenge "Find a need and fill it!" Her weariness turned to anger. A need. Indeed! She exceeded the speed limit all the way home, screamed at the kids, turned her ankle, and burned the meat. Later in the evening she did a Trackdown and concluded there were some needs she did not have to fill. Another person's Trackdown of a feeling of failure got in touch with the Parent accusation "How come you can't finish anything you start?"

These kinds of Parent statements, repeated in various forms and settings in early childhood, cause the little person to make specific decisions as expressions of or solutions to the "I'm Not OK—You're OK" position. It is important to keep in mind that the critical recording is not the face value of what the parents say but the *assumptions* that the child makes about what is said. The parents are the source of safety, strokes, *everything* to the small child. They are the magic people and it is they whom the child must please. Parental statements, thrown off the top of Mom's or Dad's head, when they themselves are weary and busy with their own internal dialogues, may, *if repeated enough times,* become fixed in a decision in the mind of the child. Mom and dad may never have said, in so many words, "Be perfect." However, they may have repeatedly dwelt on mistakes rather than on achievements: rather than praising the "90" grade on the spelling test, they may have asked only, "Which ones did you miss?" To a person with such an exacting Parent a type-over on an otherwise perfect page may produce such discomfort that the page is typed over again and again and again, until it is right. Meaning perfect.

To the assumed Parent demand "Be perfect," the Child's

decision may be "Don't try." To a Parent statement "I don't care how hard you try, people will disappoint you," the Child's decision may be "Don't trust." To the Parent dictum "Never miss an opportunity," the Child's decision may be to "Say yes to everybody." To the Parent judgment "You can't finish anything you start," the Child's decision may be "Don't start." We say *may be,* because individuals react uniquely. The above, however, have been noted as conclusions drawn from Parent messages uncovered in the Trackdown process.

The Parent statements brought into awareness in Trackdown are evidence of a *body* of similar expressions. One isolated statement by a parent is not apt to produce a conclusion in the Child. Versions of "Be perfect" have no doubt been repeated in many other ways. It is the accumulation of these expressions that finally leads the Child to conclude on some specific date how he or she must be. One woman recalled that the word *best* was sprinkled throughout all the conversations she could recall in her home. If a family member went to a doctor, he was the "best doctor on the East Coast." "This was the best way to cook beef." Someone was the "best student" in the class. Or "It never hurts to pick your friends from among the best people."

A significant aspect of the parents' communication with the child is their body language, tone of voice, rapidity of speech, facial expression, and actual body contact with the child. Frequently the "seen" communications are far more compelling than words. "You mean the world to me" can be said tenderly, seductively, flippantly, selfishly, or viciously. Therefore, as important as tuning in on what was *said* in early childhood is reexperiencing nonverbal, visualized communication and one's own body responses. Penfield's experiments in artificially evoking memory from the brain demonstrated the primary nature of the recording of seeing and hearing: "The experiential response to the surgeon's electrode is an evoked awareness of the thoughts and feelings that once moved through the subject's mind. From moment to passing moment, they move now once more with the freshness of a present experience. *The auditory and* *visual components are always prominent.* In many instances both are prominent."*

A technique for becoming aware of these visual and auditory body messages is to sit or lie in a relaxed position, close one's eyes and become aware of one's body sensations. This is particularly helpful to someone who can't recall any verbal statements or find words to describe his feelings.

A man, tracking down a feeling of being under severe pressure, reported the sensation of being shoved from behind and "could still feel his father's knuckles in his spine." Another man intensely disliked shaking hands and reported "his whole body would stiffen" when he was being introduced to someone. When he did shake hands, his hand remained limp and he withdrew it as soon as possible, all the while aware that limp handshakes did not go well in the business world. He could not make himself tighten his grip. No Parent words came to his mind as he worked on a Trackdown of his feelings, which he identified as intense fear.

He was urged to relax and get in touch with his body sensations, beginning with the top of his head and working downward through his face, neck, shoulders, etc. When *shoulders* were mentioned his entire body stiffened. This evoked the recollection of himself as a small boy being dragged by the wrist through the crowds of Christmas shoppers by his mother, a woman almost six feet tall. His feet did not touch the ground as he was jostled by oncoming pedestrians. He reexperienced extreme pain in his shoulder joint as he relived dangling from the bruising, steel grip of his mother's hand. He cried the whole way but she did not stop until they got to the car. There she beat him for crying and said Santa would not bring toys to crybabies. As he relived this experience he wept. He remembered he was frequently dragged about in this manner. (Pediatricians report this form of lifting toddlers and small children off the ground can produce serious shoulder injuries.)

*Wilder Penfield, "Engrams in the Human Brain," *Proceedings of the Royal Society of Medicine,* August 1968, Vol. 61, No. 8, pp. 831–840.

A woman reported a Trackdown wherein she could not find a word for her feeling of distress. She lay down, relaxed, and attempted to image what her body was doing. She said she felt she was being squashed into a "tiny little place," pushed from all sides and from above until she was compacted into a "tiny little corner almost disappearing into it." There was no way out. If she tried pushing herself one way she would meet resistance; the same when she tried another direction. At last she said, "I feel cornered." Which she was in fact in her life situation.

She then recalled her mother's statement about whether or not girls should have sex on high-school dates, "You're damned if you do and damned if you don't." In her memory search she recalled almost everything her parents said to her was equivocal. Straight, unqualified statements were rare. She shared a letter from her mother that was virtually one long sentence strung together with qualifying *buts* and *althoughs:* "It is important to have friends but you must be careful how you choose them although you can't always be too picky but you shouldn't be gullible either but be pleasant about it, whatever you do." Every aspect of her living was dominated by the double bind, damned whatever you do, and she was constantly in a state of indecision. *Confusion* was her predominant feeling, so much so that the word even eluded her. By examining the P-A-C of her parents she gradually discovered the sources and nature of contradictory messages. Thus objectified and put in perspective, the messages lost their power to overwhelm her, and she began to make decisions based on an evaluation of updated truth and realistic consequences.

Step 6: What can I do differently now? By the time we have gotten this far in Trackdown we actually *are* doing something different. We are in the Adult, gathering data and solving problems. We still must decide what to do about our painful feeling. A common way to handle feelings is to save them, to accumulate them as emotional trading stamps. A child learns early it is not safe to express feelings at the moment they occur, as the little boy who cried because he was dragged by the arm through the stampede of Christmas shoppers. When he cried he was beaten. Children sometimes learn it is not even safe to express good feelings. The little boy comes running through the living room whooping in glee and is told to "pipe down." Therefore the child saves his feelings to be expressed later at a parentally-approved time. Bad feelings are stored as trading stamps and pasted in books which when full can be turned in for a guilt-free prize. One book is worth a free sulk; two, a temper tantrum; five, a free drunk; ten, a free quit—tell off the boss, get a divorce, leave the country. Anyone who has had to put up with all these injustices has a right to throw in the towel! Or so the Child *feels*. But the outcome does not advance his cause. Soon he will have more bad feelings to deal with—loneliness, regret, dejection. Clearly, this is not the best way to deal with feelings.

Another option is to take up the matter of the hurt feeling with the person who triggered it. Perhaps there was a misunderstanding. A conversation can be entered into by an "I feel" statement: I felt badly after we talked this morning. Perhaps I was unfair to you; or I feel you were unfair to me. Perhaps the matter can be settled by a phone call, an apology, a reconciliation of some kind. As grownups we have considerable bargaining and reasoning power, which we did not have as small children. Perhaps we decide nothing can be done. That, too, is a decision after which we can put the matter behind us.

Another option in dealing with our feelings is to learn from them and to file in our Adult data bank the newly discovered information we have tracked down in our Parent and Child, making it readily available for the next Trackdown needed for the next hurt. The next time we feel that way we will remember, "Of course, I went all through that." Trackdowns help us build a growing body of insight about our vulnerabilities, strengths, and growing mastery.

Step 7: What can I do differently next time? This question leads us to a consideration of how we set things up to get hurt. We may feel we are innocent victims of injustice and rail against the unfairness of how "people make us hurt." There is often complicity, however, even if we are unaware of it. At this point it is helpful to go back to Step 4 and examine what part we played in turning a transaction sour, if it in fact was a transaction that triggered the feeling. It is helpful to ask, What part of the other person triggered my feeling—Parent, Adult, or Child? Perhaps we will discover we frequently hook Parent-dominated people who then come on with disapproval or rebuke. There are many ways to do this: to come on as Not OK, wearing our "Please Don't Kick Me" sign, an open invitation for just that. Or we may come across as a whining Child, or a rebel Child, or a person inconsiderate of other people's feelings. If we dump lawn clippings over the fence into our neighbor's yard, it is likely we will hear from his Parent. If we consistently fail to keep contracts with others, or never manage to show up on time, we probably will arouse a host of Parents. Being too OK, that is, flaunting one's high spirits when another person is down, may also hook his Parent. Even King Solomon observed, "If you shout a pleasant greeting to a friend too early in the morning, he will count it as a curse."* Examine your motive for whistling "Tiptoe Through the Tulips" every morning when you arrive at work! If you are a perpetual Parent hooker, figure out how you do it. You can change.

Did the other person's Adult hook you? Does the truth hurt? When a client tells you he has decided to take his account elsewhere because he needs reports on time, have you in fact done a poor job? Are you a bottleneck? Are you afraid to delegate responsibility? Are you the only one who can do the job right? Do you break contracts and let people down? If your behavior helps produce unpleasant consequences, examine your behavior. You can change.

Was it the other person's Child who hooked you? Are you terrified of other people's feelings? Do you feel great pressure to keep the peace, at any price? Do your own children's Not OK feelings make you feel a failure as a parent? Are you failing as a self-appointed rescuer when others express futility, anger, or fear? Did someone's sexy Child hook you? Are you terrified by sexy overtures? Are

---

*Proverbs 27:14, Tyndale, *The Living Bible Paraphrased*.

there options other than fright? Parent protection may have conditioned you to *Stay away from that!* Your Adult can protect you in better ways to avoid entanglements you do not want without writing off sex as bad, or people who make sexy overtures as evil.

These, then, are the Seven Steps of Trackdown. We recommend that every hurt be tracked down. In the beginning this is not possible in the middle of a transaction. Your Trackdown may have to wait until the end of the day when there is time to concentrate. With practice, however, Trackdown can be done in a matter of seconds.

Discovering Parent Messages

In addition to taking care of hurts, Trackdown has another advantage, mentioned earlier. *It is an effective way to discover the content of the Parent.* What we consciously remember our parents telling us is only a part of what they said and did. The most troubling material is generally outside our awareness, the secret messages that came from the Child part of our parents, messages such as those listed in Chapter 2. There are three ways of uncovering unknown Parent data. One way we *cannot* do it is to observe ourselves when we are in the Parent state. At the moment we are in our Parent state we do not know it, because knowing is done with the Adult, and when the Parent is on, the Adult is off. We cannot be in both states at the same time. In fact, we often are aware of a great feeling of well-being when we come on Parent: strong, right, in control, powerful. The Child has turned the transaction over to the Parent and thus feels safe in the same way that the little boy feels safe when he says, "My Daddy can lick your Daddy!" or when he actually calls Dad in to settle a fight that has gotten out of hand. Some people come on Parent most of the time, and do not know it.

The three ways this can be discovered are:

1. Reconstructing what happened after a crossed transaction:

Son: "Dad, I washed the car this afternoon."
Dad: "It's the least you can do after all the miles you put on it last weekend."
Son: (Leaves the room, sulking and slamming the door.)

When conversation ends abruptly, look for the crossed transaction. In the above example Dad effectively crossed the transaction with a Parent accusation and the conversation ended. This is not to discount the fact that Dad had feelings, too, which may have made his reply seem justified. However, what was needed was a contract about the use of the car. Contracts will be discussed in Chapter 6.

2. We can learn if we are coming on Parent by feedback from a therapy group in a setting protected by a group contract. If Dad is in the group because he wants to improve communication with his son, the group members may give him the data he needs by observing his body language, gestures, voice tone, and vocabulary, and also by reporting their own feelings in response to him. This can help him to recognize his Parent as well as his Adult and Child and provide tools for controlling his Parent.

3. We learn what is in our Parent through Trackdown, as we have demonstrated, working from the knowns (feelings) to the unknowns (old recordings, both Parent and Child).

Trackdown Example Number One

The first Trackdown was done by a woman who was upset by a feeling of not being appreciated after she had attended a committee meeting of a community organization which she had recently joined. These were the steps she reported:

1. *I hurt.*
2. *What part of me hurts?* My Child [naming herself].
3. *What feeling best describes my hurt?* Excluded.
4. *When did I become aware of this feeling? What happened? What event?* I had walked into the committee meeting room. A conversation was already in progress. I was not introduced. [She drew a seating diagram.] The board

member who had asked me to serve was not present. I had
eye contact only with one member of the seven-member
group. The others formed a circle of eye contact in which
I was not included. This persisted throughout the meeting.
I felt boredom and anger building. The contact was not
clear. What was I doing in this committee? It was not the
agenda I had anticipated from my prior conversation with
the chairperson. Some of my anger spilled out in occasional
contributions such as my statement that some kind of idea
made me want to "throw up" (a violent language form that
did not bring me the attention and response I wanted). In
later conversation, I asked if they wanted to hear about a
racial problem which existed in a school, and one impatient,
seemingly hostile man shouted *No*. I definitely felt excluded. Being dumped on, collecting stamps, made me vulnerable to a game transaction.

5. *What is my Parent saying and how is my Child responding?* Unable to tune in on any Parent-Child dialogue,
I asked myself instead, "What images come to mind of past
similar events?" I relaxed, closed my eyes and waited for
images. The image that came to mind was me, in the third
grade at Lincoln School, crawling around on my hands and
knees with the jump rope around my neck being led around
by a girl who was playing "sister." I was new to the school
and wanted desperately to play with the popular girls. They
were playing "family" and all the important spots (mother,
father, brother, sister) were taken. They decided I could be
the family dog. I was happy to do this humiliating thing
just to be included. I even had to go into the bushes to "do
my duty." My feeling was "I am the least important." I don't
count. I am a dog. Other images came to mind in which I
had been excluded when I wanted more than anything to
belong. My parents had moved a great deal and I was always
getting started in new schools.

By learning how feelings in the present evoke feelings
from the past, she recognized that past pain was often experienced in the present. She was a little girl again, trying
hard to please, but being bullied by the "in" group, laughed
at or ignored.

These feelings of being excluded were identical to what she was feeling in the present as a result of the treatment she had received in the committee meeting. By getting in touch with the little girl on hands and knees, a dog in the schoolyard bushes, she engaged her caring Parent to love that little girl and her Adult to come to her defense. She concluded, "Not all people are nice, no matter how hard one tries." She decided to let that be their problem, not hers.

6. *What can I do differently now?* I asked myself, "What shall I do with this feeling?" Should I save it and add it to my stamp collection? What I did was to tell a friend. We tracked it down together. By moving to the Adult, the old Child *hurt* tapes stopped rolling. I did not have to let this feeling dominate me, but could turn it into insight about what kinds of situations hook these old recordings. I did not have to conclude, "Nobody wants me." Instead I concluded, *"Some* people don't want me, and that is *their* problem, not mine."

7. *What can I do differently next time?* What did I do to set myself up for getting hurt? I had not understood what I was getting into. I wasn't even at the right meeting. Next time I won't be afraid to ask some questions. It turned out I was in the wrong committee, not the one I had been asked to join. When I spot Parent-type people, I will not allow them to goad me into making statements which make me vulnerable. Stay in my Adult. Do not say things like "throw up." It only makes a bad situation worse. Insist on introductions and clarification. I am not a helpless little girl. I am thirty-six years old.

I then called the chairperson of the committee and explained the misunderstanding about which committee I was to serve on. I excused myself from further attendance.

Trackdown Example Number Two

A sixty-year-old man reported he was riding his bicycle, pumping furiously, when he recognized he was full of rage.

Being a Trackdown expert, his Trackdown took only a few
moments, with the result that he stopped pumping furiously.
Reconstructed, the steps were as follows:

1. *I hurt.*
2. *What part of me hurts?* My Child. The little boy in
me.
3. *What word best describes my hurt?* Rage!
4. *What happened to trigger this feeling?* I was doing
my usual ten-mile morning ride. I was riding down the bike
lane of a residential area when a man, revving up his car
engine as he waited to back out of his driveway into the
street, yelled in a bullying, rude voice, "Get the lead out!"
5. *What past image came to mind as I tried to get in
touch with my fury?* The image that came to mind was
myself as a little boy five years old, walking up an alley
which led to the backyard gate of my home. As I walked
up the alley I was muttering furiously to myself and punching the air as hard as I could. Someone had called me
"Scarface," a hated and cruel nickname, which referred to
a burn scar on my face. When I was four years old I had
been watching my big brothers burn weeds, and a burning
gunny sack had been thrown carelessly in such a way that
it broke in half over my entire body. The blinding pain had
been compounded when an older sister had smeared the raw
burns with the wrong kind of ointment, which the doctor
later had to scrape off.

The fury was not only over the pain of the event but the
later humiliation of blame that it was "my fault," by the
cruelty of those who called me Scarface. I remembered a
bully-type neighbor man who used to taunt me by taking
out a box of matches and asking me if I would like to start
a fire. As the old image continued, I was walking down the
alley leading to my home, and one of my older brothers
was sitting on the fence watching me beat the air, and as I
approached the gate, he asked, "Who are you trying to kill?"
The painful feelings were compounded by having been found
out! My conclusion was: Keep your feelings to yourself.
Nobody cares or understands. Take it out on yourself. Hurt
yourself. *Pump harder!*

6. *What am I going to do differently now?* What I did was, I became aware of my discomfort, my chest pain and my aching muscles, and recognized I wasn't doing my body any good abusing it this way. I was aware I was involved in an uncharacteristic activity. I recognized the source of the rage—bullies who hurt and made fun of me at age four—and I immediately stopped my furious pumping and relaxed for the rest of the ride.

7. *What am I going to do differently next time?* In this I have choices. I can avoid riding by this man's house. Whenever I see him, he makes some unpleasant crack. Or, if he does, I can recognize his behavior is *his* problem. Let him take the wear and tear of feeling hostile. I don't feel any need to speed up, pump harder, or internalize his problem.

Both of these Trackdowns worked in producing change. Both the insight derived and the change accomplished recorded something new: mastery. By allowing ourselves to let the memory vaults open, we can gain *understanding* of our vulnerabilities. We can make different choices in the present. It is not true that nobody cares or understands. Some people don't. Some people do! We can choose whom we share our feelings with. We can predict responses by watching and listening. We can gain knowledge of their capacity for love and understanding, and it is to those who have this capacity that we can go for comfort. We can also predict those who are not capable of understanding and avoid further hurt by not sharing our deepest feelings with them. We do not have to waste energy *hating* them; we simply use our Adult to understand and predict, thus protecting our Child from further hurt.

Trackdown enables us to (1) identify our vulnerabilities and (2) to predict the situations in which those vulnerabilities are laid bare and expose us to further pain. We cannot erase the old tapes but we can avoid situations in which they can overwhelm us in the present. This essentially involves *decision*, an act. It is action that is the ultimate antidote to painful feelings. Therefore, feeling OK is the result of (1) understanding and (2) action. Once we have found action to be effective, we build a new store of experiences upon which we can draw, and this gives us a sense of mastery and movement toward a degree of control over our environment. We need no longer be little boys and girls, helpless in the face of cruel taunts and discounts. We can protect ourselves. This is one of the most important functions of the Adult in doing what needs to be done to feel OK. Other forms of protection will be described in Chapter 6.

5

Defuse Your Confusion

Confusion is confusing because we cannot readily see the discordant parts that comprise it. "I'm not confused," said a student, "that's just *me!*" *Just me* is, superficially, just me. Like a bucket of milk. Milk is milk, isn't it?

Milk came to mind in looking up the derivation of the word *confusion*, which comes from the Latin *com*, meaning together, and *fundere*, to pour. Poured together, that is what we are, an amalgam of experience so complex that it is easier to think of ourselves as *just me*.

On our farm we had a milk separator. A bucket of milk, white, foamy, and fresh from the cow, was poured into a large container at the top of the machine. It was a hand-operated centrifuge, which forced the milk at high speed through a set of nested metal discs to separate the cream from the skim milk, each pouring out of a spout into a separate container. The cream would have risen to the top by itself, being lighter, had the raw milk been left standing long enough in large bowls, but the separator did the job instantly.

Left standing long enough, some parts of our confusion rise to the top, but we are in a far better position if we have a mechanism to do the job faster. The necessary initial separation is to distinguish between confusion "out there" in the external world and the confusion "inside," not only conflicting messages in the Parent, but also the demands that come from the Child, and the assessment of reality made by the Adult. Unlike the milk separator, our mental separator often has flaws that compound our view of the confusion in the world around us. We must, and *can,* deal with both.

Confusion in the External World

We shall probably live the rest of our lives in turmoil. Easy answers to world conflict are suspect, and no matter how "in charge" we feel about our own lives, our destiny depends to a large degree on what happens in Washington, the Kremlin, Wall Street, and the newsrooms that report external events to us. Dr. Rollo May observed that the United States is "scared to death" of a mounting number of great problems that appear too difficult to face, and that the nation suffers from a psychological "energy crisis" and lacks imagination to deal with increasingly complicated issues, instead ignoring them, hoping "things will work themselves out." May stated we are so scared "we try to blot out the reality by withdrawing and becoming apathetic."*

From morning till night incoming signals, such as the report of Dr. May's speech, spark a brainstorm of conflicting thought patterns as we try to make decisions about getting through the day. Demands are made for decisions from the moment we awake until our final weary retreat under the covers. Shall we drink coffee or decaffeinated? (But decaffeinated *is* coffee says the kindly TV doctor who is not a doctor.) Shall we drink it black or with cream? Or with nondairy creamer? Artificial sweetener or sugar? Shall we have eggs or Egg Beater? Is bacon carcinogenic or is that just another laboratory-rat exaggeration?

Having struggled through these decisions we unfold the morning paper. Does the murderer have "diminished capacity" or is he responsible? Are interest rates up or down? Shall we sell the silverware or hide it? Shall we enroll in Weight Watchers or Slim Gym? Shall we put the kids in private school or impeach the school board? Shall we move to the country or buy better locks? The phone rings. Shall

*Rollo May, Address to the United States International University, San Diego, December 5, 1975.

we answer it or let it ring? The doorbell rings. Is it a friend or a fiend?

The kids sit at the breakfast table, listless. In response to a parental inquiry about their well-being this fine morning we are told they don't feel like talking. Shall we admonish them or give them a pep talk? Shall we keep quiet or sit on our feelings? Do repressed feelings cause cancer? Doesn't everything?

Leaving for work ends some of this cerebral cacophony as we settle into a routine that for most people has been structured by others. Even there confusion saps energy and robs many people of wholeheartedness and creativity. Shall I take a risk or play it safe? Should I delegate or do it myself? Should I confront or let it drop? Shall I use his first name or last name? At a deeper level we struggle with even more disturbing uncertainties—our health, aging, security, the meaning of our very existence. Often we utter not one word of this to anyone. It is simply a daily assault on every cell in our bodies, a continual yes-no, a binary on-off, which uses our precious energy in ruminations that produce little to promote well-being or life preservation.

Some people, unwilling to accept uncertainty as an ongoing reality, lust for the "good old days" when a dollar was a dollar, a man a man, a woman a woman, and a cigar a nickel. It is true that accelerating advances in technology, microminiaturization, mobility, genetic engineering, in vitro fertilization, and space travel have produced new and overwhelming problems, both logistic and moral. Yet we rather like Hayakawa's view that "the fact that more things can go wrong with motorcars than wheelbarrows is no reason for going back to wheelbarrows."

Other people seem to outlive their confusion because aging reduces their options. George Balanchine, the late ballet master, stated, "Old people don't get tired. It's only the young who tire. Confusion exhausts them. I've got more energy now than when I was younger because I know exactly what I want to do."

However difficult, most people attempt solutions to confusion because the mind cannot forever tolerate contradiction. In his fascinating book, *Brain,* Victor Serebriakoff writes: "Confronted by a contradiction, some drive is baulked because some sensory input warns that its fulfillment in a direct way involves threat. *A search begins*" (italics added).* The search leads different persons to different solutions, not all of which have equal life-enhancement merit. All, however, are life-*preserving*, at least at the outset, and are better than the pain of being pulled in two directions at the same time.

Confusion in the Internal World

The milk separator was always kept in perfect condition, clean, oiled, and assembled correctly. If any one disc was replaced incorrectly, the machine would not work, and the cream would not be separated from the milk. We need an efficiently working, uncontaminated Adult to separate the confusion in the external world. Some people are so confused they have lost the use of their Adult, have stopped thinking, and need therapy. Others *do* think, do have the use of their Adult, and can learn "separating" methods on their own to clarify the picture.

Disabling impairment of the Adult may result from repeated trauma at a very early age. We saw an incident in a supermarket where a little boy, about two years old, was riding in a grocery cart, being pushed by his mother. Another cart wheeled past and the boy reached out to touch a bright object in the neighboring cart. His mother, on seeing him reach for the object, hit the boy an unmerciful blow to the head. Immediately she grabbed the boy, hugged him, and said, "I love you." It was an exhibition of extreme fury followed by extreme remorse. Utter confusion showed on the little boy's face. There were tears in his eyes and a smile on his face. He was trying to please mother, responding both to her blow and her affection. Repeatedly subjected to such experiences, a young child may give up trying to get affection or to solve problems. His Adult may stop working. Why should it work?

We are not speaking of this kind of confusion in the

*Victor Serebriakoff, *Brain*, Davis-Poynter, London, 1975.

forthcoming suggestions of how to handle confusion. It is likely a person who has undergone repeated forms of this sort of erratic behavior will need therapeutic help in deconfusing the Child, a necessary intervention to allow the Adult to reemerge in its task of making sense of the world, his own and the larger world in which he lives.

Garden-Variety Confusion

Much of our confusion results from *overload,* and much of our overload results from confusion. There is a limit to neural traffic. The rate of conduction of nerve impulses varies between approximately 1,000 and 4,000 inches per second, depending on the diameter and type of nerve fiber. Another way to state this range is from a low speed of 55 m.p.h. to a high speed of 225 m.p.h. We have gotten a sense of the speed of neural messages if we have noted the time it takes for our knee to jerk in reflex to a physician's mallet tap in a neurological examination. The knee-jerk stimulus-response time is longer than most transmissions because the message must travel farther. Thinking traffic moves infinitely faster in the convoluted raceway encased in our skulls. Every second 100 million separate messages reach the brain from our senses. Simply interpreted, this means there is a *lot* and there is a *limit!*

Incoming signals can be likened to the daily mail. We are thought to be efficient if we open it on time, sort it, discard what we do not want, act on what we do want by answering letters, paying bills, and filing material in properly labeled folders so we can find it if we need to. We are thought to be inefficient if we have a growing stack of correspondence about which we cannot make decisions. Some letters cannot be answered until we get more information. Some bills can't be paid until we get more money. Some invitations do not get an RSVP because we can't decide.

If the "undecided" pile gets too high, apathy sets in. We move the pile to another room. If we wait long enough it will be too late to respond to the invitation. If we do not pay our bills we leave the decision to someone else, and the power company comes to turn off the gas. Clearly we must handle our mail appropriately and on time if we are to function socially. Similarly, we must handle incoming sensory signals appropriately and on time if we are to function mentally.

A clear indicator that most persons suffer from "too much mail," too much incoming data, too much advice, too many conflicting opinions, too much to do, too many decisions to make, is *fatigue*. We become tired, we become sick, and finally, if we get sick and tired of being sick and tired, we make a decision to confront our confusion.

What follows are two lists of ways people handle confusion, the first list being *ineffective* ways and the second *effective* ways.

Ineffective Ways of Handling Confusion

1. *Withdraw*. Alcohol and drugs, as means of withdrawal, provide immediate, though short-lived, relief from confusion. People also withdraw by removing themselves from social situations, becoming recluses or loners. Invitations are turned down, opportunities rejected, and greetings ignored. Others stay in social situations but clam up about their feelings and secretly "eat their hearts out." The ultimate withdrawal is suicide, for the person who feels that a life of continual, wrenching confusion is worse than death. Tragically, other options that could make life worth living were not explored in time.

2. *Postpone*. Like Scarlett O'Hara, postponers say, "I'll think about that tomorrow." Or this afternoon. Or in a minute. In this category fall those who smoke when they know they shouldn't, who dawdle when there is a mountain of work to be done, or who overeat. "I might as well be doing *something* while I'm waiting for tomorrow, this afternoon, or the next few minutes." Confusion is so painful to the Child that he seeks immediate, infantile gratification, something to make him feel better, something *for* him, something uncomplicated, like eating the last piece of lemon meringue pie, or lighting up a cigarette to "clear" the mind, if not the air. People who cannot sit down for a conversation without

a cigarette have many voices telling them they should be doing something else. If they are in one room, working on a noteworthy project, they feel they also should be in another room, doing an equally noteworthy project. Indecision is their constant companion. No matter what they do, there is something else equally demanding. The internal Parent message "Try harder" makes the completion of a task impossible. Therefore, why start? I'll get on that tomorrow. In the meantime, I'll feed my Child.

Supporting the notion that smoking may be linked to confusion is the 1984 report by the National Centers for Disease Control that lung cancer now surpasses breast cancer as the top cancer killer of women in eight states: California, Florida, Louisiana, Mississippi, Oregon, Texas, Washington, and Kentucky. The report also notes that while the prevalence of smoking has fallen substantially among men, it has not among women. Smoking among women rose dramatically during World War II. At that time it did not appear to have the lethal consequences we now know it has. The question now is: Since men and women are equally informed today, why does it appear that it is harder for women to give up smoking than for men? Certainly the stress, confusion, and mixed feelings over career and/or family roles among women have escalated in recent years. Does a connection exist between this confusion and the rise in lung cancer in women? We think it possible.

Alene Moris, author of *Uncommon Sense* and founder of The Individual Development Center, a career and life-planning counseling service in Seattle, agrees that girls are subjected to a severe and confusing change in expectations at the time they enter junior high school:

We know, if we have worked with first-graders, that God handed out intelligence evenly between boys and girls. Elementary schools are designed by women for girls. These girls get the idea that women are OK. They honor kids who sit still, color between the lines, and pay attention. Girls have longer attention spans and better small motor coordination than boys. They get lots of strokes up to the sixth grade. Girls are ahead of boys to that point. Around the seventh grade, little girls discover they are not people. They are girls. In counseling I see a lot of double messages that start for women in Junior High. It then becomes more important to be liked or loved than to be a leader. It is nice to be bright, but better to be gorgeous. There are exceptions, but the majority of women don't take their abilities seriously. No big deal if they are not going ahead with their God-given talents.*

3. *Speed up*. This is the attempt to speed up the mental processes to keep ahead of the confusion. In this category are people who drink coffee to excess, go on sugar binges, smoke excessively, take amphetamines, or "do" cocaine. All produce an artificial high at the expense of body functions, which, taxed to the limit, finally break down. These addictions have a point of diminishing returns in that increasing amounts are needed to produce the same euphoria initially experienced. The tremendous energy expended is what seems to make possible the "solution" of thinking fast enough to keep ahead of the confusion.

Evidence of this "salutary" effect of amphetamines is seen in the discovery that a certain mild central-nervous-system stimulant is effective in calming hyperactive children. A pediatrician colleague stated, "It amazed everybody. It was a serendipitous discovery. The children slow down and make sense. I have even seen examples of their handwriting, before and after the drug was taken. They write better. They even sleep better. The paradox is, if the children are given phenobarbital, a sedative, it stimulates them. Yet the stimulant calms them down."

If a stimulant calms a hyperactive child, what is being stimulated and what is being calmed? Is it possible that the child is calmed because his faster mental data processing is keeping ahead of confusion? With enhanced Adult functioning, is his anxiety lessened? These questions seem pertinent as we consider solutions to the problem of confusion.

*Alene Moris, Seminar, co-sponsored by the Sacramento Medical Auxiliary and the Junior League of Sacramento, March 22, 1979.

What artificial stimulation does for "clear" thinking is a matter of speculation. At the St. Helena Health Center in Deer Park, California, we saw a film about coffee consumption. Every year 137 billion cups of coffee are consumed in America; 400 million cups every 24 hours; 2.7 pounds of coffee beans consumed per capita annually. The film showed a good-sized spider spinning a huge web, an elegant, symmetrical network of repeated geometric figures, a unitary design of marvelous complexity, precise lengths of filaments, exactly reproduced angle sizes, over and over again, until the entire structure was perhaps three feet in diameter. Then the spider was given caffeine, in an amount equivalent to two cups of coffee for a 150-pound man. They set the spider in another location, and he began spinning another web. He worked fast, but there was no design. His product was a mass of haphazard, stringing, entangled "ropes," ugly to behold, compared with the web he had built previously. He appeared to have extra energy, but no design. It took him four days to recover. Then he was back to his old, beautiful pattern.

4. *Passivity.* A person's decision to give up, give in, be passive, or "go crazy" makes sense if seen as a solution to confusion. It is not a happy solution because his passivity produces new problems, which become barriers to relationships so needed for affirmation and self-esteem. His Adult gives up the effort to find workable adaptations to what he perceives as impossible double messages in the Parent: "You must take charge of your life; here, this is the way to do it." "Win! Do not be aggressive." "You are very bright, you know; that was a stupid thing to do!" "Come here this minute; don't run." These are examples of How to Be Impossible, internalized as the injunction Don't Be.

The decision to be passive affords a person the only way possible to control his environment. Also, his behavior, perhaps more aptly called nonbehavior, is a potent way to express hostility and frustrate the efforts of those who try fruitlessly to get him "self-actualized." His is a rational way, to him, of dealing with what he perceives to be an irrational internal and external environment.

Effective Ways of Handling Confusion

1. *Think*. This elementary prescription is given to those who internalized the injunction *don't think*. Do as you're told, don't ask questions, you think too much, who do you think you are? Thinking is creative work, which can produce true novelty. Thinking the "unthinkable" is the cognitive counterpart of "dreaming the impossible dream." Encouragement to think is given particularly to those who did not receive the messages Schiff claims are the most important parents can give their children: (1) You can solve problems, (2) You can think and (3) You can do things.

Buckminster Fuller believed that by the age of seven or eight a child has decided one of two ways of solving problems: with fists or with books. Anxiety is a state where unknowns outweigh knowns. Knowns, or knowledge, is an affair of words. We think because we have words. "Our humanity depends on our ability to think and communicate in complex symbolic forms," states Dr. Richard Restak.* Children who grow up in a book-strewn home are far more likely to puzzle out confusing problems than those who do not. "Looking it up" is positive action. Action dispels confusing feelings. "Fist" people do not find effective, lasting solutions. There are always people around the corner with bigger fists, sticks, spitballs, or missiles.

Emotions do not solve problems. One of the tragedies of the sixties was the escape into sensation. Many of the drug-dreary "flower children" of the "Haight-Ashbury" enclaves in the big cities of America are today victims of cults whose leaders say, "Leave the thinking to us." There may be ecstasy in turning one's life over to someone else, but there is danger also. Ecstasy does not solve problems. *Thinking does*. Whatever our early conditioning, we can learn to think. We also can learn to read, write, and spell. Anyone can enroll in a literacy program or read the dictionary. Like any endeavor, it takes a decision. Ordinary folks can act on extraordinary aspirations. One of the early teachers of Dr.

*Restak, op. cit., p. 277.

Samuel Johnson, a shoemaker named Tom Browne, compiled a spelling book and dedicated it to the universe. It does not cost any more to dream big than to dream little.

2. *Talk*. Because we can talk we can get help from others. Two heads together are better than one. Not only does talking help objectify our confusion, it is stroke producing. Because we have words we can enlist others in helping to sort out confusion. If you can't say what you mean, you probably don't know what you mean. Sometimes it takes extraordinary effort to verbalize the confusion we feel. In conversation we get outside ourselves, engage in reality testing, hear ourselves and the responses we elicit from others.

3. *Ask for clarification*. It's OK to ask questions. If you don't understand someone, ask for the statement to be repeated. If directions are not clear, say so. Often, because we don't want to appear stupid, we allow confusing statements to go unchecked, and muddle through. How many misunderstandings in marriages, schoolrooms, and world affairs could be avoided if people were not afraid to ask "stupid" questions. Confront inconsistencies. Ask for clarity. You will not only help yourself, you will help others. When I was twenty-two years old I was a press secretary to a governor. One day I was called in to a board meeting of the Governors of the Eleven Western States to prepare a news release on Northwest power policy. My boss said to the assemblage, "One of the reasons Amy is so valuable to me is that she isn't afraid to ask naive questions." They are often the questions that matter most. In the honest search for information there are no stupid questions. Stupidity is *not* asking.

4. *Write*. We can further objectify confusing thoughts by putting them on paper. We have lists for everything else—groceries, Christmas gifts, inventories, chores to be done. Why not lists for thoughts? If we are confronted with a difficult problem, when all possible solutions seem to be full of snags, it is helpful to list the comparative difficulties. In any dilemma, if all the good were on one side of the page and all the bad on the other, a decision of what to do would be simple. Most dilemmas are not like that. If we

compare difficulties, by looking at them in black and white, we can choose the way of the least difficulties. A correct decision can be made. There will still be difficulties, but we have conquered the worst difficulty, indecision.

Another way of evaluating conflicting courses of action is called "double positives." List all the positives in either direction and, if possible, try both courses at the same time, looking for the best in both. If a woman can't decide between Dick and Harry, she would, in this spirit, continue seeing both of them, giving as much energy as possible to inspiring the positive aspects of both relationships. A decision to be wholehearted may produce the needed evidence: Even at his best Harry is not as attractive or compatible as Dick. Pick Dick. Remaining indecisive means being half-hearted, and neither relationship will show much promise. This approach has an advantage over comparing difficulties in that it is a positive approach more likely to uncover surprises and buried treasure.

5. *Go to experts for more data*. We need experts, not because they are better than we, but because they have information we need. We can learn from them and become our own experts. In the beginning we needed teachers. Throughout life we need teachers, for learning is a lifelong process. From time to time we need accountants, attorneys, pastors, and therapists. Asking for help is not a sign of weakness but of wisdom. There is no one harder to abide than a person who doesn't need anybody.

6. *Practice precision*. Accurate watches, gauges, calendars, thermometers, in-tune pianos, sharpened pencils, up-to-date eyeglass prescriptions—all are instruments of clarity to reduce confusion. People who *want* to confuse us often do so by taking these instruments away from us.

Idiot lights on automobile dashboards deserve the name the public gave them. The round temperature gauge sitting as a bowsprit ornament on the Model T Ford was notice, shared by all, of the rise and fall of engine heat. In later models the information came to the driver through instruments on the dashboard, chrome-rimmed white faces with black arrows, with real arrow points, indicating real numbers painted in type styles as authentic as the country-school clock. The importance of gauges is that they make it possible for the driver to spot trends: temperature rising, oil pressure falling. Having this information, the operator has choices about what to do before it is too late. What he sees may not be good news but it is accurate news. Idiot lights tell one the temperature is dangerously hot or the oil pressure dangerously low. If the light goes on, the driver is in a state of confusion because of imprecise data, and freezes between the choices of stopping immediately at the side of the free-way or continuing on to the next service station. If he chooses to go on, his rationalization may be: It's probably a faulty light. Thus the bearer of needed information takes the blame as the engine burns up.

Another mind-deadening invention is the digital watch. It has specific advantages over regular face-and-hands watches in certain situations: logging exact times of incoming calls, clocking races, or programming video-tape re-corders. In these instances the time recorded is analyzed automatically in *reference* to other data. Precise records are made possible automatically by digital clocks.

However, a digital watch on the arm does not give the *referential* information that a watch with a face and hands does. From the face we get spatial information: "quarter [of the face] till 12; half [of the face] past three." We can judge how late in the morning it is, or about how long till supper. This data is symbolic, too, but it has added to it an element of the tangible, an area of a certain size on a flat surface called the face of the clock.

7. *Make certain big decisions that make a lot of little, daily, repetitive decisions unnecessary.* Decisions take com-puter time. They also take energy. It is important, therefore, to conserve past gains. If a woman decides to enter a con-vent, she may no longer feel the need to keep up with the latest fashion in *Vogue*. Simplicity has been achieved in at least one area of her life. If a couple decide to raise cattle in eastern Oregon, they need not concern themselves about the price of highrise condominiums in La Jolla. If a governor decides "small is beautiful," he need not furnish the gov-ernor's mansion but can live in a spartan apartment and drive a used Plymouth. If a person decides to be truthful,

he can quit worrying about what he said in the office Friday. The truth can be elaborated endlessly, but a lie takes a good memory. Retrieving it takes energy.

As stated earlier, there is a limit to the amount of neural traffic we can handle. We have to choose. Who are we? Who do we want to be? This may involve the internalization of a new model. We generally emulate the models already recorded in our heads: mother and father. This may be a blessing or a bane. Usually we do not abandon these models altogether. We will write of this further in Chapter 10, "Requirements for Change."

8. *Accept uncertainty.* We can reduce confusion, but we cannot eliminate uncertainty. We can never claim finality on our understanding of the mysteries of life, whether it be the life inside us or outside us. It is understandable that people who never received effective *how to* and *think* messages long for authority figures who will think for them. Harvard Professor Harvey Cox comments on young people who embrace authoritarian religions:

> One can sympathize with those who hope [for] a world free of complications, a world of black and white choices. But eventually they will find out that no such world will ever be found.

He is troubled by

> those who long for an absolute religious and moral authority so unquestionable and total that they will not have to make hard decisions.

People who hunger for this kind of authority over them suffer from the wounds dealt out by parents, schools and jobs where they have never been encouraged to flex their decision-making capabilities. But in order to mature, the last thing they need is one more perfect master to solve their problems for them.*

*Harvey Cox, "Eastern Cults and Western Culture: Why Young Americans Are Buying Oriental Religions," *Psychology Today,* July 1977.

We encourage people to "flex their decision-making capabilities," and to move ahead in the adventure of living, hand-in-hand with other brave souls in a cooperative, compassionate search for meaning and joy. To do so is to be fully human, what we were created to be.

6

Adult vs. Parent Protection

A three-frame cartoon shows the following: Frame 1: The scene is a delivery room. A baby has arrived. Frame 2: The doctor, holding the infant by the feet, gives him a slap to the rear side to get him breathing. Frame 3: The little guy, still dangling by the feet, strikes back at the doctor with a sweeping uppercut to the jaw.

His time will come, but not in the delivery room and not for a few years. Neither did ours. We come into this world at the mercy of our deliverers. We do have some protective equipment, certain immunities, a startle reaction, good sucking muscles, and the ability to yell for help. Some newborns have extraordinary stamina and amazingly have survived even a cold night abandoned in a garbage bin. Compared to the newborns of other species, however, most human babies are exceedingly vulnerable and totally dependent on others for survival. Most of the ways we keep from being killed in our early years are protections provided by and *experienced* at the hands of our parents. Because our very life is at stake, protective prohibitions are often experienced as harsh and loaded with emotions. Parents look up to see a huge truck about to back over their ecstatic little girl on her new tricycle. Terrible emotions propel them into action. Terrible emotions shock the little girl at the sound of their screams and the rude full-body tackle to get her out of the way. How is she to know they love her? Their anger and her fear are what she *experiences* and records.

Don't touch the stove. *Never* go near the street. *Don't* taste unwashed food. *Never* speak to strangers. To this directory of orders, which have some rationale at certain ages, times, and places, may be added superstitions that have no rationale at all: Don't walk under ladders. Don't step on a crack, you'll break your mother's back. Knock on wood. And, and, and.

A person with the above prohibitions gravely recorded in his head—provided they were never examined or modified—would go through life obediently eating cold meals; staying housebound or, on a brave day, leaning against the picket fence; washing TV dinners and having very few friends, since everyone outside the immediate family is a stranger. Such a person we no doubt would think odd, and happily most of us get beyond absolute obedience to once necessary but no longer appropriate childhood rules.

It is clear most of us update our earliest forms of protection. How thoroughly we update them, however, is a critical question. Under stress, which is nearly always present when we need protection, our tendency is to regress to early forms of learned protection, that is, *Parent protection*, specific to each of us, but generalized in the following ways.

Parent Protection

Withdrawal

Withdrawal is a Parent protection learned from all the keep-away-from warnings we heard in early childhood. It takes many forms. *Don't get involved*, thinks the doctor who passes an accident where injured persons are lying on the highway. They might sue you. *Don't get involved*, think an apartmentful of people who hear and see a young woman attacked and beaten to death in the courtyard of the complex they share with her. *Don't get involved*, Mrs. Q advises her daughter, who is concerned because she knows where her best friend is buying dope and wonders if she should tell someone. They not only fear involvement but also they fear disobeying the "wise" and also fearsome internal Parent who is prompting them. Withdrawal of this kind is generally taught by parents who are care-ful, that is full of care, sometimes uninformed, frightened, and often withdrawn themselves.

Deliberate noninvolvement is assertive in a negative way. "Why should I?" challenges a callous bystander to someone else's distress. Another kind of withdrawal is nonassertive and is called *shyness*. Generally shy people project an air of fragility, so no one dares attack them, verbally or physically. Boys so regarded are "sensitive" and girls are "precious." They invite the ministrations of "helpful mothers" and "Red Cross nurses" and aren't asked to do difficult things.

Passivity is a controlling form of noninvolvement for it "forces" others to take charge. Passivity often is used as a counter-control technique by adolescents in their relationships with their parents. Some years ago a book was published with the title *Where Did You Go? Out. What Did You Do? Nothing.* Such an exchange is just a shade more responsive than silence but maintains the respect of having answered.

Passivity is a potent form of protection but necessitates the ultimate withdrawal from others and the cutting off of stroke sources. A totally withdrawn person may be protected from most forms of external threat but may also be languishing from stroke starvation.

Intimidation

Another learned protection is intimidation: hostility, the tough front, bluster and bombast, or towering rage. "Keep away from me or else!" The playground bully or the prisonyard "Man" protects himself by toughness. Mess with me and you'll have a different face in a different place! Children learn from what they see. Parents who solve problems with belligerent voices and heavy hands teach violent solutions. Toughness is taught and usually rewarded: "See my kid? No one's going to push him around," says proud, big-knuckled father.

Some years ago in southern Sweden a mop-haired, skinned-kneed boy of six greeted us with a two-fisted salute, punching the air with first one fist, then the other, and saying, *"Lukta på den och smaka på den."* (Smell this one and taste that one.) When we got to know him he was charming and inventive in his fist-protected world. He wasn't hostile through and through, once his protective prowess was established. His behavior was learned. His he-man father beamed with pride as the kid put up his dukes, but then admonished him to shake hands politely with the American strangers.

Some people are hostile all the time, their protective mannerisms becoming set into what is seen by others as a sourpuss, a scrooge, or a bully. Some people so characterized are truly lonely, for they have told everyone to stay away. Some people may win by intimidation, but what they win is usually not friends.

Intellectualization

Intellectualization is a learned method of protection that keeps people from getting close by discounting what others say and engaging in a nonresponsive, brainy-sounding filibuster:

> *She,* adoringly: "I love the way your eyes light up when you hang the ornaments on the Christmas tree."
> *He:* "Interesting you should say that. I was just reading an article about how the pupils of the eyes dilate when a person anticipates a surprise or experiences emotions from the past. I've noticed the same thing with other people."
> *She:* "What I meant was, I love you when you seem like a little boy again."
> *He:* "Why don't you say what you mean? I was just reading . . ."

Another example:

> *Woman:* "I'm calling to tell you how much it meant to me to have you phone Monday. I was feeling blue and you lifted me right out of it."

Woman's Friend: "I'm glad to hear that. I've saved Monday mornings for phone calls to friends so I can get on without interruption the rest of the week. Budgeting your time is really the secret of taking charge of your life."

Another example:

He: "I love you."
She: "What is love?"

Ritual

Rituals, whether personal or corporate, are powerful protections because they are socially agreed-upon behaviors. Like standing for the playing of the National Anthem at a prize fight, they signal a temporary cessation of hostility. In conversation one such ritual is lighting a pipe, a fairly time-consuming way to postpone response to a personal question or evade it altogether. There is the scraping, tamping, lighting, sucking, relighting, retamping, relighting, and finally the sanctifying of the whole serious process by producing billows of smoke. Who would dare interrupt *that* ritual? Smoke has been called "white noise." It literally screens us from others, putting distance and protection between. The visual reasons for smoking are not often considered. If you are a smoker, do you enjoy smoking in the dark?

Another protective ritual is *taking off one's glasses*. When a bespectacled speaker takes his off, consider it a signal that he is about to unload a statement he is (1) afraid of (and he doesn't care to see the facial expressions of his audience); (2) unsure of ("I don't quite see what I mean"); or (3) embarrassed by (like the lecturer who, in a three-hour seminar with a group of churchwomen, removed his glasses only twice, once when he was talking about prayer and again when he was talking about sex). Taking off one's glasses is a sure way not to see "the horrified look," a highly emotionally charged image most of us recorded many times in childhood.

Neatness rituals offer protection, as when one cleans ashtrays or straightens pictures in the middle of a serious conversation. Even hugging can be a ritual if it is a way to avoid eye contact, as is sex if it is a way to avoid intimacy. Holidays and birthdays can be protective rituals: Of course you have to be nice to each other; it's his birthday!

All of the above—withdrawal, intimidation, intellectualization, and rituals—protect us from other persons. The problem is they also rob us of strokes. Stroking comes from people, and it is they whom we push away by the above protections. Living this way is like living in a fort where the entrances were boarded up and sandbagged before the supplies were taken on. We won't last long. Even so, many people live a lifetime hiding the dwindling treasures of their lives behind ferocious exteriors, all the while cursing a world so lacking in love.

Adult Protection

As little children we may have learned forms of protection other than the four listed if we had knowledgeable, caring parents who understood the importance of giving us tools for independence. Our earliest unexamined protective behaviors, however, were those just listed. We experienced and recorded the effectiveness of *withdrawal* when we ran from spankings or dodged Aunt Ethel's slobbery kiss. We experienced the effectiveness of *intimidation* when we practiced the bully role on little sister, and we experienced the effectiveness of *intellectualization* when we avoided something we did not want to do by "logical" explanation: "Boys don't kiss their daddies, just their mothers! It's sissy." We experienced the effectiveness of *rituals* when we escaped a spanking because it was Christmas Eve.

The following Adult behaviors protect us without pushing people away. Parent protections generally put distance between us and others and leave us safe, but sorry. What is needed is a way to protect the Child without losing people and the life-giving strokes they provide.

Eye Contact

A woman suffered from severe acne as a teenager. Weekly she went to her dermatologist, who administered X-ray treatments. They were standard therapy at the time and moderately effective, although they are no longer considered safe. Her acne improved somewhat, but her face wore a perpetual "sunburn" except for the areas around her Little Orphan Annie eyes, which were white since her eyes had been shielded by lead covers. As stoical as she was, she could not stop the build-up of self-consciousness and embarrassment about her face, and she finally fell apart in a tearful session with her doctor one afternoon. Deeply sympathetic to her plight, he sat her down and gave her the following memorable advice: "This is what you must do. When you speak with people, look them squarely in the eye. Lock your eyes with theirs and they will have to look into your eyes, not at your face. Then you can stop worrying about how your face looks."

She tried it, and it worked. To this day she has a directness that she sometimes has to modify by looking away. She particularly became aware of the need to do this when she learned that people from some foreign countries, some of whom were numbered among her friends, consider it rude to maintain unbroken eye contact, an invasion, she was told, of the other person's most private self. Learning cultural sensitivities, incidentally, is an important protection, becoming more so as our world shrinks and we come in contact with increasing numbers of persons of other nationalities, not only around international conference tables but at the supermarket and PTA meetings.

One reason eye contact is protective is that it keeps us in the here and now. Generally our fears are aroused by signals in the present that evoke old Parent admonitions and old Child fears. These gain volume as we stare into the distance. By focusing on the eyes of another person we are returned to today and the old fears generally stop playing.

Reading People

Not only eye contact, but *seeing* in general is necessary to
our protection. We size up a situation by noticing another
person's facial expression and body language, and changes
in both. One requirement of seeing is tuning out the internal
dialogue, so that our full attention can be focused on another.
Often we can determine if a person is in his Parent, Adult,
or Child by looking. If we see a person's face change from
"open" to "shut," if the musculature has become rigid and
stern, we have evidence that something has happened to
hook his Parent. It is as if he has dropped the visor of his
suit of protective armor. We then have information to help
us decide what to do next. It is difficult to negotiate business
when someone's Adult has disappeared, so we may need to
concentrate on ways to bring his Adult back or to "shrink
his Parent," which will be discussed in Chapter 12. At the
least we can avoid repeating what it was we did that may
have hooked his Parent in the first place. Or, if it wasn't
something *we* said or did, we can figure out what did. We
may not always learn the reason.

We can also read how a person feels by the use of our
other senses, listening, smelling, touching when appropriate, and also by intuitive hunches. When we are aware, we
can pick up the signals of fear or sadness. We can hear the
slight break in the voice that belies the cheerful words being
spoken, that "things are just fine." We can see the tremble
of the hand. Physicians learn a great deal about their patients
just by looking at their hands. We can do the same if we
learn what to look for and observe. In addition to hand
activity—tremors, wringing, playing with the wedding band,
picking at the nails, hands holding each other—*I've got to
hold myself together*—there is the condition of the hands.
Soft or hard, lotioned or cracked, blue nails or pink, clenched
or open. Many books have been written on body language
and can help us interpret what we see. Much of what we
can surmise, however, is intuitive. If we look!

These observations protect us from the error of making
problems worse by pouring salt on someone's wounds. If

we want to avoid an explosion with our children, it is important to notice "where they are"—in their Parent, Adult, or Child. We can protect ourselves from crossed transactions that end conversations. We can protect ourselves from someone's Parent by not waving red flags. If we have been observant—seeing, reading people—we will know *what* red flags incite *what* people. For instance, peace resolutions can mean different things to different people, depending on their personal experience. It would seem reasonable to suggest that *everyone wants peace*. Yet, if one were to circulate a peace petition for signatures, a Vietnam veteran might react differently from a seminary sophomore, who might react differently from the paraplegic candy vendor who lost the use of his legs at Omaha Beach.

Reading people can also help us with timing. If we want a raise and we see with our own eyes that our boss is not feeling well, we should probably postpone our request. Someone has observed that a good time to ask a favor is after a good meal, when the person we want something from has a satisfied Child with a full stomach—unless he has broken his diet resolutions, gorged, and now is in the process of an internal beating.

Sensitivity to the state of mind of one's spouse is a requirement of a good marriage. If one partner is sick with worry over a lost job, the relationship will not warm to a complaint that the house needs painting, even if it does. We protect not only ourselves but those we love, or even those we don't love, by *seeing*.

Predicting

One of the functions of the Adult is predicting or estimating probabilities. This is not necessarily the same as judging. A woman told a therapy group that her husband had been unfaithful to her. It had started four years before. He had begun seeing another woman, a friend of the family, following a Christmas holiday get-together. By summer the affair had been confronted and stopped. Things went quite well until the holidays, which "always seemed depressing," and news came to the woman of her husband's dalliance following an office Christmas party. Yet, by the time of the family summer vacation in the mountains, the illicit relationship seemed to have paled. For four years the same pattern was repeated. Tearfully, she told the group, "I simply can't trust my husband." Another group member responded, "What do you mean, you can't trust him? It sounds to me as if you can trust him to have an affair every year starting around Christmas and ending by summer." The observation rang true, and the woman, despite her unhappiness, laughed. "You're right, you know. I guess I'll just have to work with that fact."

Reality, though it may be extremely uncomfortable, helps us predict and therefore gives us a basis for determining what to *do* instead of waiting helplessly for circumstances to overtake us.

A high-school senior told a favorite teacher he would have to cancel his trip to register for university classes because he felt he was coming down with bronchitis. The wise and much-loved teacher stated, "You know, Jack, you can spend the rest of your life coming down with bronchitis." There was a mutual eye-twinkling and he said, "All right. I'll go." He went on to become chairman of the department of anthropology of a large Western university.

We can build reliability indexes on the people in our lives. Is someone *always* fifteen minutes late to meetings? Observing that fact, we can either confront the issue, stating we feel it is disrespectful of others, or we can choose to arrive fifteen minutes late ourselves. We have a choice. We may decide not to waste our time "politicking" someone who *always* votes Republican or Democrat. We may decide, as did Katharine Hepburn in *Lion in Winter,* "Save your arches; that road's closed." If an employee *always* arrives late at the office Monday mornings, we may choose not to expect that person to participate in an important conference call at 10 A.M. Monday. If a child *always* gags when served eggs, it may be wise to determine if he is allergic rather than labeling him as a picky eater.

Predicting also helps us know whom we can trust. Trust need not be blind. A woman, about to disclose a confidential matter to a recently-acquired friend, began, "I don't know if I can trust you, but. . . ." Her friend interrupted, "Until you know you can, you can't," putting the responsiblity for trusting back where it belonged. Trust does include an element of the unknown, but we can greatly reduce uncertainty by predicting from the evidence at hand. If someone says to you, "I promised not to tell this to a soul, and you must promise never to repeat it," you can pretty well predict this person will not keep your confidences either.

Other clues from which we can make predictions are our hunches about people or how we feel in their presence. People sometimes send out messages which we receive subliminally, such as subtle facial expressions or voice modulations. The Child intuitively senses these messages, and we are wise to take note. We need not make a judgment, but we can add such data to the store of information from which we make our predictions. "This doesn't feel right" is a warning signal worthy of our attention.

Options

Some things don't work. Sometimes our best-laid plans fail. We need to give ourselves permission not only to risk but also to fail. Failure is not fatal if we have options, another significant Adult Protection. Some of the ways to acquire options are to develop skills in several fields, keep more than one iron in the fire, have avocations as well as vocations, and rehearse "what would happen if." When things are going well we have discretionary time to think ahead and to prepare ourselves for what we will do if things don't go well, if the job market tightens, or if retirement is on the horizon. Diversification is as important to the investment of our time and thinking as it is to the investment of our money. We need Plans B, C, and D if our prized Plan A falls through. Bob Miller, who developed the listing of protections that we have elaborated in this chapter, stressed options as among the most significant.

We believe it is possible to commit ourselves wholeheartedly to an endeavor and still hold in reserve other possibilities for action if the endeavor fails. Having options is not "playing it cool" but living thoughtfully and realistically. As we need more than one way of solving a problem or achieving a goal, we also need more than one person in our lives. "People options" along with other options will be discussed in later chapters.

Contracts

Contracts, upon which our legal, social, and economic systems rest, are statements of mutual expectations. They are needed in personal relationships as well, in marriage, child raising, and friendships. *Contract* may seem a hard word applied to personal relationships, but it is difficult to find a better one. Heidi, as a teenager, declared one day she didn't like the word at all, stating it was "an automatic pindown." For her, at the time, contracting seemed one-sided, as it probably was. The real dependency of children makes contracts seem heavily weighted toward the desires of the parents, who are ultimately in charge, legally and financially responsible. Nevertheless, the concept is a good one if it has the following characteristics:

1. *The contract is not one-way.* The parties must base their agreement on an understanding that both benefit from a clear expression of mutual expectations.

2. *There is something "in it" for the Child of both parties.* Agreement to work together succeeds only when there is a reward in sight. If housework is divided fairly among the members of the family, the reward may be neatness and orderliness, the end of nagging over infractions of vague rules—*you never do enough around here.* A reward for children is a cheerful mother and father who no longer are harried because they never have help. Stroking for a job well done is a reward. Extra time for family picnics, a night at the movies, parties, and vacations all are possible when every member in the family shares the load.

3. *The contract is made Adult-Adult.* Contracting while emotional, Child-Child, doesn't work, for the Child is impulsive, does not take consequences into account, and is not particularly concerned about the Parent, an ever-present reality. Understanding the Parent is not the same as erasing

it. Provoked sufficiently, it can beat us unmercifully after the fact or after the act.

In this regard there are four Parents we may have to contend with. If, for instance, your Child feels like setting up a weekend tryst in the Bahamas with your married boss, you should take into account: (1) *Your* Parent. What will your conscience do to you Monday morning after it's all over? Are you prepared for that? (2) *His* or *her* parent. What will your paramour think of you Monday morning? Will he or she think you easy, immoral, or cheap, or fire you? (3) *Their* Parent, that is, society's Parent: your fellow workers, neighbors, friends, or your paramour's spouse. (4) The Future Parent, that fierce accuser down the road or down the years when you are running for the Senate, and *they* find out! The Child is not much concerned with such questions; therefore, our best protection from Child-driven impulsive behavior is a clear-thinking Adult, which takes into account the entire person—Parent, Adult, and Child—in ourselves and in other people. The Adult must also take into account what is morally right. Getting the Parent out of the picture does not do away with ethical requirements. Whether we accept or reject what our parents believed to be moral, we are not off the hook. Ultimately, learning what we "ought to do" is Adult work, not blind conformity to the Parent.*

4. *The contract is equitable: There is a mutual win if it is kept and a mutual loss if it is not.* Understanding that we stand to lose something if we don't keep our agreements is a powerful incentive to responsible participation. A good illustration is the management of money, fundamentally important to most families. If only one person in the family is the "chancellor of the exchequer," and feels he or she carries the full responsibility for making it through the year, statements about money are frequently heard by other members of the family as deprivation: *No, you can't have a new coat, you spend money like it's going out of style, "when I was your age."* Even explanations may fail to impress.

*See "P-A-C and Moral Values," *I'm OK—You're OK*, pp. 246–279.

Which reminds us of Ring Lardner's report of an exchange he had, when he was a little boy, with his father while on an automobile trip. "'Are you lost, daddy,' I asked tenderly. 'Shut up,' he explained."

Underneath depriving, accusing statements is fear. If father is the money manager and keeps his concerns to himself, he may be the only one who knows the car insurance has lapsed and that they are "going bare," or that if they have one more delinquent payment they may lose the house, or that his stomach grinds every time the doorbell rings for fear it is a bill collector. He may be the only one who knows he has an ulcer. Who is calling his signals? Is it his Parent?: *Money is a man's concern; handle it! Don't pamper the little woman. Kids must learn life is tough.*

He may not want to be tough. He may be screaming in silence, wishing his family fully understood how tight things are. The incidence of child abuse increases in times of high unemployment. Breadwinners, tired, worried, and out of work, often act out their own pain by brutalizing their children. There is another way.

Children are born problem solvers. They can help with the family budget, if there is one, and if they are told what it is, when they are age five, six, seven. A child can understand a pie chart, and can easily see how much of it goes for "our house," the car, food, lights, and the furnace, Bowser, the dentist and doctor, and donations to charity. They can share the pride of ownership in a new piano, which is being bought on installment payments of $37 a month, and which by Thanksgiving we will *own*. It will be ours to keep! Or that "by the time you are fifteen years old we will own our house." And if we stay with our budget we can build you a room of your own when you are twelve!

Not only does this teach the child fundamental lessons in how life works, it also allows him to share in the good feelings that come even from the denial of his own desires. "We can't afford it this year" is a statement he can make with grownup solemnity and the pride of *belonging* to a family that works together. It gives dignity to his later efforts as a paper boy, a baby sitter, a lawn mower. "I am helping to support my family. Moreover, I am helping Dad and Mom with their problems, *our* problems."

What this inclusion in the important matters of life does for a small child's self-esteem was the subject of an article by Ruth Stafford Peale, "Six Gifts to Make Children Strong":

> Sometimes a small child's enthusiasms may seem amusing to grownups. But laughter dampens enthusiasm. During World War II someone gave our son John, then a small boy, a book to be filled with war savings stamps. We found him one day licking stamps with gusto and pounding them home with furious blows of his little fists. "What on earth are you doing?" his father asked. "I am winning the war," cried John, hammering another stamp. We were careful not to laugh. That can-do attitude was too important.*

5. *The contract is simple, but not too simple.* Contracts should involve single issues, not a whole spray of expectations. If we make an agreement among family members about the use of the car, we need not tack on riders about the cleaning of the garage, attic, backyard, homework, and the way you cut your hair. Too many conditions might indeed constitute an "automatic pindown." If you're perfect between now and your eighteenth birthday, you can have the car Saturday nights!

I used to write long, detailed lists of kitchen chores on the refrigerator door. I even tried check-off lists and gold stars. I soon got the sinking impression they had not even been read. What I found to be much more effective was a simple sign with three points listed in bold, purple strokes: (1) PUT IT AWAY. (2) WIPE IT UP. (3) DO IT NOW. Signed: The Management. It has worked quite well.

6. *Breaking the contract is stated in terms of consequence, not punishment.* In order for this to work, family members must see the whole picture. Children learn to be merciful by experiencing mercy. How would you feel if

---

*Reader's Digest, August 1974.

someone locked you in your room every time you went off your diet? Dented the fender? Broke a goblet? Overslept? How would you feel if you were lashed with a belt? If children understand there is something in the contract "for them" they will understand it is that something they will lose when they break it. We can't have a swimming party if the pool isn't cleaned. We can't leave for the mountains until the berries are picked. We can save money for a new sound system if we don't have a large dental bill, and we can keep from having a large dental bill if we care for our teeth.

7. *It is written.* Some contracts require a lot of thought. Conserve past gains and mental energy by keeping a record. If it's vital, sign it. Recently we read of a contract which was drawn up between high-school students and their parents, promising they would not drink and drive. The promise was printed on a certificate and signed by both parents and students in front of witnesses. Some agreements are more serious than others. "Saving your life, Daughter or Son, and ours, Mom and Dad" is a solemn agreement worthy of framing, signifying the value of life and our love for each other.

8. *The contract is renegotiable.* People change. Family needs change. Circumstances change. If we think we "have it all together" we are usually in for some surprises, even disillusionment. For instance, inflation affects not only grownups but children as well. Is the agreed-upon allowance really adequate? Is the sharing of the work load fair? Realistic? If the contract isn't working, perhaps it needs changing, not because of someone's fault but because of changing facts.

What happens when we drop the ball, period? When we don't come through on our part of the bargain? A family is not a corporation run by bar graphs and productivity quotas. A family is a living, breathing organism. It is also a place of refuge where its members may come for understanding and, often, forgiveness. When love and forgiveness bind a family, we can count on acceptance, admit our mistakes, and make new starts. Change follows acceptance, and not the other way around.

The most beneficial aspect of contracts as a form of protection is that they reduce misunderstanding and accomplish the business of everyday living in a rational, efficient, and friendly way.

7

Parent Stoppers

Some days are worse than others. We have gotten behind in the Adult work of handling bad feelings and suddenly their accumulation overwhelms us. We feel we are worthless. Helpless. Hopeless. Zero. If we beat ourselves badly enough the Adult shuts down altogether and we can't even think about Trackdown, TA, Adult Protection, insight, hindsight, foresight, or anything else. We are like a boxer on the ropes, all offensive strategy gone, our arms protecting our head, dodging blows, protecting the bleeding cut over the eye, the purple lump on the ego. That's how it is sometimes. What can we do?

A boxer has learned and practiced defensive strategies, which come into play automatically even when he is about to lose consciousness. We lose consciousness, too, when we lose our Adult, which is what happens when the internal dialogue won't turn off. We can protect ourselves from an internal beating if we have a handy list of things we have learned and practiced. We call these emergency measures *Parent Stoppers* because they get us into the present, which is Adult territory. By performing Adult functions we turn off the past momentarily and the recorded accusations stop playing.

These are not analyses or thinking-through. They are things to *do* till the thinking starts. Sometimes we feel exhausted from our attempt to untangle the skeins of the past. We know, we know, we know. "I am burdened with knowing," said the Maori woman in *The Lost Tribe*, written by our friend and writer of marvelous young people's books, Louise Munro Foley. Sometimes what we know is that we're going down for the count.

Our groups devised a set of first-aid exercises to rescue the battered Child. They are not long-term solutions but do offer temporary relief from internal abuse. They turn off the Parent, engage the Adult in simple observation, and tickle the Child.

1. *Break the body set*. Carl Rogers believed that our feelings, thinking, and physical set (musculature, posture, facial expressions) tend to be congruent. If we are mad, we not only feel mad, we are thinking mad things, and our body is set for a fight, with clenched fists, tight jaws, and tense muscles. We may not be able to change our feelings or our thinking at will, but we *can,* if we are aware of our bodies, change our body set. We can deliberately unclench our fists, drop our shoulders, take a deep breath, and let our jaws sag. We have *relaxed*. After we have done this, our thinking and feelings tend to follow suit. What is it that we were mad about? What was I going to say? Who was I so mad at?

2. *Be in the here and now.* Look around the room. Say out loud what you see. A brown desk, white draperies, diplomas on the wall, two green crystal vases, a paper clip, a clock pendulum that is stopped, a blue shoe on my foot, a black notebook, mailing folders, an orange, a copper pail. During the time these items were recited the Adult was engaged in *awareness* of the present. The past could not roll. For a blessed moment there was a ceasefire. Try it. Say what you see. Say it out loud. The minutiae of life have their value.

3. *Exaggerate the problem.* You have dented your fender. Bad, bad, bad. Stupid. Dumb. Careless. Expensive. Well, you could have bashed in the whole side of the car, or totaled it and broken your leg, fractured your hip, injured a pedestrian, and lost your license. Your insurance could have lapsed. You could have had the carful of kids. You could have been charged with criminal negligence. *But none of this happened*. You only dented your fender! Sweet relief.

4. *Physical exertion.* Any kind of exertion raises metabolism. Tired? Take a walk. "Walk for life" was a prescription Tom frequently gave depressed patients. Put one foot ahead of the other, one at a time. It's easy. Breathe deeply. Think of the oxygen lighting up your brain like a fireworks display. Wonderful. Keep walking. Hit a comfortable stride. Think of the blood rushing through your arteries. Bright red. Think of your big muscle sheaths, moving in harmony, beautifully, powerfully. You're not weak anymore, or helpless. You're magnificent! (If you are over forty, on any medication, or have a history of heart problems or other illness, check with your doctor before beginning a *brisk* walking program.)

5. *Have a haven.* A place. Down by the river. Under the oak tree. A good book. A crossword puzzle. A hobby. Something tangible you can get your hands on, relief from the perplexing abstractions of life. Or a drive in the country. A place with vistas where you can look far and see deep into the wonders of the sky, the clouds, the mountains. Your own secret place. Go there, and rest.

6. *Have a sound screen.* Turn on Handel's "Water Music," Simon and Garfunkel, Bizet's *Carmen,* Abba, Tchaikovsky's Violin Concerto in D Major played by Itzhak Perlman, Jerome Kern, Larry King, when you can't sleep. It's hard to think about the leaky-faucet-that-needs-fixing-and- the- bills-that-need-paying-and-why-is-it-always-your-responsiblity-to-do-every-little-thing-and-everyone-else-couldn't-care-less, when you're listening to "Ole Man River," who "just keeps rollin' along."

7. *Go off on tangents.* I was being a bit hard on myself one day for talking too much at a meeting the night before. Why don't you just shut up once in a while? my Parent said as my Child cringed in agreement. This uneasiness had persisted all day, and finally, exhausted, I lay down on the bed and began reciting what I saw. Each sight reminded me of something else, in a more pleasant setting. Looking at the air vent, I thought of my childhood friend Betty's house. Her house had central air conditioning, and ours didn't, and it seemed like heaven to sit in front of a vent and be cooled in the ninety-degree summer. Her house always smelled of

floor wax, lilacs, cinnamon, and cedar. It was fun to go there. Now we have air vents all over the house. Imagine that!

Then my eyes wandered over to the crystal lamp on our dresser and that reminded me of Hilma Anderson's beautiful pale pink bedroom, which was cool, and smelled of home-grown lavender, and was full of crystal and perfume and silver hairbrushes. She was a beautiful, vivacious friend of my mother's whom I adored as a child.

Then I looked at our mirrored closet doors, and they reminded me of my first room-of-my-own with a walk-in closet, separated from the rest of the room by a knotty-pine wall my father built. Inside my closet was a window with lace curtains which waved in the breeze that shimmered the leaves of the enormous maple trees just outside our house. The trees were my friends, whose limbs I knew as play-mates, crotches for sitting in, limbs to swing by the knees from, hearts and arrows carved in the trunks up high, my own secret places to go and hide and plan and pretend.

Then I looked out through the door and saw the white balusters on the staircase, all in a row, orderly and shiny, and not at all accusing, reminding me we live in a house with two stories, which is what I always thought a *real* house had, when I was little and didn't have an upstairs.

Then I looked over at my clock, a quartz Picco, with the movable ring around it that tells what time it is in any part of the world. And I wondered what my cousins were doing in Sweden about then. Coffee time, perhaps, under the bowing birch trees. And I looked all around the room and thought it was beautiful, all emerald green and white and pink, and the wallpaper an Oriental print with green leaves and pink blossoms. It reminded me of apple-blossom time in central Washington State, in the wonderful little town of Selah where I grew up, where driving up through the country roads one could smell the blossoms, as if a gigantic bottle of perfume had been sprinkled all over the valley. I could hear the hum of the bees that filled all the trees, hundreds and thousands of trees and what seemed millions of bees pollinating the blossoms.

And so my reverie went, and I with it, all over the world

and through years in time. I was there. What was it that I was so worried about? At the time of this writing I have lived 20,089 days. Why should I let one event in one evening wipe all that out? Ride a tangent the way a surfer rides a big wave. It's a great Parent Stopper.

8. *Talk with someone.* Walk down the street and talk with a neighbor. Call a friend. This is another here-and-now activity that can cut off the internal dialogue. The only possible problem with this is if you dump your feelings on someone else and end up with a gloomy game of "Ain't It Awful" or "Poor Me," which is how you will feel after the conversation is over, awful and poor.

9. *Consider others.* Are you the only person in the world who's ever done a dumb thing? If you can drum up a little empathy for others, why not for yourself? Mistakes don't kill you. Misery can. Others keep going. Why not you?

10. *Make faces at yourself in the mirror.* Silly, isn't it? "Making faces at each other" was a prescription for one couple who, at the end of the day, badgered each other with a recitation of the day's woes. Annoyed by everybody else, they finally turned their anger on each other in Parent-Child putdowns and defenses. Dinnertime was always dreadful. Making faces, silly, ridiculous faces, the way little kids do, broke the pattern, and they ended up laughing.

11. *Take a nap.* Sometimes our self-abuse tires us to the bones, and despite a common Parent admonition that "you can't just sleep your life away," we need to rest. Perhaps another authority would help. Shakespeare: "Sleep that knits up the ravell'd sleave of care, The Death of each day's life, sore labour's bath, Balm of hurt minds, great nature's second course, Chief nourisher of life's feast" (Macbeth, II, 2).

12. *Pray.* Prayer, for many people, is a wonderful way to "take your burden to the Lord and leave it there," as the old hymn goes. A favorite scripture of mine is found in I John: "If our heart condemn us, God is greater than our heart, and knows all things"; I am only human, imperfect, forgiven and loved anyway. Amazing relief: God and the Parent are not the same.

* * *

All of the above Parent Stoppers are *temporary* relief from pain. They are not meant to be final solutions. Much, though not all, of our misery we bring on ourselves, and often it is we who need to change. If Parent Stoppers were taken to extremes we could, in fact, sleep our lives away, live in a dream world of tangents, be on the phone all day, or jog ourselves to death. As first-aid measures, however, the above work rather well. Rested and refreshed, we can gear up our Adult to do the work of change, change in behavior that ultimately will bring change in our feelings.

8

Stroking

Stroking is someone looking at you fondly, calling "hi" from the neighboring yard, phoning you just for the heck of it, writing you a note, calling on you in class, writing a personal note under your grade, calling you by name, touching you on the shoulder, telling someone else about you and seeing that the conversation gets back to you. Stroking is entering someone's awareness. Stroking is something our Child feels. Most stroking feels good. It energizes. It keeps us alive.

At birth, after the long, hard journey into day, stroking reassured us that life on the outside would be all right. Stroking was life-giving then. And now. Psychologist Abraham Maslow calls stroking *optimal stimulation* and lists it along with food and water as primary in the hierarchy of human needs.

We sometimes distinguish between positive and negative stroking, positive meaning it feels good, negative that it feels bad. Any attention is better than none, unless it is cruel or demeaning. In general usage, however, *stroking* has come to mean something positive, so that is the way we will use it here.

Comfort Zones

Not everyone appears to need the same amount of stroking. The intensity of our stroking hunger would seem to match what we became accustomed to as children. Given our own comfort zone (Figure 6) we get along rather well as long

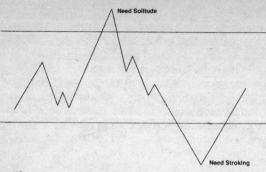

Figure 6
Stroking Comfort Zone

as we stay within its boundaries. If there is too much—too many people, too much commotion, too many phones ringing, too many demands, even too many compliments—our receiving system shuts down and we long to get away. We may retreat into our favorite solitary activity—reading a book, working in the garden, playing the piano, sitting by ourselves in the backyard, going for a walk, taking a day off, swinging in the hammock, or closing a door and locking it behind us. When we feel smothered, silence gives us breath. We may even go someplace where silence is structured, a retreat where everyone takes the vow of silence, enjoying the presence of others but not having to respond. We withdraw to think, contemplate, meditate, sort ourselves out, and make sense of life. This we do with some equanimity if we know we can reenter the world of people when we wish. Soon we wish. Most people cannot abide solitude long.

People who fall below their comfort zone get depressed. We are so constituted that we *will get strokes* one way or another in the same way that our bodies will get calories one way or another. People who are physically starving continue to burn calories at a metabolic rate sufficient to sustain life. In the absence of food fuel, excess fatty tissue is burned, then muscle. When caloric intake falls below a critical level for a prolonged period, the body, sensing danger, does not make a distinction between burning fat and lean tissue. In the last stages of starvation, vital body organs are consumed in a final effort to sustain life. Ultimately, the person dies, but the body has made every effort to continue life with whatever fuel stores are available.

Our need for stroking, both physical and psychological, is similarly demanding. When we fall too far too long below our comfort zone we begin to exhibit behaviors of distress, agitated depression, hopelessness, and often physical illness. When we look and act badly enough someone comes along and says, "You can't go on like this," which is true, and arrangements are made for crisis intervention, counseling, or hospitalization, whereupon stroking returns in generous amounts. The will to live persists in most people, and in even the most weakened condition we communicate our need. If we do not, we die psychologically just as we die physically from calorie deprivation.

The most common way to get our stroke supply back in the comfort zone is *games*, described in detail in Berne's *Games People Play* and reviewed in *I'm OK—You're OK*. A game is a series of complementary, ulterior transactions progressing to a well-defined, predictable outcome, or payoff. Games grow from stroke hunger, and people *will* get strokes, like calories, even if they must be self-destructive in the effort. Though games are basically dishonest and keep people apart, they do provide moments of highly charged confrontation *and* stroking before estrangement sets in again. All players get *something* out of games, thus their power to persist. The game is a drama. A game scenario will be described in Chapter 11.

Stroking Comes from People

True, there is power in positive thinking, but our first positive thought is often to call someone. It seems we cannot recharge our own batteries. Even in solitary contemplation our thoughts run quickly to remembered others, past glories in the setting of people, recollections of persons long dead and gone whose lives touched ours. "The good old days" usually are filled with "the good old people"—Mom and

Dad, pal Joey, the girl next door, the special high-school teacher, the kind aunt who always had time for us. Even when we insist we are communing with God alone, our understanding of who God is generally is derived by recalling the persons in whose company we first learned about God.

The People of the Past

One source of stroking is reliving the stroking of the past. The Nurturing Parent as well as the Critical Parent is part of our store of memories. We often reexperience the happiness of childhood when we "hear" Parent applause. The early, all-consuming good feeling that came from parental approval was and continues to be a powerful motivating influence in everything we do. It is as if we go through life searching for replicas of our original strokers, and if we do not find them, we recreate settings in which they reappear in our memory.

I feel a surge of great happiness when I look at our rose garden or a table nicely laid, knowing that my mother, were she still alive, would compliment me effusively, her little girl who is doing so well. I can hear her words, faithfully recorded, just the way she said them on many occasions. I can also hear my father exclaiming, "That's wonderful!" when as a child I used new and difficult words correctly; he praised me even if I used them incorrectly, but got out the dictionary so "we could learn together." We generally cannot stop doing that for which we are or were praised. This can be either a boon or a blessing, depending on what we were praised for. If a child was praised for a good job of pilfering food from the corner grocery store for his bereft family, he might set about becoming the world's cleverest thief. Mother loved me, why not you?

Our hobbies reflect our past happiness. Tom is building an elaborate O-gauge model railroad layout in a large room he recently built. It is a marvel of engineering, precisely to scale, complete with sound. Mountains, lakes, roundhouses, pumping stations, crossings, trestles, all will form the setting for the magnificent locomotives, passenger and freight cars he has been building throughout his life. Though he often spends time there alone, he is not really alone, for he replays rich memories of his father, a locomotive engineer, recalling the evenings when as a little boy he sat on his father's lap listening to the often-repeated, exciting stories about pushing the iron giant at full steam down the main line to "get her there on time."

The People of Today

Making the past come to life in the present has deep personal meaning for many people, but it is not enough. Stroking is like manna from heaven. It lasts one day. Then we need a new supply, for past happiness can seem as old as yesterday's newspaper. Whatever our past glories, however many trophies we have collected, however thick our scrapbooks and photo albums, we wake up thinking, What's for today? as surely as we wonder, What's for breakfast? Literally, we break our fast, both our food fast and our folks fast.

It is our belief that every person, on entering a room of people, a meeting, a convention, a sidewalk gang fight, a party by the pool, a trip to the moon, has surging within him or her a primary question, *the* primary question, *How do you get strokes around here?* It is as fundamental as mother's breast and "Look, Ma, no hands!"

People in Relationships

People at random are not reliable stroke sources. Therefore we form *relationships*. Relationships are to stroking what granaries are to bread, a guaranteed supply. A person is defined by the sum of his relationships. If you want to know who you are, consider your relationships. A good exercise is to list all the "people" you are. A woman may be a wife, mother, aunt, sister, citizen, teacher, friend, neighbor, student, church member, bowler, investor, philosopher, philanthropist, bridge player, or bridge builder. Make your own list. A man may be all of the above except wife, mother, aunt, and sister. Each person you are involves you with other persons in unique relationships; that is, you are a different person to your spouse than to your neighbor, and different still to your friendly folks at E. F. Hutton. A helpful way to visualize your relationship world is to draw a diagram (Figure 7) with yourself in the middle circle and the persons in your life in the satellite circles around you, each connected to you by a spoke.

Intrinsic to a relationship is that you allow it to have a claim on you, more specifically, a claim on your time. This is what makes a relationship different from a casual acquaintance, someone seen every so often on a commuter train or at the supermarket. Even a casual acquaintance, in our thinking, holds a claim of common decency or help in the case of emergency, his only credentials being that he is a human being. The claims of personal relationships, however, take precedence. If you deny the claim of relationship and chop off a spoke coming to you and say in effect, "I'm sorry, I haven't got time for you anymore," that relationship no longer exists. The person so cut off may still be around, but you do not *feel* that person's presence. Then it is you who may be lonely.

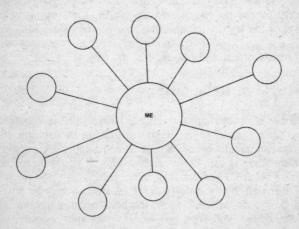

Figure 7
Relationship Diagram

During the "liberated sixties and the searching seventies" an uncommonly large number of people decided "to leave all this and go find myself." Off they went to a desert island or a mountaintop in Tibet or took a slow boat to China. Many left for good, abandoning existing claims on their lives—spouses, children, business commitments, promises to be kept. Frequently, rather than finding themselves, they found nothing, and discovered, as the old saying goes, that "wherever you go in the world, there you are." They may have found they were more lost than ever because they had cut themselves off from the relationships that defined them. Rather than finding themselves, they found nothing at all. We feel the presence of others only when we allow them to have a piece of us, a piece of our time.

Having taken a relationship inventory, we soon recognize there are competing claims. We cannot be everything to everybody all the time. We must give some thought to how many people we can be responsive to. We also must set priorities. Which relationships build a granary? Families do. Friends do. Communities of people with a common purpose do—churches, temples, and service organizations. Where will your bowling team be when you are sixty-five? Your business associates? Your buddies at Archie's Place? The answers are not forgone, but the question is important. If we distribute ourselves in small change, our emotional income down the road will no doubt be similar. Which calls to mind the sad statement of a socially overcommitted woman who said, "When my children were little I thought I couldn't stand it until they grew up, and when they did I discovered they couldn't stand me." There can be too many people in our lives.

An error in the other extreme is having too few people in our lives, thus clinging desperately to those we have, ultimately losing them. More about this in Chapter 11, "Keeping People."

Giving Strokes

To stroke someone is to give him what he wants. Not everyone wants the same form of stroking. *Stroking in its most basic form is defined as entering someone's awareness*. It is recognition. You see me. You acknowledge my entry into a room. You say "hello." I say "hello" back. It feels good. If this elemental recognition is absent we feel discounted: literally, I don't count. They don't want me here. I shouldn't have come.

Awareness is possible only after we have come to an understanding of our own internal dialogue so that our Adult is free to *see* other people. Total seeing means we see *all* of them, their Parent, Adult, and Child. We can pick up clues as to what they need. Sometimes they need to be left alone, once their presence has been acknowledged. *Stroking,* the word itself, does conjure up an image of physical activity. So understood and carried to extremes, a gathering of stroke-conscious people would be comic, with everyone going around pumping hands, slapping backs, hugging, grinning perpetually, putting *energy* into words, in a fashion so frenetic as to make sensitive people want to run. How calming to recall the words of our late friend Professor Edson Caldwell, "The greatest gift one can bestow on another is his undemanding presence."

Giving strokes to others because *we* need to, because we are supposed to, is called *marshmallow throwing:* not too bad for starters, but sickeningly sweet after a whole bagful. *Get out there and stroke someone* may be *our* agenda, but it may not be what someone else wants. Have you ever seen the overwhelmed look on the face of an infant who is being "comforted" by being jiggled up and down vigorously by an anxious parent? Of course the baby stops crying. He can hardly breathe.

The greatest affirmation we can give another is *awareness*, first of all, and then responses based on what he or she is saying or doing, not what our Parent or Child is clamoring for. Love begins by seeing another person's Child, possible only after we have handled our own agenda through Trackdown. When we see clearly, because our full awareness is focused on another, we will know what is needed: a touch on the shoulder, no touch at all, gazing silently, asking a question, not asking a question, offering to help, *asking* for help. In our need to give we may forget that others also need to give, and we become ungraceful receivers. We also may be hungry givers. It is possible to say "I love you" in such an impoverished way that the person so "loved" feels drained.

When we reach out to someone, eager to "lay on" a stroke, we need to ask ourselves, Why am I doing this? Because I should, must, have to? Is it a tradeoff? If we see giving as a guarantee for getting, a mathematical formula to get us through the lean days, the selfish nature of our giving will probably show. Certain charitable folks in times past had a ritual of getting together baskets of food for the needy and distributing them solicitously on Christmas Eve, spreading their largess with ritual warmth, then fleeing the dark scene, having done their duty. Their gifts no doubt filled hungry stomachs but did they fill hungry hearts? There is a patronizing way of giving that makes those who receive feel more impoverished than ever. The rule is always: Protect the other person's Child, his feelings and self-esteem. Charitable organizations still help the poor by stocking food closets and clothes closets, where needy people can come at a time they choose. It seems a better way.

Very often people, especially in times of grief, do not need your advice or even comfort as much as they need *you*. Being there is often the greatest gift. An open ear is often more welcome than a talking mouth. Shared tears are often a greater gift than a stiff upper lip. Lord Byron wrote, "We can see farther through a tear than through a telescope." Feelings are often more precious than facts. Again, awareness of the other person is the key. The weak do not always need the strong. It helps sometimes to share our failures.

In an article entitled "Failure at Forty" Edward Ketcham wrote: "What took me by surprise was the fact that my supposed failure opened up relationships with my co-workers. I had forgotten that every man, having failed in some area of life, will entrust himself to another broken spirit."* To cry, if that is what you feel like doing, can be a healing participation in someone else's pain, a stroke deeply felt and appreciated.

*Edward Ketcham, *Faith at Work*, August 1971.

Forms of Stroking

Assuming we are *aware* and honestly *desiring* to live in community with others, what are specific forms of stroking we may begin to practice?

1. *Eye contact*. Seeing you seeing me is like two souls entering each other. The contact need not be prolonged or intense or a "stare-down." Charles Gillett, president of the New York Convention and Visitors Bureau, stated, "Many people hardly shake hands with you before their eyes begin to wander. You think, 'For Heaven's sake, pay attention for a few seconds at least, until you finish meeting me.'" "What makes men sexy?" one woman was asked. "His eyes," she said, "if they are seeing me." See for yourself!

If you wear glasses, wear them! Wash them, too, at least once a day. If you need glasses and don't like them, ask your ophthalmologist if your vision can be corrected by contact lenses. Vanity may have its rewards, but intimate relationships aren't among them. People who wear glasses sometimes leave them at home when they go to a party, thinking themselves more attractive that way. Yet they may feel a bit "out of it" if everyone is a blur. Their preoccupation is "How do *I* look?" not "How do *you* look?" and is as counterproductive as the Good Guy's "How'm I doing?" How can you possibly see the wave of a friendly hand across a crowded room when your vision stops six feet ahead of you? We miss stroking if we don't see. Neither do we stroke others if we don't see them.

2. *Listen*. Among the greatest strokes is listening to what someone else is saying. Let other people finish sentences. Take your time. Take their time. Relax. Avoid the hurry-up body language, the up-and-down head motions that tell another person to talk faster, the impatient interruptions meaning, "Get on with it, I haven't got all day." If you do not, in fact, have all day, make a *straight* statement at some point in the conversation: "I would like to stay and talk with you, but I have an appointment at 10 A.M., so now I must

go." Variations of this can be stated courteously, protecting the other person's Child.

If you have a hearing difficulty, wear a hearing aid. If you know someone who wears hearing aids, ask how it feels. Hearing aids are not easy to wear. Tom has a severe hearing problem. He was a career medical officer in the Navy and on a ship during the Pearl Harbor attack. The hours of explosions and concussion damaged his ears. He wears two hearing aids, but he also relies on lipreading. One way to be considerate of him is to stay in place while talking, and not to start a sentence and continue it while walking across the room. One way to stroke the disabled, if we know them well enough, is to ask about their disability, not to ignore it as if it's nothing. We can then further ask, What can I do to make it easier for you? Hearing-aid wearers do not need people to shout at them. The volume is set. Shouting is painful.

3. *Ask questions*. What we ask and how we ask it must be grounded in awareness. Despite the fact that we may have been conditioned "not to pry," the reality is that most people like the inquiries of others. Not all, but most. We are introduced to persons who obviously have a rich background of experience. They may have credentials up to the ceiling, and they would love to have you know about their lives. They are not about to say, Did you know that I was the first woman to orbit the earth, swim the English Channel, vote, or receive the Nobel Prize back in aught-two? Humor helps. "I take it you are visibly and gainfully employed" generally will bring a happy response, unless you know you are talking with a racketeer. This can lead to "I would like to know how you came to be the President's Advisor on Philatelic Exchange." And so the conversation progresses, enriching both of you.

4. *Use names*. How wonderful to be called by name. How depressing to be called someone else's name or a catchall name like Sweety or Deary or Boy or Hey You. From cradle to grave your name is *you*. At age eighty-five my father was in a convalescent hospital recovering from difficult surgery. He was so weak he spoke only in a whisper, but even in a whisper his voice was indignant: "What do

these nurses know about suffering? They call me *Honey*. Don't they even know my name?" I suggested to the hospital director that patients' names be printed in large letters at the foot of each bed so every nurse would know it on entering the room. I felt that to be called by name would be at least as healing as a medication schedule. He agreed and said he would look into it, indicating such a public tag would require the patient's permission, since some people want to be anonymous.

Awareness, again, is the key to name usage. In our slapdash, All-American, cozy-up way we get to using first names awfully fast. Someone said it was a stalwart lodge brother who first called John the Baptist *Jack*. If a person has used a fourth of his or her life getting a doctorate, being addressed as *Doctor* Abercrombie will probably be deeply appreciated. It is a matter not only of honor but of identification.

Having spent considerable time in Sweden I grew to appreciate the Swedish people's use of titles. There nearly everyone has a title. Introductions are formal. If a man is a railroad stationmaster that information is included in a title at introduction. When I was there I was introduced as a journalist. People are thus identified—nurses, teachers, executives, clergy, scientists, engineers, editors, psychologists, psychiatrists, accountants, landowners, shopowners, secretaries. Therefore, on introduction you can proceed with a conversation, knowing a great deal.

When Sweden's King Karl Gustaf was visiting San Francisco a reporter asked him what he would like to be called. He said, "You may call me King." A fairly clean transaction.

In the United States about the only designations commonly used are Dr. and various forms of address for religious and political personalities. What if you are introduced to someone who is the president of the National Archives of Western Thought? "I would like you meet Joe Smith," your host says warmly. "Hi, Joe," you say, friendly-like. Would you have greeted him differently if you knew his name was Professor Joseph McGillicuddy Smith, or at least Professor Smith? With that information your conversational exchange would perhaps lead to something interesting quickly. Joe may feel something is lacking, the fact that you have no idea of his forty years of intensive research in archaeology and philosophy and another ten years in fundraising for a noble cause. This information may come out, but usually in ulterior ways. Enter, *games*. When we cannot be straight about what we do, we start showing off symbols—cars, clothes, jewelry—or mannerisms—polite smoldering, esoteric language, silence. But to someone so educated this would not matter, you say? Want to bet? People are more human than not.

A negative aspect of the titling system is that it may not seem democratic. What if you are "just a person"? There is still Mr., Mrs., Miss, and Ms. These appellations used with the last name individuate a person to a greater degree than the first name only, identifying him with a family. Once people know each other, first-name usage may proceed comfortably, based on the group protocol. Certain large companies encourage the use of first names among their employees, contending informality fosters cooperation and creativity. It is probable, however, that these employees already know a great deal about one another. Perhaps they learned some of this information when they were first introduced.

Most of us, on occasion, are somewhat uncomfortable with introductions and don't know exactly what to say, inasmuch as our rules are vague. Sad, for introductions could be the start of a pleasant transaction, even a relationship. We should decide on forms of etiquette and then teach our children how to introduce people. In our opinion children should call their elders by a relational name, such as Aunt Mary Alice or Uncle Elvin, or the neighbor by formal address, such as Mr. Huysman or Mrs. Gunderson. This is one way of establishing that grownups are in charge here. Like thanking the hostess, it is a matter of manners. Not only do manners advance friendly, orderly relationships but, as Prince Charles said, "They get you what you want."

Whatever we call people, the essential communication should be that "you count," *you're OK*. Columnist Herb Caen of the San Francisco *Chronicle* reported the following story about the late debonair Pierre Monteux, who was then conductor of the San Francisco Symphony:

"One time in New England the Monteuxes and their famous poodle Fifi were turned away from a motel by the owner, who, seeing the dog, snapped, 'We're full.' Then, suddenly recognizing Monteux, she ran after them and invited them back, apologizing: 'I didn't realize you were someone.' 'Madame,' replied the maestro, 'everyone is someone. Au revoir.'"

5. *Give yourself away.* Giving your name away is a start. It is easy to sense if someone can't remember you. Instant relief comes if you say warmly, "I'm Susan Williams, and I think we met at the PTA meeting. I'm Bobbie's mother." If the other person does not respond with *her* name, which she probably will, it is no sin to say, "I'm sorry, I feel I should remember your name, but I don't." Take a risk. It is better than mumbling through an uneasy conversation preoccupied with "What's her name, what *is* her name, *what* is her name?"

6. *Be a rewarder.* No matter how busy you are, it only takes a minute to send someone a postcard, a clipping, a note to say you appreciate his or her kindness, call, or letter. The rule is: Do it now! Then you can dispense with the long first paragraph stating how busy you've been, apologizing for your lateness, giving all the boring excuses.

7. *Carry an address book, postcards, and a pen.* One of the banes of modern life is waiting. In airports, checkout lines, bus benches, and waiting rooms. Rather than cursing your boredom or the outdated magazines, write a note to a friend. If persons are the most important thing in the world, your address book is one of your most important assets. The faintest ink is better than an intention not acted upon. Ten words, hastily written, are better than none.

8. *Plan.* Some people think happiness is a *happening* that magically occurs to them. If they just sit around and wait, the bluebird will certainly land on their sill. A bird feeder would be a good inducement. In one of our groups the subject of party planning was being discussed. A woman said, "I think things that are spontaneous are more fun." We agreed, spontaneous things *are* fun, but it became ap-

parent that more spontaneous things happened to people who also made plans.

The problem with parties is we make them too elaborate. Some admonishing voice says, "You can't serve *that* to company." If it's edible you can. Perfectionism cuts the nerve of effort. So what if it's not perfect; it may be fun.

9. *Don't allow discounting.* The opposite of discounting is *ac*counting. If you say "hello" to someone and he or she doesn't acknowledge your greeting, persist. Repeat yourself. "Hey, hi!" Maybe he didn't hear you. Maybe he is pretending not to hear you. If that person persists in ignoring you, then it's *his* problem. You will have done your part. "Give audibles" was one of our prescriptions in TA groups. If someone makes a contribution to a group discussion of which you are the leader, say, so he or she can hear, "I appreciate that" or "I don't agree with that, but thanks for your opinion." In the absence of audibles, group participants feel discounted and may feel they made stupid remarks, vowing to keep their mouths shut in the future.

10. *Loosen up.* Humor is the whipped cream of life. It can effectively sweeten another person's Child, and laughter can ease the heaviness of duty, responsibility, care, and travail. Once when Gretchen was a little girl I had unloaded a parental dissertation on her, which ended, "I don't know what I am going to do with you." "Kiss me?" she suggested brightly. I have forgotten the problem, but I remember the kiss.

11. *Doers do, and tryers try.* Nothing new will happen in your life until your intentions hit your muscles and action begins. A clear giveaway to someone's noncommitment is the word *try:* I'm going to try to get more people into my life; I'm going to try to take charge of my life; I'm going to try to be more friendly. Substitute *will* for the *tries* and the prognosis is good. Substitute *action* for *will* and the deed is done!

New feelings grow from actions, not from thinking about actions. I'll try to write Uncle Henry one of these days is just something I *have* to do. Posting the letter is an accomplishment that feels good.

12. *Don't be overnumerous in your intentions.* If you

act today on any one of the above suggestions about giving
strokes, you will have broken the long spell of non-action—
if you, in fact, have been a non-actor. It may be better to
make *one* phone call than to make a list of the fifty-five
people you are going to call this year.

9

What Do You Want?

A woman reported serving on a long-range planning committee for her church. At the first meeting, held in the evening, the committee chair wrote on the chalkboard: GOALS: *Immediate and Long-term.*

Weariness showed on the faces of the committee members, all of whom had already put in a full day. *Goals!* No way did *that* word spell relief. It seemed another way to spell *should, have to, must, ought,* even *shalt.* Feeling the heaviness, the woman asked the chair if she could amend what he had written, to which request he gladly acceded. She erased GOALS and wrote WANTS: *Immediate and Long-term.* Then she wrote under this, *I Want:* 1 . . . 2 . . . 3 . . . 4 . . .

Facial expressions changed to curiosity, three people relaxed, two sat forward in their chairs, one laid down her pencil, and one said playfully, "What you got in mind?" Enter, Child. Also, laughter.

She explained her change. *Goal* seemed Parent, *Want* is Child. Leaving the Child out of our plans, whether for a church, a school program, or a family vacation, is a guarantee our plans will falter. We generally don't meet goals if we don't want them. As the committee began speaking of wants, personal wants, the general became specific. One member told of a family difficulty and stated he would like to see a group-counseling program established on a regular basis in the church. Another was concerned for her teenage son, who didn't want to come to youth nights anymore because the youth program "seemed about three years behind where he was." One woman said she was lonely, stating she would appreciate help in finding someone to share her home, grown empty and too large since her husband died. The committee members were speaking from their ultimate concerns, which included Child fears, needs, and *wants*. After personal wants, as they related to the church program, were listed, they began to outline some steps to provide answers.

Typical of goals the Child doesn't participate in are some of our New Year's resolutions:

1. Quit drinking. (Drinking what?) 2. Quit eating too much. (How much would be about right?) 3. Get organized. (Join a union? Clean my desk? Plan a demonstration? What?) 4. Jog ten miles every morning at 5 A.M. (Have I had my health checked to see if jogging is OK?) 5. Cut TV time. (What programs?) 6. Be pleasant all the time no matter what. (If a waiter spills scalding coffee down my back?) The Child is smart. If the Child *wants* any of the above, the resolutions will be specific. Vagueness supports the status quo as in the case of politicians who promise better conditions for the poor, or more equality for women and men. Equality is equality. How can one have more or less?

Having made the above New Year's resolutions we begin with an illusion that we will change. However, by Day 3 the power supply has run out and we fall off the wagon into the potato-chip bowl, kick off our shoes and watch a rerun of the late-late show when we know we ought to go to bed.

Friedman and Rosenman wrote in *Type A Behavior and Your Heart*, "If you are to live a beautiful life, you first must begin to live beautiful days." How do we set up beautiful days? They suggest, "To live beautiful days, you also must think of beautiful things and events, even if these things and events seem silly to your . . . associates."*

As we need to divide our life into manageable chunks

*M. Friedman and R. Rosenman, *Type A Behavior and Your Heart*, Alfred A. Knopf, New York, 1974, p. 203.

of days, we also need to contemplate beauty as *we are able to see it*. Beauty to be experienced must be beauty in the context of our own life situation. If ugliness and misery are our experience and we want to change that experience, we must begin somewhere confronting the specific. We begin with want lists. For those who think wanting is selfish or hedonistic or "silly," an analysis of our wants will help us to discover whether or not this is true. Nothing can be analyzed, however, until it is stated in specific words. Here is how to start.

Take a piece of paper and start writing off the top of your head, by free association. Unedited. It's *your* list, your life. Don't share it until you have analyzed it. If, for instance, you want to take up hang gliding, don't show your list to your spouse until you have considered the consequences, a part of the analysis you are going to do. If *your* hang gliding is going to make him a nervous wreck, you may decide against it. The many parts of our life, most of which involve relationships, must hang together, unless one of our wants is to be a hermit. This does not mean that everything we want must meet with unanimous approval; yet we need to understand the consequences of disapproval. We then must figure out what to do when my want collides with your want.

First list your wants, whatever comes to mind, whether immediate or long-range, silly, salty, or salubrious. Here is one list:

1. A red sports car.
2. Roller skates.
3. A tan.
4. A million dollars.
5. A friend.
6. Twelve kids.
7. A Cross pen.
8. The Harvard Classics.
9. A word processor.
10. A dog.
11. To be President of the United States.

12. To be president of the PTA.
13. A pair of Birkenstock shoes.
14. Pretty teeth.
15. Contact lenses.
16. A gorgeous body.
17. A box of geraniums at the front door.
18. Blond hair.
19. A soulmate.
20. A water bed.
21. My name in lights.
22. A mountain cabin.
23. Food for my children.
24. A dinner party.
25. Bar bells.
26. A five-pound box of chocolate-covered, cream-filled candies.
27. A mo-ped
    [Long, isn't it? Keep writing. It doesn't cost any more to dream big than to dream small.]
28. A glorious cause.
29. Bilateral disarmament.
30. A down comforter.
31. To play the piano.
32. My own desk.
33. An answering service.
34. Peace and quiet two hours every morning.
35. Respectability.
36. To spell accurately.
37. Intimacy with another person.
38. Christmas in the Caribbean.
39. To enjoy life to the fullest.
40. A shower.
41. Find someone nice and rich to marry.
42. Youth.
43. A haircut.
44. Wake up in the morning happy.
45. A piece of lemon meringue pie.
46. Write a book.
47. A Ph.D.

48. Phone an old friend long distance.
49. Adopt a child.
50. No headaches.
51. A party.
52. Learn French.
53. Visit every state in the Union.
54. Plant a rose garden.
55. Sing in a choir.
56. A clean desk.
57. A promotion at work.
58. A divorce.
59. Live in a commune.
60. Live a long life.
61. Meet the President.
62. Run for Congress.
63. Play dominoes.
64. Laugh.
65. Go for a walk.
66. Join a prayer group.
67. Tell the boss off.
68. Memorize Shakespeare.
69. Tailor-made clothes.
70. Learn to play the French horn.
71. Plant potatoes.
72. Paint the mailbox.
73. Running water.
74. An exercise machine.
75. A banana.

The value of the above list is its specificity and spontaneity. These are the kinds of exact wants that intrude into our awareness daily as we go about our business as usual. It helps to contemplate that others go about wanting things as specific and even "weird" as we. People sometimes seek "safety" for what they want by formalizing their fantasies and sharing them with the world by pasting bumper stickers on their cars: "I'd rather be flying" or snorkeling or sailing or making love.

Some things we can do immediately, like smile or laugh.

Norman Cousins, when he was desperately ill, believed laughter would be curative, which he proved to be true.* He arranged to see funny movies and had his nurse read humor books to him. For him laughter took planning. Buying a Cross pen takes only a trip to the store and money to buy it. We can go for a walk, and it doesn't cost us a cent. A useful way to look at wants is as (1) things we can do alone and that cost nothing; (2) things we can do alone and that cost something; (3) things we can do with others and that cost nothing; and (4) things we can do with others and that cost something. These categories help defuse our excuses that "we don't have enough money" or "we don't have any friends."

Often we must break our generalized wants into manageable pieces. Possibility lies in specifics. Though we may want something as ultimate as world peace, this desire generally comes into our awareness in a group setting, in a discussion of global issues, in response to reading the morning paper. It does not generally become specific until we read we may be drafted or we watch The Day After. A sign in our office states, "Nothing ever happens until it happens to you." Actually, this is not so. Experientially, it seems so. Some of the above wants may seem trivial to certain people, perhaps to you. This brings us to the next step of our want analysis.

What Part of Me Wants It?

After each want, determine what part of you wants it: Parent, Adult, or Child, or any combination of these. This takes some time and thought, but so does any other kind of analysis. If we discover the Child doesn't want it, we probably

*"We took sedimentation rate readings just before as well as several hours after the laughter episodes. Each time there was a drop of at least five points. The drop by itself was not substantial, but it held and was cumulative. I was greatly elated by the discovery that there is a physiologic basis for the ancient theory that laughter is good medicine." Norman Cousins, The Anatomy of an Illness, Norton, New York, 1979, p. 40.

won't get it, for it is the Child who provides the "want to," the motivation. If only the Child wants it, it may not be good for us, for the Child does not consider consequences and other realities. If only the Parent wants it, we may feel a heavy *should,* and fear in the Child may provide some motivation, but fear, though it may have its roots in life preservation, does not always produce life enhancement. The Adult must also be involved in the want, for it is the Adult that provides the "how to." A team-up between Adult and Child is sometimes successful even if the Parent does not get what it wants. A combination of Parent, Adult, *and* Child, if such a configuration is possible, generally means we will get what we want. The desire to please the Parent never leaves us. Parent approval is a permanent recording, internal applause that still feels good. Therefore, we never stop trying to accommodate the Parent, as we once did, though our accommodation may have the mark of our own particular self-assertive modification. For instance, a politician's son may vow never to become a politician, but he may become a reporter on the Capitol beat, taking on the politicians *and* his Parent, but still involved in politics.

Options for Getting Each Want

If you want a million dollars there are a number of ways to go about it, including robbing a bank. Other ways include getting an advanced degree, switching from poetry to petroleum, marrying someone rich, asking for a raise, diving for sunken treasure, saving all your money, or spending nothing. You may wish to follow Samuel Johnson's advice: "Vow always to be rich. Spend less." Or you may buy a book that tells you "how to get rich the easy way," or even the hard way. Getting information, and examining it critically, is essential to getting what we want and may also have the effect of convincing us that we do not want it after all.

One option some people never consider is to ask for what they want. The more specific we are, the better the chances of getting it. You are vacationing at the home of a friend. In the midafternoon you suddenly have a craving for a banana. What are the chances of getting a banana with the following statements?

1. "I'd like to treat you to dinner tonight [maybe they'll have bananas there]." (That's hours away and you want your banana *now.*)

2. "Interesting how many fruit trees grow in California. Do you have any?" (A long conversation may ensue about horticulture. Your stomach is still growling for a banana.)

3. "I've turned into a real fruit nut since I've come here. In fact I wouldn't mind having some about now." ("Great idea," says your hostess. "I have some marvelous fresh peaches. Would you like me to fix you a bowl?" Very nice, but a peach isn't a banana.)

4. "For some vague reason I'm dying for a banana. You don't happen to have any around the house?" (Chances are you'll get what you want. Either your hostess will have a banana all ready and waiting for you, or you can offer to walk to the corner fruit stand and buy some or even treat your friend to a banana split at the ice-cream parlor.)

Other considerations apply along with your banana need— timing, courtesy, how long since you've eaten, etc. Such conditions being favorable, you will probably get exactly what you want, because you asked for it. Before you ask, however, think of the consequences.

Consequences of Each Option

It is the Adult's job to consider the consequences of each option for getting what we want. Robbing a bank may get us a million dollars for a few hours. However, the likelihood is we will end up in the slammer. Marrying someone rich may mean marrying someone selfish. Or it may not, depending on the person. Getting a divorce may lead to the discovery that the grass isn't always greener on the other side.

A consequence of being perpetually, just-off-the-beach tanned may be skin cancer. My name in lights may take away my privacy. If I tell off the boss I will probably have to forget about a promotion. Eating a five-pound box of

chocolate-covered, cream-filled candies will put 8,898 calories into my body, which is the equivalent of 2.5 pounds,
inasmuch as there are 3,500 calories in a pound. I would
have to walk 89 miles at 3 miles per hour to burn it off. To
tell myself, "You can't eat candy" is not as motivating as
"You *can* eat candy if you want to walk 89 miles, or deficit
8,898 calories in your diet over a period of several weeks."
An objective view of consequences is the function of the
Adult. The Parent may also contribute to the "discussion."
"Eat candy by the box and you'll get fat" is possibly, if not
probably, true. Knowing exactly "how much candy" and
"how fat" is more convincing. Parent *don't* messages feel
depriving. Adult conclusions give us freedom to choose for
ourselves and leave us responsible for our actions. We are
fortunate if we have good nutrition messages in the Parent,
for they reinforce good eating habits, with which the Adult
also concurs. More often we are influenced by such messages as the Pillsbury ad with the hard-to-forget song "Nothin'
spells lovin' like somethin' from the oven." There's a lot
of truth in that, but, again, it depends on what's in the oven,
and who weighs what. If everyone in your family is roly-
poly, and if walking from one room to another makes you
pant for breath, it is *not* loving to serve up Boston cream
pie after the deep-fried chicken and mashed potatoes with
gravy.

Wanting twelve kids may grow from a fantasy of having
seen *Cheaper by the Dozen,* or recalling the children's voices
in *Sound of Music*. Or we may think of touch football on
the rolling lawns of the Kennedy compound, with robust
young bodies and waggy-tailed dogs racing pell-mell in
happy contest. But are these *our* settings? Twelve children
cost money, take time and emotional stamina. So do two
children, or even one. In the case of large families both
Parent and Child may agree; the Adult may dissent. If it
does, we ignore it at great risk.

A pair of Birkenstock shoes may be frowned on by the
Parent, depending, of course, on whose Parent we are talking about. But Birkenstocks feel good to the Child, and the
Adult can list many reasons why they are good for the feet,
the back, and the personality. Who can feel they are living

the abundant life with feet that are killing them? The marketing of women's shoes appeals to the Parent and to the adaptive Child, who wants "to be attractive at any price," but ignores the Adult considerations of health, posture, and comfort. When our daughters were little, we kept them in perfect-fitted shoes, complete with inserted corrective "cookies." When we went shopping for the first pre-adolescent dress-up shoes, *at the same store,* the salesperson brought out pairs of fashionable shoes with "high" heels. They did not come in the widths the earlier shoes had. They didn't fit, in fact. The proper width was not stocked. When I objected I was told, "This is what little ladies are wearing now. They're definitely *in*." Girls, once they reach junior high school, are loaded with socially-programmed Parent messages, often from sales*men* wearing comfortable Hush Puppies. Years of healthful foot care may be wasted. Boys do not have to contend with this sudden switch, a clear, as-fundamental-as-you-can-get example of inequality. "The little old lady in tennis shoes" is still the subject of derisive humor. Sadly, many women, along with many men, laugh. Who buys your shoes? Your Parent, Adult, or Child?

When Wants Conflict

We don't have time for everything. We may have pared our want list down to realistic, possible, Child-involved, Adult-approved, and perhaps even Parent-encouraged desires. Even then, we must pare some more. One of our illusions, particularly when we are young, is that we will live forever. Clearly, priorities must be decided on, for our wants may be many but our time limited.

A twenty-year-old woman who wants a political career and ultimately a seat in Congress may not find it advisable, according to her time limitations and values, to have children. Instead, she may choose to adopt an older child who does not need as much time as is required by a preschooler. She also needs to know how much attention an older child needs. Or she may postpone her political strivings until her children are grown.

If she wants a figure like Bo Derek's she may have to

forgo the lemon-meringue pie or the chocolate candies. If one wants to wake up in the morning happy and without headaches, it is possible one must give up continuous late dinner parties. If one wants to write a book, there may not be time to be president of the League of Women Voters or organize a protest march or sing in the choir. If you want a Ph.D., the cost and time involved may require a postponement of a trip around the world. *May,* that is.

On-the-go people, whom we usually see at their best (in magazine articles, on TV interviews, and giving talks) are frequently harried and dead-tired. Super-moms are examples, although they are to be commended for attempting to do their best, having children not only to care for but frequently to support financially. Once we have accepted responsibilities, we cannot, in good conscience, walk away. Ideally, want lists should be made early in life. Unfortunately, they seldom are. If we value ourselves and respect the limitations of time and personal energy, we must not take on more than we can realistically handle. If we have not learned to say *no* we will find our *yeses* lacking in enthusiasm and, increasingly, in follow-through.

If we know what we want, we probably can get a lot more out of life than we think. Quantities of energy are released when we finalize at least some objectives and cease our endless indecision. Frequently, when we lose sight of our objectives, we work out the resulting anxiety by redoubling our effort. We are not getting anywhere, but we are getting there twice as fast. The only place change is registered is in the wear and tear on our bodies and the slow erosion of our zest for life.

As we examine our wants, we may discover they conflict with our moral convictions. Moral convictions are not necessarily Parent although they frequently have their roots in what we learned as children. As we contended in *I'm OK— You're OK,* there are *shoulds* that are Adult.* Does getting what I want leave time to help others get what they want? Will my happiness be at the expense of someone else's

---

*See "P-A-C and Moral Values," *I'm OK—You're OK,* pp. 246–279.

happiness? Will getting what I want make me happy? What will make me happy?

What Did the Child Want Originally?

One of the benefits of writing a list of our transient or ever-present wants is that we get in touch with reality. Reality is our most important therapeutic tool. If we can't say it, we probably don't know it. Once our desires are written they have a life of their own. We can study them, reorganize, delete, and amend. We have constructed a useful inventory of those inner surges of hunger, which, unexpressed, are experienced only as deficiency. "If I only had *blank* I would be happy." A home of my own, a car, a beautiful figure, a good night's sleep. Will these things make me happy?

Because it is the Child who *wants,* it is useful to ask "What did the child want originally?" We believe the original wants were three: security, novelty, and meaning.

1. *Security.* Before the beginning, in the dark, warm, rocking home of the womb, the developing child felt abiding security. Rudely evicted at birth, the security was reestablished in mother's arms. Month after month, although the newborn grew into a perceived separate personality, the desire for security did not leave him. Nor does it ever. Small children insist on declarations of certainty that this is my bed, my room, my corner of the room, my blanket, my things, my mother, my father. Strangers frighten. Mother, putting on her coat, signals her departure. The baby cries. But the growing and learning process continues, and emerging from the child's vast array of innate capabilities is curiosity. He begins to measure his security—the safe confines of his playroom—against the *novelty* of what lies outside. Security is no longer enough.

2. *Novelty.* The curiosity-fueled race for novelty is faster in childhood than at any other time of life. Fifty per cent of human skill and knowledge is thought to be gained in the first four years of life.* Consider the complexity of

*Gabor Von Varga, *Appropriate Care,* London, 1982.

learning words, sentences, words for colors, symbols for symbols. Which reminds me of the prim young mother who told her children that the "cat went number you-know-what on the rug"; you-know-what meaning *two* and *two* meaning you-know-what.

An embodiment of the curiosity and inventiveness of the child was seen in the person of the late loved futurist Buckminster Fuller, with whom we shared a podium one spring in Honolulu. We were there as faculty members of the annual University for Presidents of the Young Presidents' Organization. We sat rapt during the plenary session, to which Bucky spoke on the "Basic Physical Movements of the Universe," which he demonstrated with his own body. He once said, "If you can't build a model of it, it isn't true." On this occasion, at age seventy-eight, he looked very much like a little boy, with his snappy crewcut, thick glasses, and turned-up glowing face. He wore a white sport shirt and faded tan fatigue pants. They looked as if they had been "let down," leaving a whitish former-hem line, producing the astonishing illusion that he had been growing. Mentally, he grew every day of his life, and his marvelous Renaissance enthusiasm has left us one of the greatest gifts of the century.

It was Fuller who said that every child comes equipped with a huge collection of alarm clocks set to go off in his head, and they will ring on schedule unless someone comes along and turns them off: *You're too young to be asking such questions. Don't bother me. Never mind why it's raining; get on your galoshes!*

Because of curiosity, the child overcomes his fear of strangers and reaches out to touch the unfamiliar beard, or the car keys of mother's friend, or the white fur of the new kitten. A paradox is that the more secure a youngster feels the farther he dares roam in his search for novelty. Learning to converse greatly enhances his security. He, along with grownups, can be told what to expect and thereby reduce the anxiety of comings and goings.

A friend told us about her four-year-old daughter, Polly. Polly was blessed with a mother who believed in keeping the little girl informed. One day a visitor was expected. Mother explained, "Polly, at two o'clock Mrs. Brown is

coming to see me. She is going to tell me about a correspondence course I want to take. She will be here about
one hour, and during that time you may either sit quietly
and listen or else find something to do in your room."
Mother added, "When I see her car drive up, I'll tell you,
and you may be my butler and open the door for her. Her
name is Mrs. Brown."

Thus informed, Polly, when the time came, opened the
door and said, "Hello, Mrs. Brown. I'm Polly. Please come
in. May I take your coat?"

Such hospitality from a young child brought a warm
response from Mrs. Brown and beaming but matter-of-fact
approval from Mother. Then Mrs. Brown asked if she might
use the "necessary room," to which Polly replied she didn't
think they had one. When told that was what the bathroom
was sometimes called, she declared they *did* have a bathroom.

Mother said, "Polly, please show Mrs. Brown to the
bathroom." Which Polly did. Then, from the hallway, through
the closed door, Polly instructed helpfully, "Call me when
you're finished."

Bright, precocious children are so because they are told
what is going to happen, what they are to do, and how long
it will take. Expectations are expressed, and "how to" is
explained. *Information* makes children secure in novel situations. Though there is some risk, it is minimized.

Sadly, for most people, the security-novelty blend is not
as smooth as Polly's. The two become polarized as if each
is on the opposite end of a spectrum (Figure 8). This configuration persists through life. Most of us live somewhere
in the middle, slightly uneasy about both ends. Some grownups devote total energy to the maintenance of security, making it the number-one priority in all their dealings. They
build high walls around their homes and egos, save every
penny for a rainy day, and weigh and reweigh consequences
on a gram scale until it is too late to make a decision. The
fences that protect them also isolate them. They are secure
but dead.

Some people live at the other end of the spectrum. Throwing caution to the wind, they live for the moment, always

Security	Novelty

Figure 8
Security-Novelty Spectrum

seeking a new experience, something more kicky or kinky. Their problem is that, lacking information, their felt independence may not last long, like the LSD-expanded driver who ended up in a body cast after a head-on collision because he couldn't tell the difference between a sunburst and a Sunbeam. At the novelty end of the spectrum are the life betters, the devil-may-care risk takers, and the Russian roulette players. They do not appear to worry who will pay their medical bills, if they survive.

What makes them live recklessly? Paradoxically, it is sometimes the security they feel in obeying the Parent directive to be daring, tough or flashy—all well meant, no doubt. Or they may be adapting to the patently destructive message to "go play on the freeway." Caring parents who introduce their children to risky ventures also teach safety, thereby assuring a prudent blend of novelty and security. If this is the case, some risky activities may lead to adventure and mastery. Risk can be fun if we "pack our own parachute."

Is that all? Security and novelty? We know people who seem to have an abundance of both and are unhappy anyway. In the security department are estates and villas, at home and abroad, boats, planes, paid slaves, a *carte blanche* on things, things, and more things. In the novelty department they are experience collectors, having tried everything from nude bathing at Big Sur to "doing lines" in a strobe-lighted penthouse. They are cruise-weary, safari-sapped, and gadgeted to death. They have money to burn, and nothing to learn. Or so they feel.

What they lack, it seems, is *meaning*. What is the significance of life, *my* life, amidst the din of doing and the fear of not doing? Meaning, which is to say a conviction of personal significance with some relationship to the surrounding universe, is also a desire of the young child. When

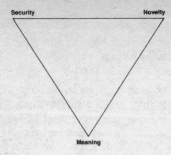

Figure 9
Wants of the Child

the little person asks, "Where did I come from?" he is as profound as Wordsworth pondering the "Intimations of Immortality." What is life for? What is death about? What am I worth? Isn't there more? Is this not the ultimate hunger? Many people would agree.

Much of my life, as a little girl, was filled with such preoccupations. Particularly do I remember Decoration Day. My family took tubfuls of peonies to the cemetery, where I helped put huge blooms in sunken metal cans on the graves of relatives and friends who had gone "home." Always there were enough flowers left over for a neglected grave, the "one over there who must have nobody." Decoration Day was a gentle way to learn about death, and as a little girl, I thought long, strange thoughts as I wandered through the marble stones, petting the sculpted lambs, staring into the vacant, reamed-out eyes of the stone angels, and wondering what the body I was standing over "looked like now."

Thus we add a third dimension to longings of the child, which remain longings throughout our life (Figure 9). Security, novelty, and meaning, and the greatest of these is meaning. Because their lives had meaning, the heroes and heroines of the world may have given up a great measure of security and novelty. We are heirs to their wisdom, and we can learn from them still.

10

Requirements for Change

Having made a want list, what do we do next? Wanting is half of getting there. The other half is change. What and who will change? Change surrounds us, but much of it seems for the worse—terrifying economic and political tension throughout the world, the national debt, the price of bread, population growth, and diminishing natural resources. Our personal contribution to this kind of change, or to stemming it, is limited, although we have evidence that individual voices crying in the wilderness have been heard and have made a difference.

What of the smaller world between Fourth and Main in Our Town, where we daily live our personal lives? How will change come about there? However much we may try to change others, the fact is, we cannot. We can influence, wheedle, and even help. If others say *no,* however, that leaves us, you and me. We can change only ourselves. When *we* change, we may effect change in others, but we must start with ourselves.

Wanting Comes First

Until we *want* to change, nothing different is likely to happen. Others may tell us we should, have to, or are "killing ourselves." We may know all that already, but our knowledge does not engage the gears of motivation unless *we decide* we want life to be different.

Three things make people want to change; pain, boredom, and enlightenment. When people hurt sufficiently, have beat their heads bloody against an unyielding wall long enough, have invested in the same slot machines enough years without a payoff, when they have hit the bottom physically or emotionally, there comes a moment of overwhelming finality. No more! They are ready and *willing* to change.

Boredom makes people want to change, going through life saying, "So what?" until they finally ask the big SO WHAT?, insisting "there has got to be more to life than this."

A third thing that makes people want to change is the discovery that they can. This has been an observable effect of TA. Many people who have shown no particular desire to change have learned TA, through lectures or reading, and this knowledge has produced excitement about new possibilities, never before dreamed of. Change was reported by thousands of readers of *I'm OK—You're OK*. A government official in New Delhi wrote: "In the absence of any coaching, I started self-practice after reading and re-reading your book. My deep-rooted fear and stress, tensions and hurry, have vanished. I am spell-bound by change, and bubble to share it with family and friends." A New Hampshire man wrote: "Your book *I'm OK—You're OK* has been, to say the least, a boon and a blessing to me in this, the worst period so far in my life. *It has got me thinking* [italics added]. I see some marked changes. As I continue re-reading and thinking about it, I hope to see more changes." A New York man: "My own marriage is near shambles with horrendous problems. Your book made me *want* to salvage my marriage, and I am grateful."

Positives Work, Negatives Don't

Often we contemplate change by planning what we are going to get rid of. Clutter, busyness, fat, fear, bills, sometimes people. *Don'ts* are depriving and account for the failure of many of our New Year's resolutions, half of which start with "Quit." Before we get rid of something, we must plan what will take its place or we may end up worse off than ever. *Dos,* on the other hand, are exhilarating. Without them we may end up with emptiness, a consummation not devoutly to be wished.

Is our motivation positive or negative? If we don't like the Parent program that is controlling us, we will not become free by flipping the computer card over and running it through our heads backward. Such reactionism is often observed in adolescents, when their behavior seems the exact opposite of everything they were ever taught. Though they seem to change, they are still dominated by the old program: they *have* to do just the opposite. They are not free for they can be controlled by any manipulator who tells them to do just the opposite of what the manipulator wants. Change designed to "show them" is not satisfying in the long run. Freedom is doing what is good for you even if your parents wanted it for you, too. Your Parent may contain vast stores of wisdom along with troubling messages such as we have described in earlier chapters. What is bad is following the Parent blindly, without ever examining it, like taking pills from an unlabeled bottle. They may be vitamins; they may be strychnine. Knowing the contents makes a difference.

Are our changes for us or for somebody else? Good weight-loss programs work when the staff members emphasize health, not the cosmetic aspects. They are *for* you, your health; they want you to live a long time; they love you; they don't imply you are disgusting the way you are. The idea is not to make a better person of you but to take better care of the person you are.

Whereas *don't* programs are depriving, *do* programs are exhilarating. *"Do* say hello to ten people a day you don't ordinarily talk to" will produce strokes, fun, and surprises. *"Don't* sit inside all day and feel sorry for yourself" will probably make you sit inside all day and feel sorry for yourself. Positive programs come from work on your want list.

Have a Reward in Sight

As we have stated, change, or redecision, requires Child participation. The Child was preeminently involved in our earliest decisions of how to get strokes and stay alive. Change will not work if it is merely an intellectual exercise, involving only the Adult. There has got to be something in it for the Child, little rewards along the way, not just one big vague reward years down the line, like "a happy and productive life." What about happy days? An important question to ask oneself when contemplating change—marriage, divorce, re-marriage, moving, selling, buying, quitting a job—is, Will I *feel* any better tomorrow because of this change? A week from now? Five years from now? Is *this* the change that will make an improvement in my life?

Every so often we vacation at the St. Helena Health Center in California's Napa Valley. Their fitness program is one of the best in the country, and a couple of weeks there is a great form of rest, recreation, and learning. The most glorious event of the day is the 6 A.M. brisk, super-oxygenated, one-hour walk through the mist-ribboned hills overlooking the vineyards in the valley, along footpaths lined with flowers, berries, curious small creatures, and ancient trees. One of the paths goes alongside a farm. This was the path Tom chose each morning. In the barnyard was a white horse who had worn a hard, shiny path to the fence where he came every morning, faithfully greeting the health-seeking city slickers, who usually obliged him with a nose rub and friendly conversation. One day Tom brought an apple for the horse, who ate it with frothy dispatch. The next day Tom again brought an apple, but called to the horse from the corner of the pasture instead of proceeding all the way to the shiny path. He whistled and held up the apple so the horse could see it. The horse started up the shiny path, as usual, but halfway along it he turned and made a direct approach to the corner of the pasture where Tom stood waiting. The following day, with another apple in sight, the horse didn't even use the shiny path, but came directly to the corner. The day after that he was waiting at the corner when Tom rounded the bend. With a reward in sight, and then in mind, he was quick to change his old habit and forge a new path, which got him what he wanted as quickly as possible.

Much of our life is dominated by habit; unthinkingly we walk the same paths, day after day, year after year. Rewards, experienced and repeated, provide a reason to change even the most ingrained habits, those we think we can never change: I am like that; that's just the way I am.

The Power of Habit

Habits are used by the body to save energy and are therefore valuable. Most of what we do is habit. Were we each morning to learn from scratch how to take a shower, the sun would be high in the heavens before we figured it out. Our getting-up rituals—tooth brushing, clothes donning, hair combing, shoe tying, shaving, makeup applying, bedmaking—are mostly automatic activities. So are poaching the eggs, eating them neatly, locking the door, starting the car, stopping for red lights, and timing the whole procedure to get us to work on time. The economy of habit is elegant, saving our energy for novel pursuits, problem solving, creative thought, reflection, and imagination.

Most often we think of habits negatively, bad habits that need breaking: a short fuse, smoking, overeating, slouching, speeding, procrastinating, frowning, compulsive spending, always saying *yes,* or *no,* or jumping to conclusions. Whether habits serve us well or ill they are automatic, programmed in primary brain circuits, producing behavior that is the path of least resistance. Unless energy is deliberately and repeatedly applied to new courses of action, we will continue to do the same thing the same old way.

The Brain Physiology of Change

How glibly we speak of change. "I changed my mind," someone says casually. "I am going to take charge of my life," says another. We speak of "turning over new leaves," starting over, becoming a "new you." Whimsically, almost, we speak of our intentions and convictions, without the slightest awareness of the incredibly complex fireworks going on in our brains as we speak.

In the dailiness of life we lost the childlike wonder we once possessed. When Heidi was three years old she fell across a barbed wire, which scratched her stomach. Awe-struck, she exclaimed, "Look, Mama, I cut into me." Her curiosity about "what was inside me" was fresh and wonderful, and to her the little cut was an opening into the inner world of her body. How often are we conscious of the blood coursing through our arteries, the faithful beating of our hearts seventy times a minute, the continual peristaltic work of our alimentary system? We forget how wonderful we are.

Yet none of these "lower body" events are nearly as incredible as what transpires, split-second to split-second, in our brains. At the moment of this writing my brain is intercepting millions of separate messages per second from my sensory receptors: information about balance, heat, cold, light, color, touch, the sound of birds singing, the hum of the air conditioner, knowing it is not yet noon, thirst, word search, that it is Thursday.

These brain events happen in actual places. There is tissue mass that corresponds to thoughts. If our knowledge and skill were adequate and our probes small enough, we might even find the Lilliputian path of an idea. At this moment some of your brain cells are firing at the rate of a thousand times per second. Where and how?

Most of us cannot think in these infinitesimal terms. I am reminded of a game my brother and I used to play as kids called "Half Way." We would stand at a given point in a room, then step off halfway toward the wall. From there we would go halfway again. And again and again. Though we always went only halfway and knew theoretically we would never get to the wall, we always *did*, frustrated and teasing each other as our feet hit the baseboard. Our game was an early lesson in the problem of matching practice to theory. We believed the theory was logical, but there was "something wrong with us" that we couldn't make it work. Our feet were too big.

The "Too-big-feet problem," as it relates to brain physiology, has been solved by the invention of electron microscopes, which in combination with computers can make pictures of "invisible" realities so large we can plaster the walls with them. Conservative estimates inform us there are at least ten billion neurons in the human brain, which by

seven years of age is almost adult in weight and size. There-
after, complexity is the result not of the growth of more
cells but of connections between cells. There are from ten
trillion to one hundred trillion such connections.

Each neuron may be likened to an electric generator.
Some neurons are running constantly while others fire intermittently as they receive messages from other neurons.
Each of the nerve cells produces about 20 millivolts of
power, and information is coded by the frequency of the
impulses. It is this electricity that we *see* on electroenceph-
alographic tracings.

The neuron has three parts: (1) the cell body, which
contains the nucleus; (2) the dendrites, which are the branches
of "receiving wires" that pick up messages from other neurons; and (3) the axon, or "sending wire" through which
messages are passed on after being evaluated by the nucleus.

The sending wire of one cell does not touch the receiving
wires of other cells. They lie on the other side of a chasm
that is a millionth of an inch wide (a far piece less than
"halfway to the wall"). The message must "jump" the chasm,
called the *synapse*. And then the next cell repeats the process. Brain messages can perform this "leap" 500 to 1,000
times per second, but average speed or frequency of firing
is 100 times per second.

There is no actual electrical connection and no passage
of electric current between one neuron and the next. The
sending wire of the cell ends in little protein vesicles called
boutons (French for buttons). The actual transmission of
the message across the synapse is a chemical reaction.
Chemicals produced by boutons "squirt" the message across.
When an action is repeated, stimulating cells at frequent
intervals, boutons at the synapse increase both in size and
number, shortening the span over which the message must
jump. *The more boutons, the less energy is needed for action
to occur, and thus habits are formed.* The more often we
perform the act, the more firmly the habit becomes established. As many as 80,000 boutons have been counted at
the edge of a single neuron. Boutons which transmit messages along habit pathways are thought to be permanent.
The name *engram* is given to the specific network of neurons

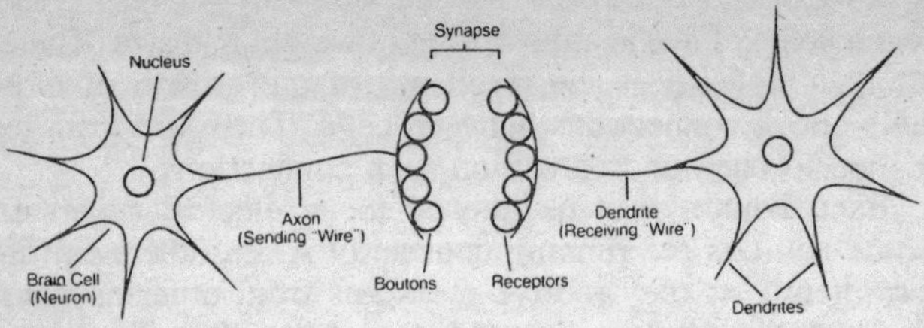

Figure 10
Brain Cell Transmission

in habit or memory chains that replay the same picture or movement with stimulation or association (Figure 10).

We Do Not Lose Our Boutons but We Can Build New Ones

Think of your habits. Then think of your boutons. How are you to change your habits if you can't get rid of your boutons, the faithful transmitters of years of economical stimulus-response messages? "How are you? Fine, thank you." See Baskin Robbins; buy double-decker coconut. Smell smoke; light cigarette. Hear phone; answer it. Boss enters; look alert. Walk on sidewalk; avoid cracks. Go to a wedding; cry. See a ladder; walk around it. See patrol car; lift foot off accelerator. With our past behavior so firmly encoded in a verifiable system of physiological reality, how can we change?

The encouraging discovery is that even though we cannot destroy the old boutons, we can grow new ones and build new neural pathways around the old ones. The most important element in building new habits is not time but *energy*.

Energy Builds New Habit Pathways

If we wish to make a new path across a grassy pasture, we will do the job faster if we dig our feet in hard, and faster yet if we do it frequently. Wholeheartedness produces maximum energy. It does not matter what kind of energy the body feels, emotional, physical, sexual; all can be used to build new habits.

Four groups participated in an exercise to learn nonsense syllables. The group lying down took the longest. The sitting people did better. Standing was better yet. The fastest learners were those who paced and said the syllables aloud. Positive emotional energy—joy, enthusiasm, anticipation, visions of glory, being stroked—is the most potent energy.

When we set about breaking old habits and building new ones, we often dissipate our energy by hemming and hawing. We are dieting. We are offered a piece of German chocolate cake. We have ten units of energy at our disposal to respond. If we put all ten into a courteous but hearty "no thank you" we will have produced a whole swarm of bouton molecules in our "no thank you, I'm keen and lean and like being seen" engram. What frequently happens instead is a dissipation of the ten units of energy because of our ambivalence:

Host: "Would you like a piece of German chocolate cake I baked this morning?"

Overweight Guest: "Would I like a piece of German chocolate cake? Is the ocean blue?" (1 unit used.)

H: "Here, I'll cut you a piece."

OG: "Uh, I really shouldn't. I'm on a diet, you know." (Tempted; "stinkin' thinkin'": 2 more units used.)

H: "But it's my birthday. C'mon, help me celebrate. One won't hurt you."

OG: "Well, just a little piece then." (Politeness sets in: 2 more units used.)

H: (Cuts enormous slab.) "How about a little ice cream with it?"

OG: "Oh, no! Well, if it's just a little." (Defeat setting in: 3 more units used.)

H: (Serves cake and ice cream.)

OG: (Eats guiltily, leaving some of the frosting, the best part, feeling deprived: remaining 2 units used.)

Had Overweight Guest put all ten units of energy into a "no thank you" response, he would have fired the synapse of a new habit path. With the ten units dissipated in indecision, the synapse did not have enough energy to fire, and the old habit, guilt and all, was reinforced. Toying with temptation drains energy. As one of the St. Helena lecturers advised, "If you want to stop going to pornographic movies, you had better stop looking at the marquees."

Evidence that change takes energy is provided by the stress scale for "Changes in Life Circumstances" developed by Drs. Thomas H. Holmes and Richard Raahe of the University of Washington School of Medicine. Even happy changes, such as marriage, a new baby, or a promotion, produce stress. Bad changes are worse, the death of a spouse rating highest on the stress scale. When many changes occur at once, raising the stress points to an overload level, physical illness often follows. Holmes suggests that we take our time arriving at important life decisions, anticipate life changes, plan for them in advance, and avoid, if possible, too many changes at once.*

It is important, therefore, to consider our timing when we undertake a move, a diet, or any other change in behavior. If bad timing turns our efforts into failure we may only reinforce our faulty assumption that (1) Happiness is for other people; (2) Nothing I do makes me happy; (3) See, I was right!

Energy Comes from People

Energy comes from strokes and strokes come from people. We rarely can change by ourselves. It is useful, therefore, to make a public commitment of our intention to change. Enlist the help of others, and, if they love us, they will not needlessly serve German chocolate cake in our presence. Group therapy is effective for the same reason. Being praised for our hard-won achievements is the apple that keeps us

*Thomas Holmes, lecture at "The Nature and Management of Stress" conference, Monterey, California, sponsored by the University of California, Santa Cruz Campus, April 15, 1978.

coming down a new path. The strength of new programming depends on how well it is reinforced by good feelings, rewards for the Child! These feelings can only be produced by experiences with others. Live in community. Ask your family for help. Join a group. Share yourself fully.

A New Internal Model

In the beginning we construct a model of how we should be by observing our parents. Children "take after" their parents, roly-poly mothers and fathers often producing roly-poly children. Happy, outgoing parents generally produce happy, outgoing children. Anxious parents, anxious children; door slammers, door slammers; and peacemakers, peacemakers. If parents are seldom seen or heard, children may model their lives after someone else—a relative, a teacher, a movie star. In adolescence peer models become important, but the old Parent model does not disappear. Some of the hairiest students of the hair-raising sixties today are close-shorn, wear banker's gray, and carry umbrellas. Even if our internal model is not in awareness, it exists in our Parent.

Internalized "persons" are more potent motivators than intellectual concepts even though the Adult may use such concepts to effect change. It is the Child who must *want* to change, and the kind of model that excites the Child is an actual person to emulate. If mothers or fathers did not provide healthy, attractive models, where can we go? Biographies are one rich repository of models. Friends and business associates may be models. Television provides models, but too often it indulges its audience in unwholesome, if not outright vile, forms of human behavior, cruelty, subterfuge, infidelity, and cheap sentiment. To its credit, television also brings us Carl Sagan, William Buckley, Alistair Cooke, J. Bronowski, Evelyn Waugh, James Joyce, the astronauts, political conventions, sports, the Olympic Games, historical documentaries, and the news.

If you want a new internal model, who do you want that person to be? Who are your heroes and heroines? Who were *their* heroes and heroines? In whom did they believe? What was their source of strength? Who makes you feel alive? Who gives you bootstraps? Who gives you hope? Anwar Sadat? Eleanor Roosevelt? Golda Meir? Lech Walesa? Henri Nouwen? Mother Teresa? Gloria Steinem? Emerson? Thomas Paine? Jean Stapleton? Pascal? St. Francis of Assisi? Disraeli? Buckminster Fuller? Billy Graham? Gandhi? St. Paul? Your next-door neighbor? Your mother? Your father? Willa Cather? Martin Luther King, Jr.? Martin Luther King, Sr.? Martin Marty? Einstein? Margaret Mead? Samuel Johnson? Samuel Gompers? Sir Thomas More? John Lennon? John Kennedy? Rose Kennedy? David Brinkley? Larry Holmes? Ralph Nader? Your big brother? Lee Iacocca? Beverly Sills?

Pick a person. Maybe no one knows that person but you. A person you admire. Find out everything you can about him or her. Try an experiment of *being* like that person for a month and see what happens. Have your feelings changed? Has your effect on others changed? When we were children we were ridiculed if we were "copy cats." What's wrong with that? When you have chosen your model, dress that way, look that way, *be* a copy cat. You are still you, but you have introduced into your personality a tangible idea of what you want to be like. A hat does not a Bella Abzug make, but if a hat turns you on, wear it. If it is fun, and does not hurt anybody, why not?

We Change a Little at a Time

Considering that it takes time to change our brain habit pathways, we do not become totally different overnight. In fact, a 180-degree change is suspect. We have either reversed the computer card, becoming a rebellious opposite, or we have merely changed loyalties, following a different leader, with the same blind conformity we once accorded the Parent. Zealots do not stop being zealots merely by changing their allegiance.

Small change, sustained, is more certain to produce different outcomes in life's transactions than the dramatic emergence of a "new you." In flying a plane, as little as a five-degree change in heading will make a significant difference in the total outcome of the journey. Although a

The difference I want	How far do I want to go?	Gain and loss	What will I do differently?

Figure 11
Behavior Change Chart

change in thinking precedes a change in behavior, it is changed behavior that counts. Action, not thinking alone, is what produces a new set of recordings, grows boutons, whose altered firing patterns sustain change.

A useful chart was developed in our groups to plan changed behavior (Figure 11). It has four parts:

1. The difference I want.
2. How far do I want to go?
3. Gain and loss.
4. What will I *do* differently?

A young man who desired to overcome his shyness used the chart in the following way:

1. More openness.
2. More openness in greeting rituals.
3. *Gain:* Strokes, getting to know people, overcoming loneliness, feeling alive. *Loss:* The protection that came from being shy, "precious," fragile: Who would dare criticize such a dear boy; "He's shy, you know."
4. Use of first names: Instead of "Hi" or a wave of the

hand, he began to say, "Hi, Bill," "Good morning, Susan."
He also began talking louder, which took energy but produced it as well, as the responses of others became more
enthusiastic.

Change Produces Loss as Well as Gain

We get paid for the way we are. How we are grows from
our early decision, "You Can Be OK If." If shyness was
the way for the little person to be OK with his parents,
shyness will persist in grownup relationships even though
it has many drawbacks. To give up shyness, or other be-
havioral armors, may mean a temporary loss of protection.
Most change in behavior produces loss as well as gain. If
the loss is not anticipated, and consequences are uncomfortable, we may feel our decision to change was wrong.

A decision to become assertive, to say what we mean
and feel instead of always sitting on our feelings, may produce discomfort in others. Losing weight may provoke others to say in word or deed, "I liked you better the way you
were." "Are you all right? You look so thin!" Change in
ourselves may be disruptive to others. That is why it is
important to talk about our intentions with those we love,
so our change does not become a threat to them.

Some change is seen as a move toward independence.
Independence does not mean we can go it alone. It means
we broaden the base of the people from whom we seek
support. We stop leaning on just one or two persons, or our
immediate family, and enlarge our community of friends,
our stroke sources. We may experience a loss of the old
comfortable, excluding "just you and me, Babe"; but we
will gain ultimately by an increase of self-esteem and a
decrease of the fear that attends putting all our eggs in one
basket. Often we feel the loss before we feel the gain. We
must, therefore, keep our goal in sight so that a momentary
dip in our self-confidence does not cause us to scrap our
program.

Everything costs. If we want more freedom we shall also
have to accept more responsibility (Figure 12). If we want
ten units of freedom we will have to accept ten units of

responsibility to make it work. As children we were free to go to the grocery store if we had responsibly learned to read road signs and grocery lists and could count money. As young people we are free to drive the car if we are responsible for paying the increased insurance premiums assessed because we have been added to the list of drivers. We are free to live in our own apartments if we are responsible for the rent, utilities, and doing our own laundry. We may lose our freedom in a hurry if we refuse to accept responsibility. A person may exult in breaking traffic laws, driving down one-way streets the wrong way, "doing as he darn well pleases." He has little freedom in the full body cast or jail cell he ends up in.

Conversely, we cannot exercise responsibility effectively if we are not given freedom to do the job. For instance, a personnel director in a large corporation is assigned the task of writing the house organ, developing job descriptions, and bolstering employee morale. He is not, however, given the freedom to hire or fire. He must therefore live with the one impossible employee who undermines all his efforts, bot-

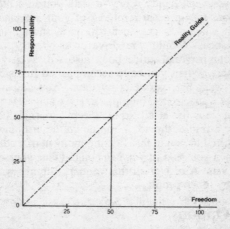

Figure 12
Freedom-Responsibility Graph

tlenecks work assignments, and snipes at everybody else. He cannot responsibly bolster employee morale if he is not free to confront, even fire, the person at the crux of the problem.

The Freedom-Responsibility Graph is useful when contemplating change. Is the responsibility you *feel* realistic? Do you feel responsible for everyone? Do you allow yourself to *feel* freedom? Have you updated the ifs in your life? If you are taking more responsibility, which may involve long hours and weekend work for a time, are you including in your plan commensurate time for rest and recreation? Does your change mean only adding and not subtracting? Whatever change you contemplate, one fact remains: there are twenty-four hours in a day.

Record Your Gains

The Child likes to *see* progress. Keeping records of the important changes in our life not only shows us what we did but spurs us on with the proof that *we can!* Keep your current want list handy. Carry it with you in a little black book as an ever-present reminder of your life plan. It will help you when you are on a trip or in strange or hostile circumstances. Would you drive cross-country without a map? Your personal guide book also will keep you from getting lost. When you have accomplished Items 5 and 12 on your want list, put stars by them. You deserve them. Add other wants to take their place. Have at least ten specific wants on your list at all times. Keep a journal. Creativity hangs by a fragile thread. Write down the brilliant thought that occurred to you in that fleeting moment of truth. A year later, when you read it, you can congratulate yourself. How bright I was. Am! Not all the wonderful things written are written by other people.

Have Options

Not everything we set out to do works. Factors outside ourselves intrude into our plans and can even bring them to an abrupt halt. Without options for getting what we want we may sink into failure. What if we lose our job? Our spouse? Our health? None of these are happy prospects, but the fact is losses occur, often through no fault of our own. Do we have Plans B, C, and D? Have we cultivated many friends with whom we can combine resources to get us through hard times? If we have only one friend, what happens if we lose him or her? While our children are growing we have discretionary time to plan what we will do when they leave the nest. Are we using that time to good advantage? Do we plan for retirement?

A useful practice is to note, alongside your want list: "When will I start?" and "When will I stop if it isn't working?" Sticking with the wrong plan proves little but perseverance, or stubbornness. Be flexible. Self-reliance need not be destroyed by adversity. Emerson encouraged starting over again and again, believing we have not one chance but a hundred chances:

> If our young men miscarry in their first enterprises they lose all heart. If the young merchant fails, men say he is ruined. If the finest genius studies at one of our colleges and is not installed in an office within one year afterwards in the cities or suburbs of Boston or New York, it seems to his friends and to himself that he is right in being disheartened and in complaining the rest of his life. A sturdy lad from New Hampshire, or Vermont, who in turn tries all the professions, who teams it, farms it, peddles, keeps a school, edits a newspaper, goes to Congress, buys a township, and so forth, in successive years, and always like a cat falls on his feet, is worth a hundred of these city dolls.*

Getting Help

Most of us need all the help we can get. Therefore, it is important that we understand our assumptions about getting help. One assumption is that if we just find the right person,

*Ralph Waldo Emerson, "Self-Reliance," *Essays and Poems*, Collins, London and Glasgow, 1954.

friend, spouse, or therapist, that person will have magic answers and will solve our problems for us. "Whatever you think best, Doctor" is a typical statement of someone looking for magic and a magician to dispense it. If step-by-step advice is not forthcoming, the likelihood is that such a person will change therapists. Another assumption is that therapists are not real people, or, if they are, they are certainly "better" than we are.

There are no magic people. We need the help of experts from time to time, not because they wield magic wands or are necessarily better persons than we, but because they have insight, skills, and information we need. Parity of fundamental worth, the "I'm OK—You're OK" position, is essential to all healthy relationships. These include therapeutic relationships. Dr. Freida Fromm-Reichmann writes:

> The self-respecting psychiatrist will keep in mind that he is in a superior category as compared with his patients *only* by virtue of his special training and experience, and not necessarily in any other way. The fact that a person needs psychiatric help in handling his emotional difficulties in living by no means constitutes any basic inferiority. Only the psychiatrist who realizes this is able to listen to his patients in such a way that there may be a psychotherapeutic success.*

Getting help is effective ony when we are willing to stop looking for magic and participate fully in solving our own problems with the help of our helper. A good therapist does not tell us what to see but where to look, not what to do, but what the possibilities are. Ultimately choices must be made, by us. As our late, loved associate Connie Drewry often told workshop participants, "TA doesn't work. You do!"

---

*Freida Fromm-Reichmann, *Principles of Intensive Psychotherapy*, University of Chicago Press, 1950, p. 17.

11

Keeping People

One of the consequences of change is that it affects other people. Others have learned to predict our behavior and often base their actions on the assumption we will "stay as sweet as we are," always go along with their ideas, or always take the lead.

Change is not likely to enhance our lives if it pushes people away, for it is from them we get our life-giving strokes. Sometimes it is others who change and who, rather than inviting us into their altered aspirations, simply walk out of our lives. That is what had happened to Dorothy.

When it was her turn to state a contract as to what she wanted from group therapy, forty-five-year-old Dorothy, meticulously groomed and self-consciously postured, sat silent for a long time. At last she said, "I don't know what I want."

"Why are you here?" asked the group leader.

"I'm not very happy," she said. She disclosed her husband had walked out ten months previously, and her two children in their early twenties had moved out into their own apartments soon after her husband had left. She had been to several therapists but they didn't "seem to do any good." "I had one really good friend," a woman with whom she had worked, "but she has practically stopped calling me." She also related she had been laid off her job a year before. "They told me it was for economic reasons, that they had to cut back. I don't think that was the real reason.

But my real problem is not me, it's my husband. He walked out after twenty-five years of marriage, just left."

"Had you picked up any clues he was unhappy or thinking of leaving?" she was asked.

"No. No clues. Everything was perfect," she said, picking lint from her blue serge skirt. "I never thought I'd have a problem keeping a husband. I did everything for him."

As she talked her voice undulated in a singsong report of what seemed to be a well-rehearsed story. Her facial muscles moved very little and she had eye contact with no one. The seven other group members looked bored.

The leader walked to the contract sheet on the easel and said, "I want you to make a contract to work on your problems. Can you state what you want from this experience, from this group, from me?"

"Well, I told you my problem. What else am I supposed to do?"

A male member of the group said, "A good contract for you, Dorothy, would be 'keeping people.' Seems you are having trouble with that."

"Keeping people?" Dorothy retorted. "John, my husband, is the only one I want to keep. I wouldn't have all these problems if it wasn't for him."

"You just told us you've lost him, your kids, your job, your friends, and several therapists," said the man. "Sounds to me like you can't keep people around."

"All I wanted was a good marriage to a good husband, and we had that, I thought."

"You're losing *me*," the man said, shrugging.

"Well, get lost then," she fired at him and slipped from the conversation into a sulk.

The leader went on to the next group member, saying, "We'll get back to your contract later, Dorothy."

After the contracts were on large sheets, taped to the walls for all to see, the leader asked, "Is that it? Anyone else want something? Want to change your contracts before we start work?"

Dorothy fumbled with her notebook.

"That it? Dorothy, how about your contract? Can you make one now?"

"I want to be happy," said Dorothy seriously.

"What would make you happy?"

"I don't know. That's why I'm here."

"Who do you expect will help you here?"

"You! You're the expert."

"What about the rest of the group?"

"What do *they* know? They're here with problems, too."

"Join the club."

"Don't be sarcastic."

"Do you care about anyone in this room?"

"Of course."

"What do you expect of them?"

"Nothing."

"You already got a good suggestion from Carl for making a contract about keeping people."

"I don't want to keep people. I want to keep John."

One and Only, None and Lonely

Relying on one person to fill all of one's emotional needs is a setup for failure. The first white heat of "you and me, darling" cools faster than a lone Presto log. This is true even if both partners feel the same way. With no one else in one's life, mutual dependency is sealed in a closed system. Love gradually becomes fear of the loss of the one source of emotional gratification. Initial closeness begins to feel the strain of *carefulness*. If you mean *everything* to me I dare not offend you. It is hard to be real with someone you need that much. With amazing speed the configuration of the relationship changes to an A-frame, both persons leaning on each other for dear life, but not close. Boredom sets in also. Soon he and she know all the partner's jokes, anecdotes, and history; and irritation sets in. "You don't tell me you love me anymore," one says accusingly, "You know I love you," comes the slightly irritated reply.

Healthy relationships require *community*: friendships, acquaintances, co-workers, members in social groups in which the entire family participates, or groups in which family members participate individually with others who share mutualities of interest and need. If your life is built on your "one and only," be prepared for none and lonely. Idolatry is built on the illusion that if we worship someone enough he or she will love us forever and ever. The reality is, sometimes people disappoint us, particularly if they prefer being real persons rather than idols. That is what had happened to Dorothy. She finally agreed to work on a contract for keeping people. Here are the suggestions the group compiled:

Want, Don't Only Need

"Can that be love that drinks another like a sponge drinks water?" wrote eighteenth-century poet William Blake. Certainly we need other people for a variety of reasons. Can we also see others as needful, like ourselves? Can we want their company for who they are as unique persons, not just appendages to our need system? Do we like the people we "love"? Someone once said, "Maybe God created people just for the heck of it." Can we like and love and want people just for the heck of it, because it feels good and natural, or must our relationships grow from careful calculations as to how they can help, support, and advance our own aspirations? "She will be good for him," someone says sagely. Will he be good for her, too? Is there community of purpose? Is the give and take fairly even, or does energy flow only one way?

Have Many Stroke Sources

Any relationship in which one person relies on another for more than 50 per cent of his or her emotional income is probably in trouble. How is emotional income measured? Time spent together? Transactions exchanged? Being in someone's mind? This is not an argument for open marriage beds. Relationships are unique. Marriage is one kind of relationship and rests on vows of fidelity. This does not mean, however, that no other relationships can exist. Many marriage contracts, set up in the first week of marriage, or even before, tragically strip each partner of those "people" resources that made each partner attractive in the first place. Rather than the total being greater than the sum of the parts, it is less: more like $1 + 1 = 3/4$.

Helen and Hal meet, fall in love and are married. Helen loves opera. Hal thinks it's "bellowing." Therefore, Helen gives up opera, for certainly "you can't go to the opera without your husband—what would they say?" Hal has a pal, Joe, whom Helen can't stand. He is "crude and loud, and dumb, too," and Helen resents the time Hal wants to spend with Joe. Hal gives up Joe. In the tradeoff Helen has lost some of her "singing heart" and Hal has lost some of his happy-go-lucky. They've changed a little already. Helen likes going to visit her parents Sundays, but Hal has tired of this weekly ritual and won't go. Helen won't go without him, so she stops going, thereby cutting off what had been a sure source of strokes. Resentful, she demands, "Well, what are we going to do *this* Sunday?" "I'm tired," says Hal, turning on the football game and opening a can of beer. Helen, sensing the onset of a three-hour discount (she might as well not exist as far as Hal is concerned), sits down and writes to her mother and daddy. Both partners *assume* facts not in evidence and are afraid to talk about their feelings. "You can't go anywhere without your husband/wife" is an assumption. "We all have to like the same thing" is another. Also, "Men understand football, women don't." Helen and Hal have assumptions about opera, Joe, football, Sundays, and probably mother and daddy, hers and his. What is needed is an examination of their assumptions with an open mind and a commitment to asking the question "What's important here?"

In marriage we tend to want to reproduce what happened in our own homes. Here is the way it was in Marilyn's home when father came home from work at the end of the day: He gathered the children around, wrestled on the floor, heard the children's reports of the day. His first hour home was devoted to the family. *That's how a family should be*, according to Marilyn.

In Bill's home when father came home from work he had the first hour to himself, read the newspaper in his favorite chair, sipped a drink, and the children were "quiet as mice." *That's how a family should be,* according to Bill.

Marilyn began to feel Bill didn't love her or the children. "The children need their father," Marilyn railed at Bill. Bill began to feel he had married a nag, but was afraid to say so. He *did* love her, but damn, why couldn't she handle the kids?

Stopping at Harry's Bar with his bachelor business buddy became an attractive alternative at the end of the work day. Then began the cover-up. "I had to work late." Once a week. Then twice.

"You certainly are working late a lot these days," Marilyn accused one night. Assumptions, unexamined, led to evasions, escape, and finally accusation. "I'm going to put a stop to this once and for all," thought Marilyn as she lay sleepless on her pillow that night, planning how she would word her ultimatum in the morning before Bill left for work.

What was needed was a discussion about *how families are* or *were* and *how we want ours to be*.

Have Fun with Each Other

Are you fun to be with? Are you fun to come home to? People are drawn to laughter, sweet relief from the duties of life. You can make fun happen if you let out your own playful Child and look for the playful Child in others. Having fun *every day* is a good prescription for keeping people. It is also a prescription for good health. A pediatrician noted that in some families there is little illness even though neither parents nor children take very good care of themselves. What she found was a lot of happiness. A bright young man of our acquaintance said, "Healthy people make healthy people." Fun is contagious.

By observing others we can discover what they consider fun. Ask questions? One of the most enjoyable forms of intimacy is sharing fantasies: What would you do if . . . you had a million dollars, owned a newspaper, had a year off from work, built a mountain cabin? Families can become dreary if problems always come first: Johnny's bad report card, the leaking roof, or balancing the checkbook. Problems need attention, but solutions come easier if people take time out *first* to relax. How long has it been since you have been silly, hopped in the car for a spin to anywhere, bought your friend a funny gift, mailed someone a cartoon, taken a day off without having to justify such "unproductive" behavior? Are you considering a relationship with someone who is serious all the time? Is that what your life together will be like? Think twice. Fun is healthy. Fun is fun!

Find the Other's Parent

What can't your friends "stand"? Most of us have certain keep-off territories, plotted by the Parent. By watching, listening, and talking we come to know the inviolate areas we can avoid. Someday we may be invited in, but until we are it is better to stay out. Politics, religion, money, certain buzz words are examples of hot spots we need to know about. If there are too many things you can't approach, you may decide this is a person you don't necessarily want to keep. A good way to approach Parent territory is to share your own hot spots. These can be mutually explored if both persons know TA. The Parent is not thereby erased, however, so don't wake a sleeping giant unless you have to.

Be Aware of the Effect You Have on Others

Do people fall asleep while you talk with them? Yawn? Fidget? Are you boring? Do you see anger building? Are you thoughtless? Infuriating? Maybe it's their problem. Then again, maybe it's yours. Do you talk too much and listen too little? While others are talking are you rehearsing? Did you hear what they said? Are you *aware* of what you are saying?

Don't Be Angry

Feeling angry is a fact. *Acting* angry often is a racket. The best way to deal with anger is Trackdown. Anger pushes people away. Do you like to be around people who are at all times ready to explode? Violence begets violence. You don't shrink a giant by feeding him. To say to someone, "I want you to know how much I resent you" is not exactly an invitation to intimacy. Some popularity has attended the notion that it is good for us to "get rid of" our anger, to be "perfectly honest," to "come on straight." We do not get rid of anger effectively by provoking others to rage. Unless we love the game of "Uproar" and find people who like to play it with us, being angry generally pushes people away.

Keep Contracts

Keeping contracts implies having them. What they are and how to set them up were discussed in Chapter 6, "Adult vs. Parent Protection." Are you as good as your word? When you agree to something, do you mean it? Do you hand out rubber checks that bounce? Do you let people down? If you do, can you apologize with the determination to change your habit of automatic agreeableness? Apology is a good thing; but a life of apologizing, with no intention of changing, is a game Berne called "Schlemiel." People finally tire of cleaning up after you, and leave.

Control Yourself, Not Others

Some people think they can keep others around by controlling them. Trying to control everybody is like trying to keep five basketballs in a swimming pool all underwater at the same time. It is tiring, precarious if you are in the deep end, and it can't be done. You can't keep even one underwater all the time without staying in there with it. People, like basketballs, keep popping up, intent on staying afloat.

A useful way to understand the transactional mechanisms of control is the Karpman Drama Triangle, devised by San Francisco psychiatrist Stephen B. Karpman to explain games. He observed that games contain the same elements as Greek drama and consist of an enclosed system, the triangle, with persons acting in the roles of Persecutor, Victim, and Rescuer, each occupying a corner (Figure 13). The "control

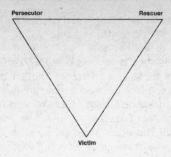

Figure 13
Karpman Drama Triangle

game," or the "action," is underway when the players switch corners.

Persecutors, Victims, and Rescuers differ from confronters, hurt persons, and helpful persons because of the switch. A person confronting someone else in a conflict situation is not a Persecutor in the game sense unless, after the confrontation, the confronted person strikes back, and the confronter then feels himself to be a Victim.

Therefore, do not confront unless the Adult is in charge. "You spend too much" is persecution, and an invitation to a game. "The bank account is overdrawn and I'm worried because we have not worked out a budget" is a confrontation, and an invitation to cooperative effort.

"Helping out" is not a rescue *if* you are asked for help or if you mean what you say when you offer help, can follow through, and define what it is you are willing to do. "You poor thing, having to live in such a rundown house and married to such an unhandy husband! You and I could paint the whole thing in one weekend," is a "game hook" you are throwing out as you set about to become a Rescuer. If, on being asked for help, you say, "I can spend one Saturday helping you paint your house," you are helping out. If, after helping out, you are mad because you ruined your new designer jeans (which you knew better than to wear), and had to give up your only day off, and your friend hardly said, "Thank you," you have chosen to become a

Victim. You are *in* the triangle and headed for the Persecutor corner: "I'll never do anything for *her* again." And you head for the phone to tell her so!

Being hurt is not the same as being a Victim in the drama triangle unless there is a switch to another corner. People are hurt every so often because people are human and, from time to time, disappoint each other. We can leave it at that and learn to protect ourselves as much as possible by predicting, and all the other steps outlined in Chapter 6. If, however, you seek revenge by planning a way to "get back," you have jumped corners.

Another jump is from Persecutor to Rescuer. Marilyn berates Bill at the breakfast table for his multiple shortcomings. He never takes her out, she accuses. Other people have fun. He doesn't love the children. They are stuck with too little money because he isn't aggressive enough with his boss about the raise. "I'll *bet* you're working late nights!" she climaxes. Husband leaves for work seething as she continues her tirade down the driveway.

By midmorning she is having second thoughts. Why did he seem so mad? What has *she* done? Bill has been thinking, too. At noon he phones and cheerfully announces, "I've made reservations for dinner tonight at Lovers Cove and we'll have a nice evening out."

"Well, how nice," she says, unsettled, and, ignoring his thoughtful arrangements, spurts, "Guess what? We're going to have dinner *here* tonight, with candlelight, just us. We really can't afford to go out. *And* guess what? *I've* written a letter for you to give to your boss. It isn't fair of me to put everything on you. I'll take care of it. You'll see!" Bill's genuine attempt to please his wife is thus snatched from the spontaneous moment, and Marilyn has taken over the matter. A rescue, following the persecution, leaves Bill a victim, feeling there is no pleasing his wife and also feeling impotent to handle his own boss by himself.

Get Out of the Triangle

The only way to stop the Persecutor-Victim-Rescuer game is to get out of the triangle. One requirement for getting out is having *other stroke sources*. You are not likely to change if "it's the only game in town." Another requirement is the decision *I will get on with my life no matter what*. This requires self-understanding, planning of options, a well-drafted want list, Adult protection, and courage. "Happiness is a form of courage," said Holbrook Jackson, most assuredly true in giving up destructive games. Blind bravado will not do, however, for courage must be accompanied by rethinking early childhood decisions about how one reacts to persecution. A child cannot leave mother. A grownup can. He also can risk experimental behaviors that break the game pattern in valued relationships.

Having planned options, Plan B, C, or D, it is essential to become *aware* of game moves. Once you bite on the hook, or let something crooked get into you, you must play the game through to the finish. It is essential, therefore, to see the hook and not bite.

Hooks are crooked and their sharp barbs are often hidden behind bushy, ever-so-natural-looking "flies." Verbal clues are: "Say, you're good at this sort of thing." (A Victim inviting a rescue.) Or "I'm going to come on straight with you." (A Persecutor about to let you have it!) A warning shot from the Rescue corner is "I know it's none of my business, but. . . ." Each of the above statements is an invitation of a romp around the triangle. Many variations of these kinds of phrases signal the onset of a crooked transaction, which you can cross by an Adult response, and thereby stop. Humor, appropriately expressed, also helps.

Options for the above overtures, to keep you out of the triangle, include the following:

Stimulus: "Say, you're good at this sort of thing."
Possible Responses:
1. "What sort of thing did you have in mind [with a twinkle]?"
2. "OK, I'll *say* it: 'You're good at this sort of thing.'"
3. "Tell me more. I need all the compliments I can get."
4. Listen for details. It might not be a crooked hook, just a manner of speaking.

* * *

Stimulus: "I'm going to come on straight with you."
Possible Responses:

1. Run.
2. "Don't you always?"
3. "Would you like a cup of tea first?" (Play for time).
4. *"Straight* is an interesting word. I was reading something only yesterday by Alfred North Whitehead, who said, 'Straightness can be perceived without measurement.' You've read Whitehead, haven't you? An absolute genius who also said, 'Moral education is impossible without an habitual vision of greatness.' He has meant a great deal to my concept of the 'internal model' and. . . . What do *you* think about his ideas?" (Go off on a tangent.)
5. "That's what I've always liked about you, your ability to see the problem accurately and get to the point without beating around the bush. Shoot!" (Stroke his Child; while he basks in your compliment, he'll forget what he was going to say. If he doesn't, prepare to duck.)
6. For other responses, see the next chapter, "Parent Shrinkers."

Stimulus: "I know it's none of my business, but. . . ."
Possible Responses:

1. "What did you say your business was?"
2. "Well, if it isn't yours, then it isn't mine either."
3. "How do you *know* it's none of your business?"
4. "Hey, buddy, I'm up to my ears in business, and if this is going to be about business, I'm leaving."
5. If you aren't able to chop off the prelude before the contents are sprayed forth, and if the contents are about somebody you both know who said something about you, there are other possibilities, as: "Well, she always speaks very highly of you!" Or grab a pencil and say, "Hold it. This I want to get! What was that she said again?" This generally produces a quick retreat and a change of subject.

The above examples certainly do not exhaust the possibilities. The point is, we have options. The more successful we are in extricating ourselves from our own internal dialogue, the more efficiently our Adult works for us, taking clues from the fleet-footed Child, and dodging bullets and game hooks. We do not have to go along with every come-on. The art of saying *no* the "I'm OK—You're OK" way is to do everything possible to avoid hurting the Child in another person at the same time you are looking after yours. Sometimes *silence*, while looking thoughtfully and kindly into another's eyes, searching for a Child somewhere in all the gamy mire, is the best game stopper of all. But even that has its risks. Sir Thomas More, on trial for his life, pleaded in his defense that he had not spoken against the supremacy of Henry VIII and that "nowhere in the world is there any law that makes silence punishable." Then he lost his head. On the scaffold.

The moral of the story: Don't lose your head, that is, your Adult. Know what you are doing and keep an eye out for Child-ren.

Stop and Think

The above options are examples of responses when you are in the middle of a transaction, when *you* have been engaged verbally by a Persecutor, Victim, or Rescuer. Sometimes it is you, or I, who is about to be the instigator. Useful precautions to avoid stepping into the triangle of our own volition are:

1. If you feel the great urge to jump in and solve someone else's problem, to rescue him, cover for him, be a helpful friend, *stop and think*. Why do you feel the great need to do this? Whose problem is it? Do you know how to solve it? Is it your business? How will you feel the next day? Here is a place to do a "Future Trackdown," using the same steps of Trackdown described in Chapter 4. Set up a "what if." Predict your feelings. Will they begin "I hurt"? If so, don't be a Rescuer.

2. If you feel the great urge to let someone have it, give him a piece of your mind, nip his bud, nail him good, *stop and think*. Why are you about to do this? What are you going to get out of it? How will it help the relationship? How will you feel after you've emptied both barrels? If you

predict that you will feel the need to patch it up (Rescue) or feel sorry for yourself (Victim), don't be a Persecutor. Let it be. Get on with Plan B, C, or D.

3. If you feel the great urge to drown your sorrows on a weekend binge or call a friend for an evening's "Ain't It Awful," *stop and think*. Why are you about to do this? Because you hurt? Hurting is not a game, but indulging in sweet self-pity is. Trading on your misery is a racket, wherein the hurt becomes valuable as stroke-getting currency. Then you are a Victim. Instead, get on with Plan B, C, or D.

Don't bring your triangle into a new relationship. This is easier said than done. A wife whose husband stops persecuting, rescuing, or being victimized by her may find someone else to play the game with her. A husband may leave his wife and go looking for someone else who plays by the old rules.

The reason games are hard to give up is that they provide strokes, prove our position, produce transactional trading stamps, avoid intimacy, structure time, or all of the above. Therefore Plans B, C, or D must offer substitutes for these advantages. A knowledge of TA, along with knowing the important "ifs" in our lives, is a requirement for letting go of what it is we must prove. According to Berne the aims of all games are among the following: self-castigation, justification, reassurance, absolution, revenge, alleviation of guilt, and vindication. One way or another the Child asserts "I am *too* OK!" Even in self-castigation, the assertion is "I am OK," i.e., "doing what you want me to do, Parent." In this case the Parent message is "You will be OK *if* you fail; then you will need me."

Games are such a significant part of time structuring that we recommend *Games People Play**, a rereading of it if necessary. Seen as a defense to the "I'm Not OK—You're OK" life position, games make sense. In the beginning, they were the Child's attempts to get momentary relief from Not OK feelings by controlling others. The payoff, unfor-

---

*Eric Berne, *Games People Play*, Grove Press, New York, 1964.

tunately, leaves him as he was, separated from, yet dependent on, those he wants and needs.

Manipulative stroking is another form of controlling behavior. Because strokes are the most valuable units of personal exchange, they frequently are used as instruments of manipulation. Withholding strokes is an effective way to control behavior. Particularly vulnerable to stroke withholding are people who are driven by the Parent directive "Please Me." Ignoring such a person, because he has displeased you, is a game ploy that rather quickly "brings him into line." Eager to please, he will do almost *anything* to reinstate a stroking relationship.

A three-handed way of amplifying the message "you have displeased me" is for stroke givers to ignore stroke seekers while, in their presence, effusively stroking someone else they like better. "See how good I can be! Too bad you missed out." As in sibling rivalry, jealousy and anger follow. New ways must be devised to put down the rival ("Let's You and Him Fight") and be returned to the place of favor (mama's sweetheart, daddy's darling, teacher's pet, or boss's only intimate).

A person arrives at a board meeting one-half hour late. If the chair takes this as a personal insult and handles it by stroke withholding, he will avoid eye contact, discount contributions made by the latecomer, or entertain a motion two-thirds of the way through the meeting that latecomers be dropped from membership after three infractions. This is a duplex transaction with a ricochet to the offender while still ignoring him.

A straight way to handle the latecomer is to acknowledge his arrival, question his lateness by asking if something went wrong, and then include him in the proceedings. Perpetual lateness should be confronted personally, again in a straight manner: "You have been late three times in a row, and I feel it is disruptive to board proceedings and unfair to those who arrive on time. What is the problem?"

It is then up to the latecomer to account for his behavior and state his intentions for the future: "The timing of this meeting always interferes with the only evening our family can spend together. Therefore, I think it best I resign from the board." If no accommodation can be worked out, "We are sorry, we will miss you" from the leader is still a straight transaction.

Confrontation, with care taken to protect the Child in another, is a healthy way to attend to problems. Ignoring, discounting, or ricochet putdowns are not.

People with "Please Me" scripts need to accept the reality that they cannot please everybody. Once convinced, they can pick and choose, drop some activities, attend fully to others, and simplify their lives. If not they become harried and are so beleaguered they couldn't recognize a stroke if it hit them between the eyes. Though they spend their lives being "pleasing," as Good Guys and Sweethearts, they are so anxious no stroking registers, and they go through life depressed. Though they attempt to control others by trying harder they *feel* unappreciated because the internal dialogue preempts incoming signals from others.

Controlling others, whether from a top-dog or bottom-dog position, is not working from the "I'm OK—You're OK" position.

Conflict Resolution

Keeping people requires conflict resolution. Learning TA together is a sound way to approach conflict. Had Bill and Marilyn understood the power of their differing Parent recordings of "what fathers do when they come home from work," the ensuing misunderstanding and uproar could have been averted. They could even have discovered the ways in which their parentally-derived ideas agreed. They could have kept some, discarded some, and constructed their own unique plan for how they wanted *their* marriage to be.

We are indebted to Dr. Louis Normington of St. Helena Health Center for his presentation of the following methods of conflict resolution, which we have elaborated with examples and additions. As he indicated, some are effective, and some are not.

1. *Consensus. Consensus* sounds respectable and means general agreement or collective opinion. If everybody has

had his or her full say in the matter, *and* equal potency, the agreement may be real. Often it is not. Frequently the covert message of the more powerful person is "I want you to do what you want, but I want you to want what I want." What really happens is:

2. *Concession*. One partner habitually gives in, until it seems natural to do so. Therefore the family always go to his folks for Christmas and to her folks for Thanksgiving. If she is the giving-in sort, this arrangement may last for years, and then one happy holiday season, out of the blue, she erupts, "I'm leaving you." Comply, comply, comply, explode!

3. *Compromise*. Compromise is often a mutual concession in which neither party gets what he wants. Something has to be surrendered by both sides. Often it seems the only way a conflict can be resolved, but it may not be the best way. John wants a sailboat. Judy wants a mountain cabin near the ski slopes. She gets seasick, and heights make him dizzy. They compromise by buying a cottage on the seashore. They take long walks on the beach, she missing the ski slopes and he missing the rolling and yawing on the high seas. Neither gets what he and she wants. A compromise, but no fun.

Retirement comes. A nest egg has been saved for a long-awaited celebration. John wants to see the ruins of Athens and take a tour of the Greek Islands. Judy longs to travel to Australia and visit her brothers and sisters, whom she hasn't seen in thirty years. They compromise by a cruise to Alaska. Neither gets what he and she wants. Compromise often has the quality of disagreeing parties both giving up what they want most and settling for "neutral" territory. In these two examples, a better solution might have been:

4. *Cooperation*. This means working together to make possible the greatest measure of enjoyment for everyone concerned. In the first example, a cooperative solution would have been for John to join a sailing club and Judy a skiing club, making it possible for both to enjoy the sports they loved. In the second example, they could have gone their separate ways, he going to tour Greece and she flying to Australia for a reunion with her family.

Essential to acting cooperatively is the willingness to examine the assumption that "they must do everything together." Caring and understanding one another could certainly sustain their relationship during the brief periods of separation. People can cooperate by agreeing to disagree. They can be together on what they're together on, and apart on what they're apart on. They can still be close. Closeness is not measured by identical wants, but by identical caring. Caring involves trust.

Allowing our loved ones to be themselves is a way of keeping love alive. There are plenty of "together" activities that also can be planned, and these should not be neglected. If every conflict is solved by going one's own way, then no relationship exists. Generally, however, a bit of separation now and then makes the heart grow fonder, if the relationship is sound in the first place. If it is not sound, perhaps all that will be left, as Dr. Normington suggested, will be "ruins and relatives."

Who brings home the "emotional bacon" in your family? John and Judy could have both brought home twice as much excitement about the world out there if they had been able to fulfill their deepest longings, each reporting on the separate adventures. As it was, all they could do was grumble about what the salt water was doing to the seashore cottage neither really wanted, and overeat on their cruise to Alaska, compensation for not being at the Acropolis, for John, and Adelaide, for Judy.

A practical way to find out how much you or your spouse wants to do something together is to state, first, what you would like to do. "How about a game of dominoes?" Tom asks. Loving dominoes, I'm generally ready to play. If I'm in the middle of something else, I'll ask, "On a scale of one to ten, how much do you want to play?" If he says, "Eight," I'll probably drop what I'm doing, if I can, and play. If he says, "Oh, about three," we'll talk about that, and maybe postpone the game. If I'm "two," he'll suggest we play later. It sounds a bit statistical and even comical, but it works. We not only let each other know what we want to do, but how much we want to do it. It's more fun to do things together when there's not the stressful feeling that the other person is doing it only to be accommodating. Try it. "Let's have dinner out tonight!" Sounds like a ten to me. (Helpful hint to dieters: Dominoes is a good substitute for dessert.)

5. *Confrontation.* Confronting conflict is healthy if the Adult is in charge. "There is a real problem here, and I feel we have to sit down and work on it together. I feel terrible and can't go on this way." Here, the Adult is reporting on the Child's feelings, and also enlisting the help of the other person to solve the problem.

Having confronted a problem, complementary communication, even friendly talking, can take place provided the Parent does not take charge of the conversation with blaming, placating, or lecturing, and if the frightened Child does not run from the problem with distractions, changing the subject, or laughing it off, as if it's just a tempest in a teapot or "the wrong time of the month."

Among the most difficult problems many people face today are economic, whether it is unemployment or not enough money to go around even with employment. Perhaps the most unsettling problem is about work division in the home when both husband and wife hold jobs outside the home: what is fair, and who does what? "Hell hour" is the name given to the period between 5 P.M. and 7 P.M. in homes where both partners have just arrived from a day on the job. Who props his or her feet up and is left alone? Either, or both, or neither? What about the children? Who talks with them? These are significant questions producing painful conflict in many families. We shall write more of this in Chapter 14, "Building Children."

6. *Conciliation.* Conciliation is what you do to smooth the rough edges after confrontation. *Conciliation* means to overcome hostility or suspicion and to secure friendship. Remarkable to hear were the words of George McGovern at the 1984 Democratic convention, when the party stalwarts were mending fences after the battles preceding the primaries: "Conciliation must walk hand in hand with conscience." Since the "conscience" we hear is mostly Parent recordings, his statement provides a model for personal problem solving. Conflict resolution and conciliation are

possible through confrontation and cooperation if the Child
wants them and the Adult knows how. All are ways to keep
people. And keeping people around has always been a want
of the Child.

Unhooking

Many people seek counseling because they are involved in
relationships that are destructive. They are hooked either in
illicit relationships, cruel marriages, or alliances that can't
possibly work out. Or they are young people trying to ex-
tricate themselves from parents who don't want them to
grow up. Other defeating relationships involve dependency,
either on drugs or alcohol or on the manipulation of "Pied
Pipers."

Reason tells emotionally enslaved people they should get
out, but they are in fact hooked by unexamined sentiments,
such as were expressed by a woman who withdrew charges
of assault and battery against her abusive boyfriend because
she "loved" him. Our groups devised a list of things to do
in an exercise of unhooking. They appear calculating, and
they are, but provide several ways to end impossible relationships, or to alter their nature. Young people who unhook
from their parents do not necessarily stop loving their parents, but are able to achieve the independence to become
persons themselves.

1. Don't give or take "emotional trading stamps." Don't
put down the other person or let him put you down. Don't
be angry. It only heats up the relationship.

2. Give low-value strokes. "You are looking well" is a
modulated compliment that doesn't point toward the bedroom. "Your shirt is gorgeous and matches your baby-blue
eyes" does.

3. Don't be a Persecutor, Rescuer, or Victim. Keep out
of the triangle. That's where the hook is.

4. Stay OK but don't flaunt it. "Things are going pretty
well with me, how about you?" is a neutral statement said
to someone you have been away from for a couple of weeks.
"Terrrrific, never felt better!" (who needs you?) overdoes it
a bit.

5. Keep transactions in the Adult. Child seductions or whimpers or Parent putdowns set the stage for more fun and games.

6. Stay in the now. Bringing out the photo album of the sizzling tryst at Wits End is not going to cool the affair. Talking about the future—how will I ever get through the next week without you—doesn't help either.

7. Protect the Child in the other person, if possible. Do not heap abuse on the person you're unhooking from. Do not boast of your new romance. For whatever reason your relationship can't go on, don't be cruel. Be kind and courteous to your parents, even while you are preparing to slip your leash. You may impress them with how grownup and thoughtful you've become.

8. Develop other relationships. Loneliness and stroke hunger provide a wonderful excuse to "get things going again." You can't get out of the game triangle, or any other kind of triangle, if it's the only action in town.

9. Be consistent. When we part company with someone, it is easy to remember all the good times. Remember why you are unhooking. This is one situation in which it is well to remember the bad times. What will happen if this relationship does not stop? The decision to unhook is hard enough. Do not make it harder by wiping out past gains with just "one phone call that can't hurt."

10. If possible, stay friends. If not, don't. Encumbering yourself with destructive relationships will only stand in the way of finding the people you want to keep.

Unhooking is made easier if you recognize that "being hooked" is essentially an emotional condition. The Adult is often left out of initial infatuations. Get the Adult working by asking yourself hard, realistic questions: Where is this relationship going? How much punishment am I willing to take? What are my values? What will I be doing five years from now unless I change? Ten? When I am old?

Do switch horses in the middle of a stream if the horse you're on is going under, and you with it.

12

Parent Shrinkers

Keeping some people is difficult if their primary source of communication is the Parent. Our inclination may be to run. This is not advantageous if that person is our boss, spouse, mother, father, daughter, son, friend—folks we want to keep in our lives. Parent Shrinkers were devised by group members as a method of getting others out of the Parent and into the Adult or Child, in order that relationships may be sustained without the continual hazard of Child beating.

Talking with a person who is a constant Parent is like trying to talk with the time operator. "At the sound of the tone, the time will be. . . ." Every ten seconds the same interminable statement proceeds. Try interrupting.

It is just as hard to interrupt a person continually in the Parent state because you are listening to a recording. The Parent has neither eyes nor ears and is interested, first and foremost, in preserving the institution of the Parent, not the whole person. The point of this chapter is not to shrink people, but to shrink the Parent in people in order to get on with transactions involving the Adult and Child, where listening, cooperation, and novelty are possible.

People constantly in the Parent state most often have chosen this mode of behavior for a defensive reason. "The Constant Parent, the constant Adult and the Constant Child all result primarily from defensive exclusion of the two complementary aspects in each case."* The Constant Parent

*Eric Berne, *Transactional Analysis in Psychotherapy,* Grove Press, New York, 1961.

does use his Adult, but it is a Parent-contaminated Adult, that is, the computer is turned over to the Parent for its exclusive use, for the running of Parent programs. What seems to this person to be realistic is his own unexamined dogma externalized in what our pastor Robert Ball calls "God-almighty statements."* Prejudice, that is, prejudgment, or applying no Adult inquiry to one's beliefs, characterizes the content of the constant Parent.

Why are people this way? Parent-dominated people were rewarded in childhood for perfect conformity, compliance, and unquestioning obedience. To them, as grownups, the path of wisdom still appears to be total conformity to the Parent and continued blocking-out of childlike behavior or impulses. Sometimes mindless or terrified conformity is ensured by severe corporal punishment of little children, such as reported today among certain religious sects. Children in one such church "can be beaten by any adult who cares to," according to one woman who had left the fold. She stated they were to "spank the children until their spirit was broken." The leader of the church was asked, "At what age do you feel that your children are accountable and must be disciplined?" He replied, "We believe that if you wait until a child is able to reason, you have waited too long."

Parents who practice dehumanizing conditioning of children are cloning themselves, producing automatons doing exactly as they are told, being perfectly obedient (at Jonestown even unto death), terrified of questioning authority, in fact rendered *unable* to question authority, for they never learned to think for themselves. Physical threat is not the way to build thinking, creative human beings. What is communicated is that power is in the parent who wields the rod, and that when all else fails, hit. Bomb. Destroy. Ravage. Kill. It is a somber reflection that children who are beaten are often people who, when grown, beat not only their own children but their elderly parents as well, those from whom they learned their lessons in corporal control. We reap what we sow, a fact that hopefully may intrude into the con-

*See Robert R. Ball, *Why Can't I Tell You Who I Really Am?*, Word Inc., Waco, 1977.

sciousness of those heavy-handed parents who abuse their children "for their own good."

How We Hook Parents

Everyone, even nice, thinking folks, has a Parent, capable of being hooked. If we are continually confronted by someone's Parent, it is useful to ask what our contribution to the situation is. Do we bring Parent wrath on ourselves? What hooks the Parent? If we are always whiny, cranky, obstinate, sloppy, late, and unreasonable, we may drive a person to engage his "internal higher power."

One time in a therapy group, in which everyone was sitting on large pillows in a circle around the room, every member of the group was glowering at one young woman. She had effectively hooked everybody's Parent. The scene was called to the group's attention. What was this woman doing that had been able to elicit such a concerted response?

Her hair was in her face, so no one could see her facial expression. When she talked she spoke rapidly and slurred her words, many of which were drug culture expressions. Everyone had to strain to hear her. She discounted the statements of others by looking at the floor when they talked. She was slouched down, resting her weight on her upper back and shoulders, a postural statement that she couldn't care less if she took charge of her life—which was a fundamental part of the group contract. She thus invited the others to do her work for her, and because she refused to use her Adult, acting only as a rebellious Child, the other members were finally "forced" into a Parent position. Her passive-aggressive behavior shut out the Adult and Child of the other group members and, frustrated, they turned to their original source of ideas, protection, and power, the Parent. In this case, the young woman had brought the Parent on herself. We sometimes do the same. When we hook another's Parent, we may arouse not only the Critical Parent but also the Nurturing Parent, neither of which may be desirable in the long run.

The Critical Parent

A person constantly in his Critical Parent state is experienced as prejudiced, powerful, intimidating, controlling, and cornering. He frequently demands yes or no answers, thus reducing one's choices to *two*, either-or, leaving no creative options beyond this limited response. "Did you or did you not make the phone call I asked you to make?" Yes or no! Perhaps you did not, but for reasons you would like to explain, which might even have been in the questioner's interest: "I decided to wait till you returned because while you were gone this letter arrived that I thought you would like to see first, before you responded to Mr. Jones." A Parent-dominated boss may feel obedience is more important than his own self-interest, again a case where the Parent is more interested in preserving the power of the Parent than of the whole person.

Some of the threat we feel coming from a Parent-dominated person is diminished when we recognize that underneath he is afraid. "The person who is scaring me is capable of being scared," Steinbeck, the master of people study, observed.* The same Parent that beats outwardly at you also beats inwardly at him. One way for him to escape a Child beating himself is to turn the wrath outward. When he does so, he *feels* powerful in the same way he did when he called on his father to rescue him from the neighborhood bully. It is better to feel powerful than afraid. It is not only fear that floods the Child of the Parent-dominated person, but also mistrust of his own thinking, or Adult, which, as a child, he was not encouraged to use. Therefore he has great difficulty engaging in cooperative, Adult-Adult problem solving with others. He trusts neither others nor himself. Instead, he cites authorities.

*John Steinbeck, *In Dubious Battle*, Viking Press, New York, 1936.

The Nurturing Parent

The Parent is not only critical but nurturing. There are times we long for a nurturing Parent, like Mama used to be, feeding us chicken soup and apple pie, tucking the down comforter around us and letting us indulge in being little again. When we are sick or sad, this feels good. For a while. But in time, in the same way the Critical Parent is oppressive, the Nurturing Parent is depressive. Dr. Craig Johnson reported what happened at a state institution where he had been a staff member when a new program was instituted to put all "depressed patients" in the same ward. The administration asked for volunteers from each discipline to staff the ward. The people who volunteered, not surprisingly, were for the most part Nurturing Parent type therapists and attendants. The unit quickly filled with patients and had the most constant population in the institution. Nobody got well and left. Within six months the unit was discontinued. The depressed patients were then moved to other wards of the hospital, improved quickly, and were discharged. The average stay in the regular units was three weeks. Johnson's conclusion was that solicitous nurturing, however well intended, kept these people depressed. They improved at once when non-Parental staff members confronted them with the requirement to exercise responsibility for their own lives, to think, to use their Adult.

For some people, going home to mom and dad for a visit can reproduce feelings not only of happiness but also of helplessness. At first there is the wonderful sense of protection and the good old days, but after a while depression may set in. Good and ongoing relationships between parents and their offspring are based on a flexible use of the whole personality, including the Adult and Child, which make possible a relationship of parity concerned with the present as well as the past.

Is Parent Shrinking OK?

Three observations underlie Parent Shrinking. The first is that the Parent does not think. Like the time operator, it is a recording. A person in the Parent is not operating in his Adult, and therefore is neither thinking nor listening. We usually recognize a Parent when we run into one, mostly because of the oppression we *feel*. Here are some other clues. *Physical:* Frowning, pursed lips, the pointing index finger, head wagging, the "horrified look," foot tapping, impatient pencil tapping, hands on hips, arms folded across chest (closing you out), wringing hands, tongue clucking, sighing, patting another on the head. *Verbal:* I am going to put a stop to this *once and for all;* I can't for the life of me . . . ; Now always remember . . . ; How many times have I told you; If I were you . . . *Always* and *never* are usually Parent words, which reveal the limitations of an archaic system closed to new data. The frequent use of clichés also is a clue to the Parent.*

The second observation is that when a Parent-originated transaction is crossed by an Adult response, communication cannot continue in the same vein. This may or may not be desirable. It is one option and may be desirable if you wish to get off a painful subject and on to something else. The Parent is aiming at your Child, so if your response is Child (fear, confusion, anger, compliance), the transaction is complementary and encourages the Parent to keep coming at you. Two choices are open. One is to come back with your Parent in an attempt to hook the other's Child. This is called an argument, which is really a conversation of the deaf, since neither person is listening. The other option is to come on Adult, with statements of fact relevant to the situation. Father to ten-year-old son: "Shut up and eat your banana!" Son: "That's an awful mixture." (How can I shut up and eat my banana at the same time.) Children are good at this kind of disarming statement, although sometimes they are rewarded by a smart slap for being sassy.

*See *I'm OK—You're OK*, pp. 89–91.

The third observation is that coming on Parent is the way many people protect their Child. Underneath all the bluster is a real, live person we would like to reach. In shrinking Parents we are not giving up on the "I'm OK—You're OK" position, but seeking to make it possible in our transactions.

Parent Shrinkers

One way to escape the attack of an abusive Parent is to run. What if the Parent is our boss, our spouse, our parents, even our children, all those important "others" in our life whom we wish to keep. Are there options other than running?

There are. The following Parent Shrinkers were developed in our groups. *Decommissioning* is perhaps a more accurate word than shrinking, for the content of the Parent is a permanent recording, always available for replay. *The purpose of Parent Shrinkers is to get the other person out of his Parent and into his Adult or Child ego state, so that here-and-now communication can proceed.* They differ from Parent Stoppers, described in Chapter 7. Parent Stoppers are used to turn off our own Parent when it is beating us internally. Parent Shrinkers are used to turn off someone else's Parent when it is beating on us externally.

Parent Shrinkers must be used with care, and *by the Adult,* for there is a fine line between protecting your Child and manipulating people. Yet, as in love and war, deliberate defensive transactional responses seem fair when our task is to protect the Child within us from child beating by self-righteous, abusive Parent types. Would you fault a little child for kicking and spitting and clawing his way out of the hands of cruel parents? We are not suggesting kicking, spitting, and clawing: we are suggesting nonviolent Adult responses, using your mind and not your molars to protect yourself and, if you are successful, to even build bridges of communication.

One way *not* to shrink the Parent is to tell a person, flat out, his Parent is talking. This will only add fuel to the fire. Another way not to shrink the Parent is to put the person down, that is, if you wish to keep a relationship going—

unless, of course, the relationship thrives on fun and games. It is funny to contemplate what we might like to say or, as an afterthought, what we could have said if we had the eloquently instrumented tongue of Churchill, who when being scolded by his housekeeper about his over-much drinking one evening said, "Madam, I am drunk and you are ugly, and in the morning I will be sober." Churchill was Churchill. You and I are you and I. For us, the following are no doubt more appropriate.

1. *Cross the transaction.* Some Adult responses to a Parent putdown or tirade might be: "I can see you feel strongly about that. Would you care to tell me how you arrived at that conclusion? I appreciate your willingness to let me know your thinking. That is one way to handle the situation, but it does raise problems. It would be helpful to me if you would write a short report for our next meeting." Each of the foregoing statements is a single response, which would then await the next statement by the Parent person. Generally about three such Adult statements will force a person into his Adult; not guaranteed, of course.

If a Parent persists, another response is: "It would be helpful to me if you would let me know what it is you plan to *do*." The Parent is good at talking, but action is something else. He will either back down, leave, or engage his Adult, since thinking and time are required for action. Variations of this type of Adult response must fit a particular situation. With a fast-working Adult in charge, you can predict what may or may not happen, based on past experience and the clues of the moment. The secret of having a fast-working Adult is to have done your homework with Trackdown and the other tools of insight described in this book.

2. *Agree.* Variations of agreement are "You're right!" "You've got a point there," and "I see what you mean." This is only useful if he really is right. For instance, if a highway patrol officer stops you for speeding and you were doing 80 mph, he may have a full head of Parent steam all ready to read you the riot act, especially if he's had it with reckless drivers all day. When you roll down your window and he says, "You were going a little fast there," he has

shot you the prelude for what may be the big lashing he's going to lay on you. He doesn't get to deliver it, however, if you say, "Yes sir, I was. I'm really sorry." (You're going to get a ticket anyway, so you may as well shrink his Parent and avoid some of the tongue-lashing.)

One day I was in a supermarket and had left my purse in the shopping basket while I looked for something on the shelf. When I turned back a woman with a mean and angry look scolded me abusively, "You shouldn't leave your purse in the basket." I said, "Good advice, I shouldn't. You're absolutely right!" She was. And I went on my way, chastised, but without open wounds. Sometimes you might find a point of agreement with a Parent person, even though you feel that much of what he says is off base. If you can fish out that one point, and respond favorably to it, he may lose his desire to hassle over the other nineteen points.

3. *Go off on a tangent.* This one is a little risky, but may work in getting the other person out of his Parent. Parent statement: "I simply couldn't believe it when I heard you had put Jeremy Furbermeister in charge of the Family Building Fund Drive when he's only been a member two years and isn't even married, so they say." Response: "Jeremy? Say, I was talking with him just this morning and he said some very complimentary things about you and really appreciated what a great help you were when he first moved here. Did you know he is one of the Denver Furbermeisters? Have you ever seen that marvelous park down there his family donated? We had a rally, etc., etc."

4. *Cheers.* When a Parent has made an impassioned statement about some issue, draw him out. "That's marvelous! You really put words to that one. I wish everyone had that kind of enthusiasm. I'd love to have you present your ideas at our meeting so we could get a good discussion going. I wish you would fully develop your ideas, perhaps even write them up."

5. *Silence.* A puzzled or intrigued stare with a friendly crinkling at the corner of the mouth is disarming. The person may even hear what he just said. Five to ten seconds of silence will raise his discomfort level to a point where he

may feel he must say something else. Most people can't handle silence. Chances are they will modify what they just said. If they call you on your silence you can say, "That really deserves some deep thought." You're not lying. Everything deserves deep thought.

6. *Move in.* Parent types get very uncomfortable if you invade their space. Remove barriers. Move from behind your desk. Get about two feet away from them—or however far their bubble extends. They will back away. They will actually retreat, or be forced to think (Adult), "What's going on here?"

7. *Change your mind,* if you mean it. If you are being criticized because of something you said six months ago at the twenty-fifth annual convention of Button Collectors, declare you have given your statement serious thought and believe this was not the best approach at all, and you truly appreciate your confronter's sensitivity to the broader picture. Then ask him for his approach. The Parent is often critical of someone else's idea. It takes the Adult to come up with a better one.

8. *Could you please state that another way?* If someone has just delivered himself of a mighty load, has just put his total energy into it, you, with considerable perplexity, can say, "I want to be sure I followed your thinking correctly so I don't misunderstand your meaning—could you please state that again?" Since his Parent proclamation is a recording, he'll have to rewind the tape and play it back, and that takes some time and some thinking, and may engage his Adult. His second delivery will not have the impact of the first.

9. *Ricochet.* If there is a third party present, your response can be to that third party but may be heard by the Parent person. "This guy is really something! Did you know he led the protest for the Save Our National Monuments Association back when they wanted to carve Archie Bunker's bust in Cathedral Rock, without Edith?" This is the buckshot approach, and makes for a merry melee.

10. *Write it down.* When someone is reporting the dirt on someone else, make a big to-do about "What was that

name again? Hold on a minute. How do you spell *Penelope?*" A handsome leather-bound notebook and gold pen make a driving impression.

11. *Find his Child and feed it*. This is the most commendable Parent Shrinker. Everyone has a hungry Child, even if it is buried under tons of Parent compost. If someone is forever criticizing what is going on, in your church, PTA, business office, family he might be led into a discussion of his own deep need by questions such as: "I'm not asking you to, understand, but *if* you had the opportunity to plan the annual picnic (family budget, worship service, Christmas party) in a way that would really make you feel good, what would you change?" Perhaps you already know something about the other person's deepest needs. For instance, you may know that your boss, the business tycoon, really wanted to be a sculptor once upon a time, or that he had to give up his music career to support the family after his father died. Be aware of his daily routines, including how much Alka Seltzer he takes. Is he hurting, lonely, afraid? Did he lose a child in a traffic accident? Was he an orphan? Is he dreading retirement? Is he afraid of the future? What are his hobbies? Does he secretly do needlepoint? Is he a closet liberal? Have you ever seen tears in his eyes? On the basis of what you learn by daily observation, can you *see* his Child hidden somewhere behind his forehead, even though the Parent has taken over? Kindness, born from your knowledge that he needs love too, sometimes melts the hostility.

12. *Be OK*. Self-esteem is the requirement to make any of the foregoing effective. It is a tall order for most of us, and requires that we daily replenish our inner resources, through meditation or regularly being in the company of people who value us. Being OK does not mean a constant display of euphoria, or whistling Dixie, or wearing a perpetual grin. Rather it is a calm self-esteem that holds the flapping canvas in place during stormy weather. Parent types like to move in whenever there is a sign of perturbation. If it isn't with criticism it may well be with nurturing. Sometimes this is pleasant, sometimes it isn't. A "there there" can be every bit as discomforting as a "here here." Some people are like ambulance chasers, eager to be in on the

excitement, help out, give advice, take charge, even when it's morbid. Sharing your problems with disaster addicts will not make you feel better. Sharing your problems with *thinking* and *feeling* people will.

It is not possible to shrink the Parent in everyone. For many people, when things get tough, the tendency, and sometimes the only assumed option, is to retreat to the old safety, the Parent. They do not understand why the Parent has such a hold on them. TA provides this kind of knowledge, and the insight that grows from it is the ultimate Parent Shrinker. When you know what others do not, you must carry the burden of insight alone, hoping that a time and place will come when it will be possible to share your insight with them. Until such time arrives, the foregoing measures may get you through many an emergency unscathed. Whatever you do, be gentle, courteous, and *open,* ever ready to greet the Child when it finally breaks out of the prison of constraints in which a Parent-dominated person lives.

13

Take Charge of Your Time

Staying OK means taking charge of your life, and taking charge of your life means taking charge of your time. Most of us, until we feel that tight turn of the screw called the "midlife crisis," don't pay much attention to time, for our illusion is we will live forever. In our open-ended youth we often kill time, as if it were our enemy, getting through days, weeks, and years without recognizing time as our most valuable gift. Of money, William Sloane Coffin said, "There are two ways to be rich: one is to have a lot of money; the other is to have few needs." The first option, having more, is not open to us where time is concerned. We have so much and can't increase it substantially. But we can reduce the demands we put on the time we have, and we can arrange our lives in such a way that we use time in rewarding ways.

This requires that we use time deliberately, planning our lives, and, as Dr. Elton Trueblood suggests, "living our lives in chapters, and knowing what chapter it is." Using time deliberately does not come naturally to us. We have to learn how. In our early years, most of our time is structured for us, by parents, teachers, professors, job-placement bureaus, bosses, spouses, then children. Not many people make a want list early in life and set about making their dreams come true. Most of us are far down the path before we stop and smell the roses.

A useful exercise is to draw a time line representing the span of your life, from birth to how long you expect to live.

Our own expectation has something to do with how long we will live, for it influences how well we take care of ourselves. The actuaries give us average figures, which serve as a guide, but we can look at the up side of the figures and hope to extend our days beyond the predictions. Life expectancy for people born in 1980 is 70 years for men and 77.7 years for women, or an average of roughly 74. Don't despair if you are 74 today. If you are, your life expectancy is yet another 13.3 years, according to predictions. In the same way that the rich seem to get richer, the old seem to get older.

Having drawn your line, where are you on it? If you are fifty, and a woman, you have about thirty more years to live. Do you have a plan? How long is thirty years? Think back on the past thirty years and consider what has taken place. Thirty years is a long time. Will you do time or do life? The answer depends on whether or not you own your life, treasure it, and plan its use.

Learn from Your Heart

The best model for time-structuring is your heart. During the three-phase cardiac cycle of each heartbeat the heart works one-third of the time and rests two-thirds. Faithfully it does its unerring job from before birth until our final day. For a healthy person this adds up to nearly 3 billion beats in a lifetime—or 3,000 million, if that helps your grasp of its miraculous labor.

Were we to follow our hearts we would divide our twenty-four hours into three segments, working eight hours, sleeping eight hours, and using the remaining eight hours for life-renewing activities. What a revolutionary change would come over us individually and as a society if we followed our hearts.

Some people insist they don't need eight hours of sleep, and perhaps this is true, give or take an hour or so. Or they divide sleep time into naps here and there through the day. However we manage our sleep, we know if we get enough. That leaves the other two segments, work and recreation. Some people believe their work to be recreational, fun even, and for them there is some overlap. But for most people work is work for eight hours a day, unless they are working mothers or moonlighters, whose toil is never done. The significant elective time, therefore, is the eight hours between work and sleep.

Who is in charge of your time? A friend of ours told us she awoke one night, thrashing about, unable to sleep because something was bothering her. She suddenly discovered that Mrs. Smith (her boss) was "in charge of my sleep." Enough of that, she decided, and promptly dozed off. Who is in charge of your sleep, your work, your free time? Often it is not free because we have left a vacuum into which swoops someone else's agenda; or we blindly follow what is expected of us, whether it is rewarding or not.

I was preparing an outline for a lecture about "hurry sickness," which was to include a review of Meyer Friedman and Ray Rosenman's *Type A Behavior and Your Heart*. Gretchen walked into the room, and I asked her to give me some ideas. "Gretchen, what are people to do about Type A behavior?" She replied at once, "They've got to decide if they want it or not." I gave her an A for astuteness and a hug for help.

Taking charge of our time involves decision. Even if we are living with impossible pressures based on past decisions, not well thought out, we still have options. If we think we don't, we must make them, for the alternative may kill us. The Latin word for anguish, which certainly attends severe time pressure, is *angustia,* meaning "narrowness" or "tightness" as in asthma. Sometimes our narrowness is the real crowding of demands upon us, but sometimes it is a narrowness of thinking. Our hope in this chapter is to open up some of our thinking so we can breathe a little easier. One way we can gain time is to eliminate time wasters, those things we do that produce no enjoyment, only worry.

Time Wasters

1. *Things*. Even if we can't get through the house without falling over the latest carton from UPS, we keep on buying. Many of us are inveterate collectors, gift buyers,

gadgeteers, catalogue and coupon addicts, shoppers, and, when the money runs out, window shoppers. How much is enough? The cost of things is not only what we pay for them, but also time. Everything we own takes our time, even if we don't enjoy it. Things must be dusted, rearranged, closeted, hung up, stored, mothballed, catalogued, protected, and insured. It even takes time to feel guilty, as when we look at the gadget on the shelf we paid $76 for and have never used, but there it sits. And every time we look at it, zap! A moment of guilt stolen from our day.

How much time do we spend nagging our children to put their things away? Do we feel guilty for being bad parents because our kids don't use their things either? My hometown newspaper *The Selah Valley Optimist* featured this statement by Bill Vaughn: "A three-year-old child is a being who gets almost as much fun out of a fifty-six-dollar set of swings as it does out of finding a small green worm."

Little things seem more fun than big things sometimes. A favorite book is Pascal's *Pensées,* a collection of tersely stated thoughts containing gigantic meaning. Each segment is short, stands alone, and has more meat than the average bear. T. S. Eliot said of Pascal, "His mind was active rather than accumulative." Are our minds active? Do the things we buy stimulate our mental life or do they just accumulate like dust on a log? There is a place for the aesthetic, beauty for its own sake, paintings on the wall and primroses along the path. We do not discourage the enjoyment of beauty, but raise the question of whether or not it is enjoyment we feel. Since we are paying a price, time, is that next thing we get worth our time? Queen Elizabeth I gave her answer in her dying words, "All my possessions for a moment of time."

2. *Confusion.* In Chapter 5 we dealt at length with the energy drain and time consumption of confusion, not only in the world "out there" but also in the mental world inside us. Unmade decisions rob us of sleep and wholeheartedness in our work and can reduce us to apathy during our eight-hour recreation segment. The critical question is not whether or not we have perplexing problems, but are the problems we have today the same ones we had a year ago at this

time? If so, how many hours of the past year have gone
into worry about them? Can we finalize at least some of
our decisions and get on with new matters?

We can narrow our choices. One of the great things about
traveling is looking in the hotel closet and seeing three
outfits hanging there. It takes but a moment to decide what
to wear. When we pack, our choices are reduced by the
limitations of our luggage size. Closets at home are not
nearly as appealing. How many clothes do you keep that
you haven't worn for ten years? Do you have wardrobes in
different sizes, depending on your fluctuating weight? Perhaps you need to make a decision about your weight. Do
you keep shoes that hurt your feet and haven't been worn
since you bought them because you can't bear to get rid of
something you paid so much for? Do you wear them in
agony every now and then to justify keeping them? Who
says you have to go through life with sore feet? Get rid of
painful shoes. Pick out Wednesday's clothes Tuesday night.
No need to start a brand-new day hemming and hawing
between the gray suit and the tan. Have a plan. When in
doubt, throw it out. Into the Goodwill barrel. You will make
someone happy and be relieved yourself.

A sign once hung above my desk that said, "A clean
desk is a sign of a sick mind." It was pure rationalization.
Clutter means unfinished business. How many times do you
handle a piece of paper? How many pieces of paper are on
your desk? Perhaps you need a system. Perhaps you have
a problem delegating or asking for help, living by that ver-
sion of the 11th Commandment that states, "Thou must do
it all thyself." You have as many hours in the day as the
President of the United States. A country cannot run without
delegation. Why should you?

3. *You can't say no*. Days upon weeks are wasted getting out of tasks we shouldn't have taken on in the first
place. We knew at the outset we didn't have time, didn't
want to, and had fifty other commitments still hanging fire.
A helpful way to break the *yes* pattern, at least on the phone,
is to decide never to make a decision on the spur of the
moment. It takes a little time to say, "I'll have to check my
schedule, think about it, and call you back," but not nearly

as much time as muddling through an acceptance you didn't mean.

4. *You don't know how to interrupt.* Politeness can eat up your day. Have you ever listened to a long one-way conversation that proceeded without pause, like a steady stream from a fire hose, knowing all the while you are late for an appointment? We can learn to interrupt without being rude; that is certainly better than to listen impatiently with our body language yelling "anger."

5. *Dulling sensation.* People do what they do for reasons. Weary and worried, we often seek relief in ways that are momentarily satisfying but rob us of the very thing that could make us feel good, strokes. That celebrated institution, the cocktail party, has the fastest point of diminishing returns of any of our social rituals. As stroke-hungry as most of us are, it is ironic we spend time together dulling sensation as quickly as possible. "Can I get you something to drink?" is a question that beats "How are you?" to the door. England's sherry hour at least has some restraints, and small glasses. A spot of sherry may warm the cockles of the heart and relax work-weary muscles, but how many spots are enough?

A hostess spends a week preparing a gourmet feast, and no one tastes the food. What a waste. I remember my childhood days on the farm when company came. Alcohol was not served. Company was enough. Talk came naturally. Just being together, even silence, was pleasant, warm bodies sitting peacefully listening to the faraway frog concert, or the Doppler-bent steam whistle of the Northern Pacific freight headed for the mountains. No one needed "oiling." When people of all ages talked, great aunts *and* children, everyone listened.

When we kill sensation we kill time. How many evenings are lost, conversations forgotten, strokes unregistered, when people slowly drink themselves into oblivion. Berne believed the reason people drink is to diminish the control of the Parent, allowing the Child to come out and play. According to him, the Parent is the first to go. Our observation is that all three parts of the personality are affected by alcohol simultaneously. Adult functioning is also diminished, often with disastrous results because of impaired judgment. The Child, with no protection, may feel high but then must feel the low the next day because of what he said, did, or forgot. The better way to remove the constraints of the Parent is by Trackdown. Drug takers are equally dulled and often dull. Euphoric, their communication is like a spillway, which allows nothing upstream. The contributions of others are not heard. No strokes, which register, are exchanged.

6. *Television*. A recent survey found that the TV set in the average American home is on more than seven hours per day every day. There goes the eight-hour recreational segment. Although TV can be good, relaxing, entertaining, and educational, it provides no strokes. We are not watching people interested in *us*. We are watching a large, inanimate box, about fifteen cubic feet in size. The sad thing is that though we may love Lucy, Lucy can't love us back. For some people the "soaps" have become more real than their own lives. One man argued that he wasn't that much influenced by TV. Asked what kind of toothpaste he used, he named a brand. When asked why, he said, "Because I can't brush after every meal."

One of the serious problems of TV is that it robs us of the opportunity to perform one of the most important functions of the human mind, *imaging*. When you are watching TV you are *in* the experience, and the work of the mind in imaging is preempted. The image is there for you. The work of imaging is one of the most important in the developing mind of children. Two broomsticks, a tree, and a blanket are all that are needed to make a house on the back lawn. In the child's mind it can be a palace, a pirate's cove or a doll house. It is hard to pretend anything when one's senses are captured by what emanates from the TV set. When you read a book *you* bring something to the experience, imagining what the heroine and the villain look like, attributing to them your own rich store of past experience. Have you ever been disappointed at seeing a movie based on a book you had already read? Did the pictures match the ones you already had in mind?

This is not an argument against TV, but it is an argument

against the mindless watching of anything that comes on the screen. A useful antidote is to review the TV guide that comes with the Sunday newspaper and deliberately choose those programs you wish to watch, giving some thought to how you could spend the time in a more rewarding way if you wish.

7. *Using prime time for second-rate tasks*. When is your best, most creative time of the day? For many it is the morning. Do you spend one-half of the morning reading the newspapers when you could be making your own news? Save them for later in the day, when you need to put your feet up and take a breather. The news will keep. Perhaps you need a review of the front section to be up on what's the latest. Perhaps the last six sections can wait. You have a choice.

8. *Untimeliness*. Whether asking your boss for a raise or your spouse for a favor, timing is of the essence. Your well-rehearsed request may be wasted if your timing is off. We learn timeliness from awareness. When the other person is hurried, harried, and hassled, your perfectly reasonable request may be the last weightless snowflake that breaks the branch.

9. *A perfectly clean house*. Cleaning the house, says Erma Bombeck, is like putting beads on a string that doesn't have a knot in it. Buckminster Fuller, always eager to prod sacred cows, painted the all-American domestic picture:

> I figure that because cleanliness is popularly accepted as next to Godliness, daily routines tallying by categories one-and-a-half hours of dishwashing, one-and-a-half hours of clothes, towel and bed linen washing, one hour of house cleaning, two hours of cleaning and preparation of food, one hour of self-cleaning, externally and internally, interspersed with an hour for back-resting, all add up to an eight-hour day devoted to yesterday's dirt, lest that dirt become today's filth and tomorrow's disease. And in all those eight hours devoted to the clean-up of yesterday, not one constructive act nor forward gain in the standard of living is accomplished.
>
> I figure that it takes a seventh day, hallowed for rest-

ing, and considerable preaching, praying and psalm-singing, to keep a mother-housekeeper in good humor as she progressively relinquishes her own potentials to the next generation.*

Whether or not we agree with Fuller's assessment—*someone* has to scrub the floor—we need to ask a significant question. Do we have a choice? Is there some other way to get things done? A Labor Department survey found that 84 per cent of fully employed women have prime responsibility for home and family. Add the above attention to yesterday's dirt to a full-time job, and you have a very tired woman. There appears no time for recreation; yet people who cannot find time for recreation will, sooner or later, have to find time for illness.

10. *Worrying about aging.* Wrinkles can kill you if you cringe every time you look in the mirror. Another zap. Another bad moment. Wrinkles are interesting for they tell your history. They are like scars, which tell you two things, that you have been wounded and that you healed. The most arresting personality studies are found in art photographs, which show, in stark contrast, the crags and gulleys of the human face. Is it fair that it is OK for men to have wrinkles but not women? It was reassuring to me, on one occasion, to contemplate that Golda Meir probably did not spend an inordinate amount of time plucking her eyebrows. What is wrong with being who we are? This is not to say that our appearance doesn't matter at all. Grooming is a political statement and also an expression of our self-esteem or lack of it. Also, there is truth in the aphorism "You never have a second chance to make a good first impression."

11. *Staying up late.* Your body needs regularity. We can induce our own jet lag by staying up and, as Dr. Trueblood says, "chewing the fat long after the grease is gone." Being awake makes a good first impression.

*Buckminster Fuller, *Ideas and Integrities*, Collier Books, New York, 1963, p. 114.

How to Take Charge of Your Time

If you don't take charge of your time someone else will. In addition to the suggestions already given to plug the energy drain of wasted time, we suggest you try the following.

1. *Plan*. Planning seems such an obvious answer that it hardly seems helpful. The problem is we usually don't plan for long enough periods. Did it ever occur to you that you could plan your whole life, in orderly chapters, including retirement? First we must have a want list and a set of priorities based on an ethical evaluation of the meaning of our life. We must make *decisions* about whether or not we want to have children, make a name for ourselves, be good citizens with time given to community service, make a million dollars by the time we are twenty-five, or work for our ultimate dream of a cottage small by a waterfall. Some of what we think we want is Parent-programmed. Will our Child get something out of it, and does the Adult see our strivings as realistic or possible? A life plan isn't made in a day, but we can start by at least planning by the year.

2. *Have a fuller calendar*. More useful than New Year's resolutions is a day spent contemplating a year-long date book. Mark off the days you want for yourself. Enter birthdates, anniversaries, and vacations. If Monday is a good "be alone and organize" day, mark it "filled." Make an appointment with yourself. Then if someone calls you to do something on a Monday, you can truthfully say, "Sorry, Monday is full." Or we are busy in July. It's your date book. It's your life. If mornings are creative times for you, don't clutter them with appointments that could as well be made for the afternoons. Days are a precious commodity. Don't let people steal them.

3. *Count the cost*. How long will it take to have a baby, raise a child, get a degree, finish a project? How much time can you realistically spend commuting? How large a vegetable garden do you have time for? How many evenings can you give up to the co-op board? Little League? How

many children, committees, jobs do you have time for? Do you have time to finish what you start? Are you starting too late? Dr. Trueblood tells a story about a couple who had driven cross-country on an anniversary pilgrimage to visit the Stanford Chapel, where they had been married. They arrived at the chapel at 5:15 P.M. on a Friday, and to their dismay, found it had been closed at 5 o'clock. They implored the caretaker to unlock the chapel and let them in, stating they had driven six days all the way from New England, especially for this nostalgic experience. "I'm very sorry," the caretaker replied, "you should have left New England fifteen minutes earlier."

What is the cost to your health of your life plan? How long can you burn the candle at both ends? Are you willing to consider seriously the heart model, working on count one and resting on counts two and three? Coronary artery disease is present in 100 million Americans, according to Friedman and Rosenman, authors of *Type A Behavior and Your Heart*. That is one out of every 2.25 people. They describe Type A behavior as a "particular complex of personality traits, including excessive competitive drive, aggressiveness, impatience, and a harrying sense of time urgency. Individuals displaying this pattern seem to be engaged in a chronic, ceaseless, and often fruitless struggle—with themselves and others, with circumstances, with time, sometimes with life itself."* They concluded that serum cholesterol, which contributes significantly to coronary artery disease, "may be determined just as much by what a person feels as by what he feeds himself."

The most significant trait of people with Type A Behavior is time urgency, or "hurry sickness." Another is a quest for numbers. They lack a sense of their own value: "The type A person has either lost or never had any intrinsic yardstick by which he can gauge his own worth to his own satisfaction and begins to measure his value in terms of the *number* of his *achievements*. Thus, pace becomes a primary measure of success. The key reason for the insecurity of the Type

*Friedman and Rosenman, *op. cit.*

A person is that he has staked his innermost security on the *pace* of his status enhancement. This pace depends upon a *maximal* number of achievements accomplished in a *minimal* amount of time."*

J. Paul Getty at age eleven made this notation: "I now have 275 marbles. Counted my stamps—305."† Type A starts early.

The cost is too high if you constantly exhibit the following behaviors, listed by Friedman and Rosenman:

•Vocal explosiveness, accentuating various key words, hurrying of the end of sentences indicating impatience with spending even the time required for your own speech.

•You *always* move, walk, and eat rapidly.

•You feel *impatience* with the rate at which most events take place, hurrying the speech of others, head nodding, yes, yes, yes . . . and finishing other people's sentences for them.

•You do two or more things at once. Do you always automatically grab for something to read when you sit down to eat a sandwich? People can go through their whole lives not *experiencing* eating.

•You *always* find it difficult to refrain from bringing the subject around to what interests you. "We've been talking about me all the time. Now tell me, what do *you* think of me?"

•You feel guilty when you relax.

•You don't observe well, and because you are preoccupied, you don't see a sunset or a garden or the dimpled hands of the little child.

•You do not have any time to spare to become a person worth *being* because you are so preoccupied with the things worth *having*.

•You schedule more and more in less and less time.

•Your body language includes a clenched jaw, grinding teeth, and tight muscles.

*Ibid.
†K. Lamott, *The Money Makers*, Little, Brown, Boston, 1969.

•You are afraid to stop doing everything faster and faster.
•Your free choice has been supplanted by a sad enslavement to the acquisition of numbers.*

If the above pattern fits you, would you like sweet relief, or as Gretchen suggested, can you *decide* not to live that way? Some people declare they like pressure, get more done that way, enjoy the rat race, or even feel it is the morally superior thing to do. It is not forgone that you will want to stop this frenetic kind of life. We are suggesting, however, that you count the cost. What is driving you? What are the "ifs" in your life? Are you killing yourself to prove something to your Parent? Something you have never examined? Can you retrieve your whole personality, including your Child?

4. *Take charge of your space.* Looking for the Scotch tape for a half hour is pure torment. Whether we live in a ten-room villa or a one-room flat, we lose quantities of time by not being able to find things. "A place for everything and everything in its place" is one of the more life-enhancing adages that have come through the generations. We generally know where important things are kept—deeds, birth certificates, automobile ownership titles, credit cards, and income-tax returns. It is the little things that steal our time— the can opener, the stapler, the dog leash, the extension cord, coat hangers, sprinkler heads, umbrellas, and sunglasses.

Also, our homes are becoming increasingly engorged with paperwork: health-insurance forms, government documents, magazines, newspapers, letters, notes to ourselves, notes to other family members, clippings, correspondence in answer to unfeeling computers, college catalogues, notices of phone rate changes from many sources, birthdate books, baby pictures, graduation notices, and a flood of junk mail that grows exponentially if we have fallen prey to the mailing-list exchange. Every home needs an office with big desks, several good filing cabinets, book shelves, office-supply cabinets, and counter space. It is ironic to see

*Adapted from Friedman and Rosenman, pp. 82–85.

a costly new home, with everything from a sauna to a satellite dish, equipped with a built-in desk about the size of a serving tray wedged into a corner of the kitchen from which the "little woman" is to run her household.

Many people use extra bedrooms for home offices, but few houses are designed deliberately with a brain center where home planning, indeed life planning, can take place in an orderly fashion. We are encouraged to let our fingers do the walking through the yellow pages. Much of our confusion could be eliminated, and time saved, if we had space to let our brains walk through the paperwork. Where do you keep your stationery, your encyclopedia, your dictionaries, your typewriter, your computer, your files? Can you find your homeowners' policy or do you have to move several stacks of boxes to get to the "house stuff"?

Think realistically. A home should contain not only a hearth but a brain center. The vocation of homemaking would be imbued with immense dignity if architects would take women seriously, and if women would take themselves seriously. They need space—even in a small home. Yet the attitude prevails that women can't balance a checkbook. Actually, the balance has to do with whether or not it will fall off the table.

Every home could use a good copy machine. How many trips have you had to make to the local library or supermarket to photocopy a document? How can you conduct business with the growing number of credit-card companies, government agencies, and all the organizations involving yourself and your children if you don't keep a copy of the complicated form it took you half a day to fill out?

If you have many books, how are they organized on the shelves? Can you find what you're looking for? How are your files labeled? Could you run a business from your home? Your home *is* a business, a very important business, and deserves better equipment and space than most households provide.

5. *Be prepared*. Much of life is spent waiting. We can experience waiting as wasted time or we can see it as a gift, an extra moment in the day away from the usual demands of life. Use waiting time, don't stew over it. As mentioned

before, get in the habit of carrying an address book, pen, postcards, and stamps. So you're stranded in the doctor's waiting room for an hour. You can write several postcards and keep your friendships in repair. Don't swear at the doctors. They cannot cut an unexpectedly difficult surgery short to get back to the office to be on time for your appointment. They encounter emergencies all the time that require their full attention. Few doctors *mean* to keep you waiting. Look at the rosy side. Use the time to your advantage. Bring a book. Be in the middle of two or three good books at all times; then you have a choice. Bring a notebook. You could be *writing* a book when other people are reading old magazines. Do you commute by car? Bring cassettes. Learn Spanish, brush up on economics, or the history of jazz, whatever turns you on. Get out of the dependency habit. If you don't like what your local stations serve up, have your own menu.

6. *Be precise*. Among the best things to come out of our technological age are inexpensive accurate watches. Wear one. You're upstairs and planning to watch the Monday Night Movie, which starts at 9. If you know your watch is accurate, to the second, you will know you have ten minutes before show time. You don't have to waste energy worrying about whether you'll get downstairs for the beginning of the show, the first scene of which may be the key to the entire drama. If you *know* it is exactly 8:50, you have ten minutes, and there is a lot you can do in ten minutes: change into something comfortable, make a phone call, straighten a drawer, water a plant, exercise, play the piano, pick a bouquet, clean a flat surface, make an apology, look at the moon, sit and do nothing, or hug your kids. All without anxiety.

7. *Do chores in terms of time*. Cleaning house isn't fun but has to be done every so often. Our friends Craig and Joanne Johnson are always figuring out imaginative ways to make living fun. It was Saturday and they and their children wanted to go to the park. But the house needed attention. They set a timer for thirty minutes, and everybody pitched in full steam to get things picked up, quite willing to do their part, knowing that the painful business would

be over in thirty minutes. The agreement was, when the timer rang they would stop. You can get a lot of house cleaning done in thirty minutes if you know a reward is waiting.

8. *Enjoy something in terms of time*. When we go to Baskin-Robbins, which is an occasional treat we try not to overdo, I get twenty minutes' worth of ice cream. That is, whether it's one scoop or two, I make it last twenty minutes. Don't gulp your food. Don't eat while reading. You won't taste a thing, and you may as well not have eaten.

9. *Preventive time-saving*. An impressive TV ad suggests you change your oil filter so you won't have to change your engine. The first takes some time and money, but the second takes much more. Fix a leaking faucet. It takes far less time than ripping out a wall of dry rot two years later. The time you spend caring for your teeth will save you many hours in the dentist's office. A brisk daily forty-five-minute walk not only makes you feel good, but may put quite a few years on your life.

10. *Break the body set*. Once we are aware of the bodily symptoms of hurry sickness, we can deliberately change our pace. We can talk more slowly, walk and not run, and relax tight muscles. The effect of this was discussed in Chapter 7.

11. *Have something to SHOW for your time*. For many people the greater part of the day is spent in the abstract, the world of words, numbers, and ideas. This is the world of the Adult, data processing. The Child thrives on tangibles, those things that please all the senses—touch, hearing, smell, sight, and taste. Christopher Morley said "no one is lonely eating spaghetti." If your work time is spent mostly with abstractions, revive your Child after work with busy, spaghetti things. Paint on a fence, sew on a quilt, bake bread, plant a geranium, work on a model railroad, play softball, build a swing in your back yard, swing on it, pet a puppy, buy a puppy. The Child in us still likes to show and tell, "Look what I did!"

In more sophisticated ways we feed our touch hungers, like working our hands around a fine leather-bound book, not necessarily because of its contents, but just because it feels good, like an amulet. The hunger for the tangible in the vast world of the abstract may give a clue to why people smoke, hold cigarettes in their hands even after they've quit, doodle, scribble, draw stick people and smiling faces on their conference notes. So they can do something with their hands. And see what they've done.

12. *Live in the present moment.* So much of our life is spent preparing for the next day, the next year, the next promotion, the next generation, that we may forget that *this* moment, which will not come again, is when we live. Do we worry about eternal life, all the while throwing away the life we already have, piece by piece, in daily exercises of anxiety about tomorrow? Most of us give that incomprehensible span of time called eternity some thought, now and then. It generally is thought of as a religious concept, rather uneasily by some, or cynically by others. Can it be thought of in practical terms?

Perhaps eternal life is when time stands still, when we are so consumed in the awareness of the present that the past and future cannot put parentheses around it.

Kierkegaard wrote, "One who rows a boat turns his back to the goal toward which he labours. So it is with the next day. When a man is eternally absorbed in today, the more decisively does he turn his back upon the next day, so that he does not see it at all. Faith turns its back to the eternal in order precisely to have it with him today."*

Perhaps we experience eternal life precisely when we do not think about it, when it is enough to say, "Thank you for today," and live in celebration of the moment.

*Sören Kierkegaard, *Christian Discourses Etc.*, Princeton University Press, Princeton, N.J., 1971.

14

Building Children

A Swedish expression to describe a rude, uncouth person is *han är obildat*, meaning, "he is unformed, or unfashioned," in a sense, *unbuilt*. The expression implies no one took the time to put the proper personality blocks in place. The meaning is not so much that he was built wrong, but that he was not built at all.

Since the most important building of the personality takes place in childhood, it seems worthwhile to share some ideas about how to build children. Early building blocks are those parental teachings, demonstrations, standards, admonitions, permissions, applause, and how-to information that a little person records in his Parent. Since everyone comes out of childhood with a Parent recorded in his brain, what can parents do to make that body of internalized experience as life-enhancing as possible to the child?

This chapter is for everybody. Even if your children are grown, some of these ideas still apply. If your children are little, all the better. If you have no children, these ideas can be applied to yourself if you wish to internalize new permissions and possibilities to benefit the little person inside you, *your* Child. Just as we can develop new habits at any age, we can build new personality blocks and renovate the house in which we live. We can gradually become what we want to be, provided we have some models and blueprints.

What Is Good Parenting?

In our view there are three kinds of parents:

1. Those who mean well and who parent well.
2. Those who mean well and parent poorly (because of lack of information, insight, planning adequate time, or their own preempting need).
3. Those who don't mean well and don't parent well.

We shall speak to the first two kinds of parents, with the cheerful hope that the majority of our readers mean well.

The following suggestions are ideals we invite you to consider creatively as they pertain to your particular family situation. Most of us have a hard time living up to the ideals we already embrace. Not living up to ideals is one thing; not having ideals is a worse thing. Therefore, these suggestions are offered as desirable guidelines against which to measure our efforts. We think they are good ideals, although they certainly do not exhaust the possibilities of things parents can do to build children. If our children are grown, and we missed the boat more often than we embarked, all is not lost. We have second chances. We have forgiveness. We have tomorrow, and we have each other.

Awareness

Berne wrote, "The aware person is alive because he knows how he feels, where he is and when it is. He knows that after he dies the trees will still be there, but he will not be there to look at them again, so he wants to see them now with as much poignancy as possible."*

Seeing your children with as much poignancy as possible, knowing what age they are, seeing them for who they are,

*Eric Berne, *Games People Play,* Grove Press, New York, 1964, p. 180.

individual human beings of infinite worth: *that* is awareness of children.

Acceptance

Unconditional acceptance comes next. Even though the small child assumed conditions for getting parental approval in the beginning, parents can override the initial uncertainty by repeated expressions and actions of unconditional love as the child grows. Everyone needs to know there is someone on his side, no matter what. That is what parents are for. Children can survive dreadful events if they are sure of their parents' presence, love, and protection.

I shall never forget my first first-grade report card. In three places, the teacher had written in bold letters and underlined "NO GOOD." After one "NO GOOD" she had added, "Idle too much." In shame and agony I looked at the judgment: NO GOOD. NO GOOD. NO GOOD. I hid the report until the night before it had to be returned. Exhausted and crying, I showed it to my parents. They were outraged, not at me, bless them, but at the teacher. I felt their unconditional acceptance of me. *She* felt their wrath, as they confronted her with the crude and cruel judgment of their six-year-old daughter. What mattered was that *they* were for me, no matter what. Knowing that, I not only survived first grade, I began to feel I could survive anything. I still believe it!

Children learn their value from their parents. A friend of ours told us about a three-year-old boy who was playing in the neighboring front yard. The gate to the swimming pool had been left open. Alarmed for the tot's safety, our friend crossed the street and closed the gate and said to the boy, "You must always be careful, John, and not go near the pool when no grownups are with you." To which the boy said squarely, "You don't think I would do anything to hurt my precious little body, do you?" What a fortunate little boy to have been told his body was precious. He knew his worth. Precious! Acceptance has frosting on it when it is accompanied by rejoicing in the magnificence of the body, mind, and being of our children.

Honesty

Good parents do not lie to their children. They may protect them from information that is too hard, at a very young age, to handle. Knowing this fine line comes from awareness. What do you say to a six-year-old who asks you if he "will be burned to a crisp when the bomb comes"? Do you say, "No." Or "No, you'll just disappear." Or "No bomb is coming, silly." What do you say?

Children as young as five years old worry about nuclear war. "What is it like to grow up thinking that you won't?" asks MIT psychiatrist Eric Chivian. "We heard a six-year-old boy say he wonders every time he hears a plane overhead whether that's 'the war plane,'" Chivian says. Massachusetts psychologist Steven Zeitlin states, "Silence about the issue of nuclear war not only intensifies children's despair and negativity, but also leads them to be suspicious of adults, who have not been able to adequately protect them." In the opinion of Milton Schwebel, a Rutgers University psychologist, "very young children should be reassured and told not to worry, because that's all they can deal with. But from mid-elementary school on, it's important not to misinform them. Adolescents find the most reassurance in being told that parents also feel afraid, although not helpless." A positive, fear-allaying response to this gruesome concern is suggested in the story about a teacher who asked her students if they believed that there would be a nuclear war in their lifetimes. Everyone except for one boy raised his hand. When asked why he didn't think there would be a nuclear war, the boy replied, "Because my daddy is out every night trying to prevent it."*

Talking Straight

As we should with anyone, we should think before we speak to children. Good parenting requires simple, unqualified

---

*Marcia Yudkin, "When Kids Think the Unthinkable," *Psychology Today*, April 1984, pp. 18–25.

statements that do not confuse the child. "Come to me, Billy" is straight. So is "It is time to put your toys away, Billy. Please do it now." Not straight is "Mommy sure would like you to come sit on her lap when you've put your toys away, darling." Susan says, "Mom, can I go swimming with the kids at Taylor Ditch?" "OK, you can *this* time" means mother doesn't have time to make a decision and therefore makes an exception. A straight answer would be "Yes" or "No" or "I don't know if it's safe. I'll have to find out but I don't have time now. So for now, the answer is No." *Yes* and *no* make sense to a little child but they lose their impact if they are mucked up by the addition of a lot of hemming and hawing words like "Well, oh, I would say you could, if you're careful, yes, I suppose it's all right, but, no, you'd better go ask your father first." *No* also loses its impact when it's preceded by "How many times do I have to tell you?" Oaths are even worse. "No, by God!" communicates a lot more information to Billy, or Bobby, or Susie (anger, leave me alone, get lost) than a simple *no*.

The most important straight messages, already mentioned, are (1) You can solve problems; (2) You can think; (3) You can do things.

Consistency

Said one person of her mother whom she adored, "She was dead wrong about some things, at least *I* thought so, but she was consistent. We always knew where she stood." Consistency makes prediction possible, as well as efficient planning. "I know they won't let me go, so count me out" is a declaration that saves a lot of time and uproar. Soon the peer group begin to plan around the fact that Rachel doesn't party on the Sabbath, and Peggy doesn't eat meat, and George doesn't miss family birthday gatherings.

Consistency doesn't mean we are planted in cement. A foolish consistency, which Emerson called the "hobgoblin of little minds," needs to be changed. Parents who discover they were wrong and change their minds should be honest about it and explain the change to their children. Lillian Hellman said, "People change, and forget to tell each other."

Children can accept the mistakes of their parents. What they cannot abide is a coverup. Changing one's mind is no sin; in fact, it gives permission to the child: *Change is all right*. Frivolous change without good reason, however, *is* inconsistency. It confuses the child and undermines the authority of the parent.

Hope

"Hell is a place where no one believes in solutions anymore," said Johan in Ingmar Bergman's *Scenes from a Marriage*. Good parents solve problems, and if they can't, they have faith that a solution is possible if they keep searching for it. We will find a way! In *I Remember Mama*, when the "sugar bowl treasury" was nearing empty, Mama would say, "We can always go to the bank." There wasn't much in the bank, as I recall, but the children believed a "bigger resource" was always available. Whether the resource is material or only the parents' self-determination and faith, it keeps hope alive. If it is a religious faith that sustains parents, they should share it with their children, not only the commandments but also the blessings. St. Peter said, "Be ready at all times to answer anyone who asks you to explain the hope you have in you; but do it with gentleness and respect." Among the most important "anyones" are our children. We don't have to have all the answers to talk about the questions.

Repetition

Little children love repetition, the same favorite book read over and over again, the same rules applied with consistency, the same rituals engaged in in just the right way. Reinforcement of learning is enhanced by repetition. "Mama, *that's* not the way it goes. It's the white rabbit who hides in the cabbage patch, not the spotted one." Repetition builds sure neural pathways in a child's brain, and he experiences a sense of mastery when he can match what goes on "out there" with what he knows to be true inside.

Tradition

Tradition is one of the most powerful motivators throughout life. It is passed from generation to generation through the Parent. What pride shines on the face of a child who says to his playmates, "In *our* family we..." (go to the beach, spend Christmas at Grandma and Grandpa's, have a green tree with twinkling lights, go to church Sundays, have a seder, sing around the piano, play Trivial Pursuit on Sunday afternoons, go to the family conference, deliver May Day baskets to the neighbors, make birthday cards, go to the art gallery, plant a garden every year). The how-to of tradition is recorded in the Parent, but the enjoyment and anticipation are gifts to the Child.

Friedman and Rosenman suggest that one way to change Type A behavior is to take time out to enjoy ritual and tradition. So much of our time is spent in cerebration that we have little time for celebration, observing the mileposts of life with a demonstration of respect and rejoicing. It isn't what we have that makes life good, but what we enjoy. Celebration is how we share that enjoyment. Birthday parties; anniversaries; celebrating a raise, a new refrigerator, a new tree, ennoble the common things of life and make us feel rich even if, in material things, we are not.

When I was little Christmas was the biggest event of the year. All the relatives, who numbered about twenty-five, arrived at noon of Christmas Eve, when the celebrating began. Some of us sat on wooden apple boxes, for there weren't chairs enough to go around, but the table was laid with the best linen and silver, and the traditional Swedish Christmas food was served the same elegant way year after year. Every day until New Year's Day we had dinner at the home of a different relative. It was one continuing party. As little children we looked forward to seeing what the "other Christmas trees look like this year," and felt great happiness to see the same ornaments, the funny Santa Claus, the light that looked like a house, on Aunt Elma's tree, or Aunt Anna's tree. Though my childhood unfolded in the years of the Great Depression, I felt we had great riches. Tradition was the reason.

If you bring little tradition to your own family you can start your own. One family we know lets each child pick out one new Christmas ornament each year, which is purchased and added to the accumulating store of memories. Saying a table grace can be a new tradition even if you were not brought up to do so. A friend reported she had visited a family where no one ever sat down together to eat. A table was not even set. Dinner was served haphazardly and usually eaten before the TV set. The children walked around the house eating "something" from a bowl.

In our harried world this kind of randomness invades most of our homes more often than we like. Yet we can minimize its demoralizing effect by making some things inviolate. We will *always* eat dinner together Sunday after church in the dining room. Or we will always eat breakfast together. Or dinner. Or Dad will always make waffles for the family Saturday morning. Or popcorn for the Forty-Niners game. Or. Or. We have choices. Do you long for a family like the Waltons? If you do, start doing what they did. It's your life. It's your family. Have you ever really believed you can have what you want? Go for it.

Anticipation

Looking forward to a good time is half the fun. With tradition this is possible. When our girls were little we prepared them for tonsillectomies by playing a record over and over. I remember the words to this day, "Peter Ponsil and his Tonsil." Even though there was some dread in their anticipation, they were prepared. In a more pleasant vein, are you going for a summer vaction in the mountains? Start planning in the spring. Plant the seed. Let the children look forward. Indulge their fantasies of what it will be like, what they will take. Who will do what. Working people look forward to Friday. What can little children look forward to? Do they have special days?

Rules That Give the Child a Break

One of the rules firmly implanted in my Parent is that "we do not work on Sundays." I still enjoy Sundays, feeling no pressure to do anything particular except go to church, which was also a rule. It was a day of rest, and still is. Can we share the heart model with our children: work eight hours, sleep eight hours, and play eight hours. Does that sound ridiculously impossible in your frenetic life? Can you make it possible? Can you give it a try? Were that model implanted in the Parent of people, think of the permission to relax, live well, play, be healthy and assertive, and enjoy life. Would it not be wonderful to hear a firm Parent voice saying, "Well, that's it for today. Time to knock off!"? What a gift to give our children!

Actions Expressing Values

What we tell our children when they are little makes far less impression than what we do. If we do not believe in violence, an action to express our belief is to *turn off the TV set* when violence starts, or change channels: In our family we do not believe in violence. A good and sorely needed dogma. The media, particularly some movie and TV critics, are incredibly naïve or downright stupid in some of their evaluations. In a recent "Guide to Current Films" the critic said of *Star Trek II: The Wrath of Kahn* (PG), "Some violence and a scene of torture might upset little ones." *Might?* Should there be the slightest question about torture upsetting little ones? Another critic, announcing the replay of the TV production about Jim Jones and Jonestown, called it "powerful entertainment." Entertainment? Just 913 gruesome suicides and murders in one of the most shocking, horrifying episodes of recent times. That, too, might upset little ones.

Leave books around if you value reading. Read yourself. Look it up. Does your child know his ABCs? Teach him if he doesn't. Drill him. Make it a game. How can anyone make use of a phone book, a dictionary, an index, an encyclopedia, if he doesn't know *m* comes before *n*, or *h* after *g* or "*i* before *e* except after *c*."

Cheerfulness

Cheerfulness and humor also express values. A father was telling about holding his infant daughter every morning, walking through the house saying, "Good morning, clock; good morning, refrigerator; good morning, stove; good morning, flowers; good morning, table." Not only was the baby feeling her father's strong arms, she also was learning the names of things, and also learning that "good morning" is what you say first thing in the morning. To everything. And everybody. Do people say "good morning" to each other in your home? Never too late to start. How wonderful to also have "good morning" in your Parent. What a marvelous antidote to people who feel like the sweatshirt slogan we saw a man wearing one early morning on a cruise ship in the Caribbean, "Another Lousy Day in Paradise."

Being willing to change is also important. Consistency is a virtue, but examining it is another. When baby brother arrives, when mother takes a job, when father works the swing shift, when you move to a new town, some things may need to change, hopefully not too many all at once. Saying "good morning" doesn't need to change, unless father's swing shift has him in bed when everyone else is getting up. Perhaps "good afternoon" must take its place. Either way, it's *good* that's important.

The family is out of work. The annual summer vacation at the beach will have to be postponed this year. Tell the children not just the facts, but also your feelings; you are disappointed, too. Let them feel their feelings. Then ask them to help plan a substitution—camping parties in the backyard, wiener roasts, a whole week of things on a "silly" list. Change is possible and can be life-enhancing if "good morning" and "I love you" stay!

Humor

"Belly-laugh" families do not have nearly as many belly aches as families who are dead serious all the time, *dead* being an accurate descriptive word. A story I am a bit reluctant to relate, for fear of hooking someone's Parent, but will anyway, is an example of what seemed to be effective parenting the hilarious way. One late afternoon I was driving Heidi and Gretchen home from choir practice. They were ages ten and six, respectively. From the back seat I heard giggling and the whispering back and forth of a word I didn't think particularly decorous or advantageous in polite society, a judgment call, to be sure, by a parent, me. In a burst of abandon I started singing the "Toreador Song" from *Carmen* at the top of my lungs, using only that word repeatedly as the lyrics for this boisterous tune.

*"Mu-*thur!" they yelled in embarrassed concert. "*Muthur!*" The more they protested the louder I sang. *I* was bringing shame on the family, and in the rear-view mirror I could see them looking horrified at the passing cars. They finally hid on the floor. At last I ceased and desisted, and we all cracked up together. Thenceforward, if a "bleep" word was spoken, I would begin my operatic assault. We have not had much trouble with four-letter words around our house, except for *love, book, help, hope,* and such.

Expectations

To ask a toddler to help you is to tell him he can do things. Parents often seem to be about two years behind their children in their estimate of what the child is able to do. Observation and awareness make the difference. Lifelong neatness comes from expectations that "you will take care of your things" expressed to a little person when he can understand words and demonstrated even earlier. He may need help, but as soon as he learns how, he will want to do it himself. There are lapses, to be sure, but the "you can do" message, along with your confidence in his ability, will be firmly implanted in his Parent along with reinforcing praise.

Being There

It is not necessary, or even desirable, to solve all of one's children's problems. Being there to listen is. Sometimes parents must make a decision. Other times the child must. Awareness, again, is the key. A parent cannot be aware if he or she is not there. There is much talk about "quality time" for children. This must be examined from a child's point of view. *Now* is quality time for the small child: when he has a bright idea, hurts himself, needs a Band-Aid, brings home a good paper, or a bad paper.

Family Planning

Families are off to a good start when parents-to-be think through what they want their families to be. As mentioned in earlier chapters, we bring into new relationships, including marriage, the tradition or lack of it that was a part of our own childhood. Even if we bring little tradition to the relationship, it is never too late to start our own.

Family planning starts ideally before marriage. Persons asked to perform the ceremony often make premarital counseling a requirement. A pastor we know engages in the following practice. He first meets with each partner individually. Each is asked, "What do you see yourself doing five years from now? What will your spouse be doing? What will your house look like? What city will it be in? Who will be in the kitchen most of the time? What will you do Sundays? Saturdays? Monday through Fridays? Who will pay the bills? Who will make the money? How many cars will you have? Have you made a budget? How many children do you want? When will you want them? Where will you spend Christmas? Summer vacation? How often will you see your parents? What will you be doing ten years from now? Twenty? Where will you spend your retirement years? What will you be doing then?"

Then he meets with the couple together, reviews their individual fantasies (with the permission of each), and confronts inconsistencies. Frequently about-to-be marrieds have given little thought to many of these issues. Some bring unresolved and difficult personal problems into the relationship, assuming blissfully that marriage will solve everything. Which it won't.

One of the most serious disagreements has to do with children, how many, when, and who will take care of them. If there is more disagreement than agreement on most issues, he may suggest they rethink their plans for marriage. Are they ready? Will their love overcome the differences? If they think so, exactly how will this be done? Often, because of conflicting experiences and role models, the young couple have little knowledge of how long it takes to raise a child. Time is an essential requirement.

Time

A young executive proudly announced he was a new father. His wife and the baby were doing fine and would arrive home from the hospital the following day. He stated she also was an executive in a large firm, then added confidently, "But she is taking time out to have the baby. She doesn't have to go back to work for six weeks."

The wife of a rapidly ascending corporate officer asked, "What do you think about the effect on our one-year-old daughter of my going to work?"

"Why do you want to go to work?" she was asked.

"We just bought a $400,000 home at Plush Pointe and we must both work in order to make the payments," she said.

"Is that the only reason you want to work?" she was asked.

"Yes. I would rather be home with Elizabeth. In fact, we want three children."

"Why do you need the new house?"

"All the up-and-coming company men live on the Pointe."

"But what about Elizabeth?"

"That's what I'm asking. Will she be OK?"

The answer is, Probably not. A day in the life of a working woman with small children is a mixture of fantasy, frustration, and frenzy. It probably also contains a sizable portion of failure. A reasonably healthy family life can evolve *if* there are sufficient funds tó buy the personal services of a caring and *constant* nursemaid. How many couples can afford that? Where are such nursemaids found? Realistic, fair divisions of mother-father responsibilities are uncommon. Supermom tries to pull it off, deficit-financing her health, energy, and emotions. Does the executive father or the rapidly ascending corporate officer really cook for the family 3.5 nights a week? Does he spend his days off vacuuming, grocery shopping, taking the kids to the dentist, and arranging for preschool? Even if he does, chances are everyone becomes harried. As pressure builds, the children sometimes become a source of resentment. *You* wanted them! You mean you didn't?

In many families there is often no choice. Both parents work outside the home to put bread on the table. In other situations both parents have invested years of their lives in careers that provide a significant measure of fulfillment and self-esteem. Must all that be forfeited to have children? Compromises appear to be working in some families. What is ideal?

It is our belief that the *minimum* requirement is that one parent should be at home, or constantly available to the child, until the child has made a decision about whether or not he is a good reader. A child makes such a decision about the time of first or second grade, sometimes later, occasionally earlier. He may not be able to read a lot but he knows if he is a "good reader" or not. He also knows if he "can't read." Reading is the primary tool of the child's independence. When a child reads well, and *knows it,* he or she can, with confidence, read instructions on the refrigerator, shop from a grocery list, and do homework by himself. If a child reads poorly, and even worse, thinks of himself as a "poor reader," all of his schooling will suffer. Even if he takes remedial reading, other subjects like geography, history, and civics proceed at a regular pace, leaving him behind.

Some parents today are pushing the process, introducing infants to flash cards, foreign languages, and Flaubert before they have even discovered their feet. "Superbabies" as young as two years old are being sent to nursery school. Perhaps they can "read," a little. But what of their emotional development? Have they had time to learn *their* way, by unhurried exploration and creative playing? Is the force feeding of the facts of life a parent need or a child need? The pursuit of excellence in child education seems a welcome trend, and we do not feel in a position to be reactionary with regard to early learning opportunities. Yet we feel it is a development that needs careful monitoring. Pediatrician T. Berry Brazelton states, "Parents have to be disabused of the notion that there's a magical time for learning and if they miss out, it's lost." He suggests that we may get so caught up in things we can measure, like intellectual development, that we may miss out on emotional development.

We believe six years off to have a baby is minimal. Six weeks off is tragically short of the ideal. Considering that one-half of a child's knowledge is thought to be attained in the first four years of life, it seems of the greatest importance that he or she be maximally cared for, guided, instructed, and loved during those years. What will be recorded in the little person's Parent? Impatience, hurry, absence, weariness, anxiety, irritability, mixed messages, and strange and changing "parents" in the form of sitters and questionably qualified nursery tenders? The Parent recordings can be otherwise: tenderness, availability, surprise, stroking, safety, reliability, nurturing, teaching, patience, showing, helping, cooperation, a good father-mother relationship, kissing, hugging, and fun along with the powerful Child recording "I belong!"

Who will be recorded in the little person's Parent? Will it be mother and father or someone else who has provided most of the care in the critical formative years from birth to five? Parents understandably want to pass on their genes and their names to offspring. Do they also wish to pass on their personalities, themselves? This takes time. This takes *being with*. What is a baby for? Is it only for having? Like a possession? Or is it for building a life that will bring joy and build a family? Ideally, these are questions people should ask before they bring a new life into the world.

If possible the six years should be stretched to ten or twelve, the "taking-off" years, when parental guidance is needed as much as ever. It seems cruel, in a way, to encourage young women to seek careers without giving them adequate information about what it takes to raise a child. With that information, if they *want* children, they could perhaps modify their career ambitions so that they could work from their homes. Options are available. Many women and men today are doing a commendable job raising a family and working outside the home at the same time. Not all latch-key children seem to suffer. Other factors apply. We still believe, however, that the period up to the point of knowing how to read well, and having that knowledge affirmed in a social setting, school, is a minimal time for one parent to be continually available to the child. Whether this is mother or father or a responsible, caring, constant person who shares the parents' values, is a matter for the parents to work out. The essential point is that children need care. Someone must provide it.

15

Knowing and Daring

"When you're getting to the end of the runway and you don't know how to fly, you're in trouble," Heidi said one morning at the breakfast table when she was sixteen years old and gathering speed down that bumpy runway toward high-school graduation.

We had owned a small plane when the girls were little, and Heidi's remark beat in my temples as I felt again the exhilarating terror just before liftoff, markers flitting by, the wheels thumping the runway's asphalt seams, faster and faster, throttle to the board, commitment total. One engine, one chance. Up or out.

Early in our flying years I was given to clawing the upholstery. Tom was the pilot and I the navigator. For him, flying was a breeze. He had become a pilot to get over his fear of flying. And he did. But I never quite got rid of the knots in my stomach, even though I knew the manuals, had a navigation certificate, was a whiz with the dead-reckoning computer, unfortunately named, I thought, and had even taken off and landed many times myself, with an instructor at my side. In fact, I knew how to fly. Also, I knew legal altitudes, compass and magnetic deviations, weather-report codes, the Morse code, navigation, wind-correction angles, radio frequencies, restricted zones, terrain, the "rules of the road," and all the information about our plane, its structural limitations, stall speed, load limits, range, equipment, and instrumentation.

Yet I was terrified when I was at the controls, with the

end of the runway coming at me like a flowing Kafka wall.
What saved me, and what I remember most vividly about
our flight instructor was his often-shouted command, *"You
fly the plane, don't let it fly you!"* All I lacked was the
courage to *do it*. But I did it anyway, and then I felt courage.

In living, as in flying, we may never get off the ground
if we think the courage must come first. We learn all we
can by diligent study and review, and then in a leap of faith
we do hard things because they're fun and exciting even
though sometimes they scare us to death. Like Jonathan
Livingston Seagull we want to soar!

Living joyously means living not only by knowledge but
also by faith. Once embarked, courage is available. Here
are some ways we have found courage, and we invite you
to think about them. We need to tell each other what helps
us stay aloft. Not everything that helps us can be written
in easy-to-follow formulas. Some things are more myste-
rious and elusive than "how to lose your fear in ten easy
lessons."

Solitude

Has your life become one dreary thing after another, flying
you? Does your week proceed in the way one man described
his life: "Getting up every day and feeling pretty good about
it and getting the familiar strokes during the day sprinkled
with a few novelties and knowing the bank account isn't
overdrawn and I don't have a headache. First day, great!
Second day, yeah, great! Third day, well, I have no com-
plaints. Fourth day, ho hum. Fifth day, Yawn. Thank God
it's Friday. Fifth night, tie one on. Sixth day, ghastly, my
head. Seventh day, rest and recovery."

Is that all there is, micro-misery week after dreary week,
a morning newspaper poorly thrown, one's personal coffee
mug used by somebody else, a hangnail, a scratched fender?
"I'll just *die* if it rains tonight!" Whatever. Given the fact
of the briefness of our life's journey, some of our fears seem
terribly silly. Why should we worry all the time when we
can be self-confident most of the time? Why should we

"peep or steal," as Emerson asks, "or skulk up and down with the air of a charity-boy, a bastard, or an interloper in the world which exists for us?"

One way to break the pattern of dwelling on the trivial is to start the day differently. How we start our day determines our day. Do you think it might be worthwhile doing an experiment of spending as much time sitting silently somewhere and *doing nothing* as you do reading the morning paper? A half hour perhaps?

One morning I sat in silence, relatively free from the need to intend, request, implore, or even think; and I became aware of two things. One was the clock ticking and the other was the furnace coming on. I let my mind roam and I became aware that everything I have is a gift. I have the gift of time, and I have the gift of natural resources, such as the fuel coming up from the bowels of the earth to warm me. Nothing I did caused me to deserve these gifts. I didn't bring myself about either. I was filled with wonder when it occurred to me that in the slow unfolding of the millions of years of the existence of the universe, I, a person with a name and unique history, got in on a little piece of the action. It was a moment I profoundly felt what it means to worship. I had nothing to say about my coming into this world, nor do I have charge of my going out. Life is a gift. What do you do with a gift? You say "thank you," and I did. The day was different because of it.

Gratitude

Gratitude is a sure cure for envy, an emotion guaranteed to keep us from soaring, seeing, loving, and living. Aleksandr Solzhenitsyn, from the depths of solitude and suffering, discovered

> it is enough if you don't freeze in the cold, and if thirst and hunger don't claw at your insides. If your back isn't broken, if your feet can walk, if both arms can bend, if both eyes can see, and if both ears can hear, then whom should you envy? And why? Our envy of others devours

us most of all. Rub your eyes and purify your heart and prize above all else in the world those who love you and who wish you well.*

Imagination

A little boy was playing "announcer" with an expensive miniature tape recorder his father had recently purchased. Father, coming on the scene, shouted in fright, "Give me that. It's not a toy!" Father's fear that his new recorder would be mishandled was understandable. Yet the little boy's fascination was understandable, too.

In the same way that we don't allow small children to play with expensive equipment, it seems as if the high-capacity computer, the Adult, is often off limits to the Child. Do we use the Adult, with all its immense capabilities, solely to process the programs of the Parent? What would happen if the Child had computer time, too? The Child, playing with the computer, produces imagination, invention, something new under the sun. What if the Child could try all the "what if" possibilities, in the same way that we feed random variables into our personal computers? What kinds of novel graphics would appear? Solutions? Possibilities? Can we dare to be naïve once in a while? Can we dare to be a Child?

Are we too old? Some people, on the downside of life's age curve, may think the possibilities are all behind them. We may not be able to sprint and leap as we once did, but our feelings can! Some of us are pretty good marathon runners and time and again enter new races and new challenges completely different from anything we've tried.

At one hundred years of age Grandma Moses was painting. At ninety-two George Bernard Shaw wrote another play. At ninety-one Eamon de Valera was president of Ireland. At eighty-seven Konrad Adenauer was Chancellor of Germany. At eighty-nine Albert Schweitzer headed a hospital in Africa. At eighty-three Goethe finished *Faust*.

*The Gulag Archipelago, Harper & Row, New York, 1974.

Cato learned Greek at eighty, and at that same age Plato wrote *The Laws* and George Burns won his first Academy Award. At eighty-five Elton Trueblood lectures and writes for several periodicals even though he already has written more than thirty magnificent books. To Bernard Baruch old age was always fifteen years older than he! You are old only when you think you are.

Conserving Past Gains

As much as we value imagination and the novelty it produces, most of our knowledge is a gift from the past. Imagination is not unique to the present. Creative minds through the centuries have done the important work of adapting past gains to an ever-changing present, a work which we must continue. To accomplish this task effectively we must accord respect to the thinking of the past, and the best way to do that is to know what that thinking is. The way to pursue excellence is to become acquainted with what has worked as well as what has not. Truth will not be ruined by scrutiny. The greatest tool for scrutiny is reading critically, and the greatest repository of truth is in books. Having done our homework we are then ready to ask questions, in the same way a child asks questions. In the process we become thinking human beings, living not by whim or dogma, but by our own evaluation of what has gone before and what we can contribute to its preservation, correction, or enhancement.

Conserving past gains also is an important value in decisions affecting our personal lives. For instance, how much is lost when a marriage is dissolved and a home breaks up? A home is more than community property, things. It is the product of days and weeks and years of personal investments of energy, love, thought, and being. How much of the very lives of persons is lost when that unique relationship called a family is shattered? Whether we ask this from an ethical or a pragmatic point of view, it is a question that should be considered seriously before people walk away from each other. It should be asked for their own sake. Sometimes forgiveness is a better way. Forgiveness is not being a doormat, but a door. It is a door through which we can enter into another person's pain and try to understand how it feels to fail, to grow old, to hurt someone, to have one's dreams shattered, to be afraid, to strike first in defense, to hurt the one we love. To walk through a door of forgiveness we open what has been shut, a relationship closed by silent resentment, stored angers, and remembered affronts. Forgiving is for *getting,* getting back what has been lost, getting rid of guilt, getting another chance, changing behavior, and conserving past gains.

Forgiveness is not righting a wrong, but righting a relationship. Sometimes we must right wrongs other ways, by confrontation, correction, even conflict. Some things ought not to be tolerated—life-threatening behavior, cruelty, social oppression, and using persons as things. We need wisdom and grace to know the difference between what may be tolerated and what may not, to pray, as Reinhold Niebuhr did, that "we be granted the serenity to accept the things we cannot change, courage to change the things we can, and the wisdom to know the difference."

Faith

In *I'm OK—You're OK* an entire chapter was devoted to morals and religion. In this book very little has been said about religious faith. This is not to imply that our faith has diminished. Yet it takes more than an esoteric phrase, a currently popular buzz word, ricocheted to someone who "knows what we mean," to explain the basis of one's faith. Many religious communities today have become divisive and exclusive. Carl Sandburg once was asked what the worst word in the English language was. He thought awhile, and then said, "Exclusive." To sort sheep from goats, saints from sinners, us from them does not seem to be the loving invitation to redemptive relationships we understand the good news to be. "God will love you *if*" is as graceless as "I will love you if." The best prayer we have heard lately is attributed to a little boy who said, "Please make all the bad people good and all the good people nice." The most reassuring credal statement we know was written by Dr.

James Wharton, "We're all in this thing together, and God is in this thing with us." We can soar with that.

Preparation

Before a pilot leaves the ramp and heads for the runway, there are five checkouts that must be performed. These are given the mnemonic CIGAR.* Failure in any one of these means takeoff should be postponed.

C is for *Controls*. Brakes, ailerons, flaps, wheels, elevator, all movable equipment is tested.

I is for *Insruments*. Gauges, altimeter, radio, and navigation equipment are among the instruments checked.

G is for *Gasoline*. Do you have enough fuel to get where you're going?

A is for *Attitude*, which means the tilt or tip of the nose of the plane which must be adjusted or "trimmed" to compensate for load distribution so the plane will fly level, not nose-up or nose-down.

R means *Runup*, revving your engine at full throttle to determine if you have maximum power. If all the "Cigars" check out, you are ready to roll. If they do not, you cannot take off safely.

Here is a CIGAR for living. Before you undertake a journey, a new exploration of life, perhaps based on something inspired by the possibilities set forth in this book, check the following:

C is for your *Controls*. Who is controlling your life, your Parent, Adult, or Child? Who's in charge, you or somebody else? Is there any control at all?

I is for your physical *Instruments*. How is your health: vision, hearing, heart, blood pressure? Do you know how to read the health gauges which warn of malfunction?

G is for your *Gasoline*. Emotional fuel. How is your stroke supply?

---

*We realize that this mnemonic dates us. New technology requires checking out many other systems and instrumentation. However, during our days in the wild blue yonder, CIGAR served us well.

A is for your *Attitude*. Is your head up or down? Are you dragging your tail because you are overloaded, or because your load is distributed unevenly? Have you made compensating adjustments? Are you on the level? Does your nose point in the direction you want to go?

R is for your *Runup*. Have you tested your maximum capabilities, rehearsed, practiced? Are you ready to lift off?

Soaring

Every so often an unexpected updraft surprises us and, quite beyond our control or intention, lifts us to extraordinary heights of emotion. Those are the rare, golden moments of ecstasy and wonder we find hard to describe, when we are transported by a power that seems not of our own generation. We cannot manufacture these moments. All we can do is to be open to them, to adopt an attitude of expectation, to let ourselves be lifted, to soar, to laugh, to cry, to feel all there is to feel. Sometimes our most magnificent feelings are tinged with melancholy, for we know the intensity will not last. Yet duration is not a measure of height or depth, and we feel most profoundly when we unashamedly live that moment as if there were no other. It is enough. Though we cannot make the moments happen, we can put ourselves where they happen—in flight, underway, airborne, having risked liftoff, having decided to live courageously and expectantly.

Most of us have known such a moment. It may have been a time when we were all by ourselves, sitting on a log in a redwood forest grove, looking straight up to the towering, converging treetops, splitting the sun's rays into a great, spoked nimbus, blessing us. It may have been when we were at the seashore, or walking on a country lane in the autumn, or sitting in a candlelit sanctuary. What had moved us may have been the lonesome strains of Dvořák's "Going Home," the measured, sweet dirge of Handel's "Largo," or his triumphant *Messiah*. It may have been when we stood at a graveside and came to believe in the promise of eternal life, because we could do nothing else. It may have been the recorded voices from the past reminding us of the triumph of the human spirit, "I have a dream . . . ," "Ask not what your country can do for you . . . ," "We have nothing to fear but fear itself." It may have been Ethel Waters singing "His Eye Is on the Sparrow," or the sound of children's voices singing "Silver Bells" in a mid-Manhattan holiday shopping crush. It may have been when you first saw your baby. It may have been when somebody loved you.

It may have been in your living room on the night of July 29, 1984, when with millions of people around the world you watched the opening ceremonies of the twenty-third Olympiad and saw tens of thousands of men, women, and children from hundreds of nations let their voices, bodies, and feelings flow together in one trusting childlike oratorio. "Reach out and touch somebody's hand, make this a better world if you can."

That people throughout the world can be moved to trust, to aspire, and to love each other is cause for hope. We know we must be realists in our longing for a better world. Therefore it is important that we take into account not only the difficult realities but also those that hold promise. Among the most promising are that love is real and that hope is real.

Index

abuse of children, 24–25, 105,
  187–88
achievement:
  discounting or belittling, 29,
    37, 39, 40
  discouraging, 29
  happiness associated with,
    38
  parental expectation of child's,
    24, 37–38, 225–26
  unhappiness associated with,
    38–40
acceptance, unconditional:
  child's need for parents', 217
  See also love
acquaintance, defined, 120
adolescence:
  denial of, 29
  passivity in, 94
  rejection of Parent programs in,
    148–49
Adult:
  alcohol use and, 203–4
  in breaking triangles, 176–77
  change and, 149–50
  confusion and, 80
  definition of, 14–15
  imagination and, 234
  Parent Shrinkers and, 192–93
  protections, 97–103
  regaining, Parent Stopper
    techniques for, 109–14

  shoulds, 141
  in Trackdown, 61, 63, 67
  in unhooking, 185
Adult-Adult transactions, 179–80
  contracts as; 103–4
aging:
  anxiety about, 206
  new challenges and, 234–35
agreement, as Parent Shrinker,
  193–94
alcohol:
  as time waster, 203–4
  withdrawal from confusion
    through use of, 82
amphetamines, 84
anger, Trackdown for handling,
  171–72
anticipation, in building children,
  222
anxiety:
  confusion and, 84
  definition of, 86
apathy, indecision and, 81–82
appearance, 206
approval:
  Good Guys' transactions for,
    53–54
  See also acceptance
arguments, defined, 191–92
assumptive reality of child, 7, 24,
  37
  I'M NOT OK—YOU'RE OK as, 26

241

conversation, as Parent Stopper,
113
cooperation:
in conflict resolution, 181–82
togetherness distinct from, 182
courage, 231–32, 236
Cousins, Norman, 136
Cox, Harvey, 90
criticism, Parent versus non-
Parent, 45, 60
crossed transactions, 49
breaking triangles with, 175–
76
Parent mode and, 70–71
as Parent Shrinkers, 193
cults, 86, 90, 187, 223, 236
cultural differences, learning
about, 98
curiosity, *don't* messages and, 143
cutting-out transactions, *see*
discounting transactions

daily living, confusion and
decisions about, 78–80
death, thinking about, 146
death of a loved one, 29
decisions:
accepting responsibility for, 34
accumulation of experiences
and, 26–27
confusion in making, *see*
confusion
Trackdown and, 60, 68–69
wholehearted, 88
dependency:
as critical reality of childhood,
5–8, 24–25, 92–93
in love relationships, 167–68
overcoming, 22
depression:
nurturing and, 190

stroke deprivation and, 117
destructive relationships,
unhooking, 184–85
determinism versus free will, 33–
36
dialogue, internal, *see* internal
dialogue
dieting, dissipating energy and,
154–56
digital watches, 89
dinner time, 223
directness:
in building children, 218–19
See also straight transactions
disabled persons, stroking, 125
discipline, humor and, 225
discounting transactions, 49–52;
diagram, 50
absence of audibles experienced
as, 129
of achievement, 29, 37, 39, 40
intellectualization as, 95–96
lack of recognition or strokes
as, 121–23
divorce, 235–36
do messages, 28, 30–31, 225–26
building children and, 86, 219
as motivations for change,
148–49
negative, 30–31
positive, need for, 37–38
don't messages, 92–93
change inhibited by, 148–49
child's curiosity and, 143–44
examples of, 28–30
as internalized injunctions, 26–
27, 28–30
double messages, 31–34
Drewry, Connie, 164
drugs, 82, 84, 203
duplex transactions, 49, 179
Durant, Will, 21

keeping people *(cont.)*
  Parent orientation of other as
    obstacle to, 186–88
  self-awareness and, 171
  wanting as well as needing and,
    168
Ketcham, Edward, 123
Kierkegaard, Søren, 52, 214
Kissinger, Henry, 31
Kübler-Ross, Elisabeth, 23–24,
  25

Lardner, Ring, 105
laughter, Cousins's experiments
  with, 136
life expectancy, self-evaluation of,
  199
life positions, 4–5
  redeciding, 8–9, 149–74
  See also OK (positions)
life script, 25
listening, as stroking, 124–25
loss, as result of change, 160–62
love:
  conditional, 23–24, 25–28
  unconditional, 7, 23, 25, 27–
    28, 217
Lynch, Gary, 16–17

manipulation, 178–79, 192–93
marriage:
  break up of, 235–36
  conflict resolution in, 180–84
  as emotional trap, 168–70
  family planning before, 226–27
  as reproduction of parents'
    relationship, 169–70
Maslow, Abraham, 115
master, 7, 37, 220
  See also achievement
May, Rollo, 78
meaning, as basic Child want,
  145–46

meditation, 233
memory(-ies):
  brain physiology of, 153–54;
    diagram, 154
  earliest, as most powerful, 18–
    19
  Penfield's experiments on, 15–
    16, 18–19, 65–66
  as record of experiences and
    feelings, 16, 18–19
messages:
  do, see "do" messages
  don't, *see "don't"* messages
  double, 31–34
  freedom of choice and rejection
    of internal, 34–36
  if, 22, 23, 25–28
  nonverbal, 42–43, 65–67
  Parent, 60–61, 70–71
  warning, Child and, 102
midlife crisis, time as issue of,
  198
Miller, Bob, 102
money issues, 105
moral values, 223–24, 236–37
  wants in conflict with, 141–42
Moris, Alene, 83–84
music, as Parent Stopper, 111

names:
  difficulty remembering, 54
  diminutive, 29, 125–26
  giving your own, stroking and,
    128
  using correct, as stroking, 125–
    28
napping, as Parent Stopper, 113
neatness rituals, as Parent
  protection, 97
neurons, 152–54
New Year's resolutions, as Parent
  goals, 132